INDIGENOUS MEMORY, URBAN REALITIES

Indigenous Memory, Urban Reality

Stories of American Indian Relocation and Reclamation

Michelle R. Jacobs

NEW YORK UNIVERSITY PRESS

New York

NEW YORK UNIVERSITY PRESS
New York
www.nyupress.org

References to Internet websites (URLs) were accurate at the time of writing. Neither the author nor New York University Press is responsible for URLs that may have expired or changed since the manuscript was prepared.

Please contact the Library of Congress for Cataloging-in-Publication data.
ISBN: 9781479837588 (hardback)
ISBN: 9781479849123 (paperback)
ISBN: 9781479832460 (library ebook)
ISBN: 9781479833382 (consumer ebook)

New York University Press books are printed on acid-free paper, and their binding materials are chosen for strength and durability. We strive to use environmentally responsible suppliers and materials to the greatest extent possible in publishing our books.

Manufactured in the United States of America

10 9 8 7 6 5 4 3 2 1

Also available as an ebook

CONTENTS

Introduction

The truth about stories is that that's all we are.
—Thomas King (Greek and Cherokee descent)

I asked Berta,[1] a woman in her sixties who identifies as full-blood Lakota, what it means to be Indian.[2] She responded,

> I think, um, what it means to me is the right to be who I am. Everybody in this country has a right to be who they are and I want to be, I want to feel that I have the right to be who *I* am—without, you know, without people bothering me about it. I don't tell people how to be white. I don't tell people how to be black. And I don't like people telling me how to be Indian. I know what I'm supposed to be. . . . I know *how* I'm supposed to be, and I want the right to practice my own way without being bothered about it. Leave me alone. I don't want to be like you.

I admit I was not expecting this response. When I think back, I guess I was expecting Berta to say she was proud to be Indian. I thought she would talk about her struggles, her ancestors' struggles, to *remain* Indian despite all the hardships being Indian entailed. But that was only part of Berta's story. Because Berta was not just Indian. She was an Indian who lived most of her life in Northeast (NE) Ohio. And in NE Ohio, people know a *lot* of stories about Indians. The problem is that most of them are not true.

Berta said these words more than a decade ago. She has since walked over into the spirit realm, but her words, stories, and memories remain significant. They help us understand Berta's experiences as an Indigenous woman living more than a thousand miles from her reservation home, the home where she was born and raised—until, at age thirteen, her family picked up stakes and moved to Cleveland as participants in the federal government's Indian Relocation Program. Even then, before

Clevelanders knew *any* Indigenous people, they (thought they) knew who Indians were. "I remember people would say, 'You're Indian?' And they used to pinch me and my sisters [and say], 'I heard Indians don't feel pain.' . . . I used to get into fights all the time because people would tease me or try to bully me," Berta said. "It was hard, you know, coming from the reservation."

It was hard for many reasons, but one reason in particular stuck with Berta. People would not stop "bothering" her about being the kind of Indian *they* wanted her to be, the kind of Indian white people knew stories about. Berta was not that kind of Indian, and that made people unhappy.

* * *

This book, about urban Indigenous people, communities, and identities, centers the stories of Indigenous residents of NE Ohio. It also engages with stories, memories, and histories constructed and remembered by settlers in this same contextual sphere. As Métis scholar Chris Andersen articulates, analyses of indigeneity require interrogations and critiques of the colonizing society because colonialism is not *external* to Indigenous communities. It is not external to *any* communities inhabiting colonized space. Still-existing structures of settler colonialism impact all human understandings and experiences. This book merely attempts to expose *some* complexities of urban Indigenous realities that emerge within the specific colonial context of Northeast Ohio.

Settler-constructed images of Indianness dominate this space. They inspire non-Indians to "play Indian" and consequently create ambiguous boundaries between Indians and Indian impersonators. *This* complexity of urban Indigenous realities is fundamental to many stories shared here, and this book, as a result, features stories of Indigenous and Indigenous-*identified* people. The latter are people *unclaimed* by long-standing Indigenous communities. I discuss the important distinction between claimed and unclaimed persons more fully in chapter 1. For now, a caveat: to avoid excessive wordiness, I sometimes collapse these categories into one. When I discuss all project participants as a group, for instance, I occasionally use the term "Indigenous people" to refer to Indigenous *and* Indigenous-identified people. I recognize the fallibility of this linguistic contraction, but assure readers it is not my intention to validate the Indigenous identities of people unclaimed by tribal nations or other long-established Indigenous communities.

> Those who tell the stories rule the world.
> —Native American Proverb

Indigenous peoples across the Americas understand this indisputable fact: white people came, claimed, and eventually possessed nearly all Indigenous lands. To justify their possession, the white people crafted stories—heroic tales of brave (white) men who defeated savages and conquered wilderness to bring godliness and civilization to the Western hemisphere. The white people, pleased with their stories, repeated them again and again until they transmuted into memories that transmuted into History. Generation after generation, this settler-colonial history is *re*presented as Manichean ideology and definitive "truth"—the inevitable triumph of light over darkness, sophistication over savagery, technology over nature. This imposed history is not comprised of factual or objective recollections of settlers' experiences but rather incorporates fragmented constellations of manipulated memories that serve an ultimate purpose: white domination.

Settler Colonialism, White Supremacy, and Colonial Unknowing

Well into the twenty-first century, white people continue to overwrite the stories of Indigenous peoples. Efforts to understand the mechanisms underlying such overwriting are ongoing, but contemporary explications and excavations are stunted and disrupted by the very processes scholars seek to understand. In spite of this fact, this book—which is a white-settler-trespasser-woman's attempt to illuminate (as in brighten, make more visible) stories of urban Indigenous people, stories shared with me to be illuminated, and stories I believe can help many white people understand how they are complicit in Indigenous peoples' oppression—rests on a foundation of (imperfect) ideas contributed by Indigenous (studies) scholars, sociologists, philosophers, and others. They are imperfect *because* they exist within settler-colonial structures that renovate landscapes of learning and understanding by hiding and destroying evidence and fabricating facts. They are illuminating because they make *more* visible the means by which settler colonialism makes meaning of whiteness and reproduces whiteness ideologies. I believe the stories illuminated in this book are more illuminating because they are supported by knowledge produced by and in support of scholars, authors, and activists working toward the goal of decolonization.

It is difficult to start at the beginning because so many beginnings have been displaced or erased. Instead, I begin with the most likely starting point(s) of these displacements and erasures—i.e., the related but unique nation-state formations of imperialism and colonialism. Imperialism is an ideology, or structured system of beliefs, that foments the creation of empires and extension of dominance over peoples, communities, societies, and nations. Colonialism, in contrast, refers to actions taken in pursuit of imperialist rule. Not all imperialisms leverage colonization to achieve political goals. Colonialisms, however, always bolster imperialism through processes of possession. In contrast to *classic* colonialism, in which colonizers possess another people's resources, *settler* colonialism involves the possession of another peoples' lands. Settlers accomplish the goals of seizure and permanent "settlement," or occupancy, of Indigenous territories by *eliminating* the Indigenous inhabitants.[3] In territory now called the United States, white European settlers utilized various violent modes of "transfer," including genocide, forced removal, internment, enslavement, segregation, forced assimilation, and representational obliteration, to eliminate Indigenous peoples.[4]

Settler colonialism relies on ideologies to justify violent and *enduring* strategies of Indigenous elimination. Settlers reinforced their sovereignty over Indigenous lands through the promulgation of *racial* ideologies defining white settlers as superior/dominant and Indigenous peoples as inferior/subordinate.[5] These subjugating notions were solidified by (ongoing) projects of Indigenous race making, or "racialization," which connotes the social and political practices used to construct rigid yet arbitrary boundaries between groups with differential access to power and resources.[6] Continuing processes of racialization make the subordination of Indigenous peoples and the possession of Indigenous territories seem natural, inevitable, and moral.[7] Settler colonialism, thus, is never a singular event, but more precisely described as "a structuring event, an ongoing elaboration of a structure, a suspension of time, tense, and timeliness."[8]

Racisms, predicated on white possessive logics, are therefore "inextricably tied to the theft and appropriation of Indigenous lands" in settler nations like the United States.[9] In such contexts, *whiteness* extends beyond phenotype. As the work of Aboriginal scholar Aileen Moreton-Robinson reveals, whiteness acts as "a form of power, as supremacy, as hegemony, as ideology and ontology."[10] Whiteness, accordingly, structures (and subverts) understandings of racialized social relations by defining and constructing whites/settlers as natural, "common sense" proprietors of Indigenous territories. Whites become wealthy by accumulating stolen lands, and their wealth reinforces their position at "the pinnacle" of their "own racial hierarchy."[11] Whiteness, thereby, incentivizes whiteness and maintains white supremacy.[12]

White supremacy is characterized by all-encompassing assemblages of structures and stories that preserve the material and psychological interests of white people. White people in settler-colonial, white-supremacist societies not only have privileged access to crucial societal resources, but they also (generally) understand their privileges as merited. Similarly, they understand oppressions experienced by people of color as merited. This perverted dis-orientation occurs because white supremacy institutionalizes racialized hierarchies of knowledge, or what some scholars refer to as "epistemic apartheid."[13] Epistemologies are basically theories of knowledge. They are understandings of how humans know what they know and how people delineate facts from fictions. Epistemic apartheid, then, is the colonization of knowledge, such that what passes as white/settler "knowledge" is determined to be factual, whereas ideas generated by racialized others are deemed mythological.

Histories, for instance, are arbitrary, fluid, and contested interpretations of the past. *What* people remember, *how* people remember, and *who* people remember are strongly influenced by the societies, cultures, and groups to which they belong.[14] Constructed "rules of remembrance" also dictate *when* people remember—not only with respect to when they should commemorate certain people and events, such as honoring US veterans on Memorial Day,[15] but also with respect to *which eras* are deemed worthy of remembrance and which are relegated to perpetual obscurity. In settler societies, Europeans/settlers have literally possessed *time* as well as territory, creating systems of periodization that reify ideologies of whiteness and epistemologies of ignorance.[16] In the United

States, for instance, "discovery" narratives locate the beginning of US time in 1492, i.e., when "Columbus sailed the ocean blue." Such narratives mnemonically eliminate Indigenous populations by placing them outside "memorable" settler history.

Philosopher Charles Mills refers to this phenomenon as "white time." Time *could* be apportioned in innumerable ways, but white-supremacist structures have *racialized* time.[17] "The White settler state," Mills contends, "'sets the historical chronometer' at zero, to signal that before its arrival, no history has taken place, no real passage of time, since a time in which no history passes is a time that has not really itself passed."[18] Racialized white time excises settler violence against Indigenous peoples, and thereby purges "modern Western liberal Euro-states" of their "actual history . . . of genocide, slavery, aboriginal expropriation, and absolutist colonial rule over people of color."[19] As Moreton-Robinson asserts, "Repressing the history of Native American dispossession works to protect the possessive white self from ontological disturbance."[20] (Ontologies are peoples' beliefs about the nature of being and existence, so removing Indigenous peoples from history affirms settlers' assumed rights to Indigenous territories.) White possession is continuously justified through the construction of the Americas as *terra nullius*, meaning empty or unused land, to rationalize settlers' appropriation of other peoples' lands.[21] The ubiquity of this taken-for-granted untruth reveals how deeply *possession* is rooted in white/settler subjectivity.[22]

> An odd thing occurs in the minds of Americans when
> Indian civilization is mentioned: little or nothing.
> —Paula Gunn Allen (Lebanese, Laguna, Sioux,
> Scottish descent), *The Sacred Hoop*

Settler colonialism and white supremacy are vastly misunderstood *because of* their vast influence on human realities and subjectivities. The "ongoing elaborations" of these "structuring events" obscure the conditions they create.[23] Indigenous (studies) scholars invoke the concept of *colonial unknowing* to describe an epistemological orientation that disguises and disregards colonial and racial simultaneities to manipulate understandings of indigeneity and whiteness.[24] Importantly, the past is not forgotten. Rather, some Indigenous studies scholars suggest that ignorance of the past "is aggressively made and reproduced" to justify the continuing oppression of Indigenous and other racialized populations.[25] Colonial unknowing advances "epistemologies of ignorance" by "*presenting itself unblushingly as* knowledge"[26] constituted through settler-constructed accounts of "reasonableness," "evidence," and "proof."[27] Continuing colonialism, for instance, is constructed as *un*reasonable while the taken-for-granted "historical 'fact' of colonization," which purportedly disappeared Indigenous peoples, eradicates Indigenous futures and affirms white domination.[28] White possession of Indigenous territories is normalized, and white/settler people benefiting from the still-existing structures of settler colonialism righteously, *ignorantly* proclaim "innocence" in an environment that conceals how and why settler privilege/ownership exists in relation to Indigenous peoples' oppression/dispossession.[29]

> Signs of white possession are embedded everywhere
> in the landscape.
> —Aileen Moreton-Robinson, *The White Possessive*

Cleveland, Ohio, and the Cuyahoga River Valley

In Northeast Ohio and across the United States, settlers legitimate and maintain white domination by telling repurposed, regionally relevant stories that obscure local Indigenous peoples' histories. This book elucidates some of the specific stories and particular manifestations of white possession operating in the NE Ohio region. Like other regions across the nation, many Ohio cities, villages, townships, counties, streets, and landforms evince Indian names, like Akron, Ashtabula, and Chillicothe (cities), Delaware, Seneca, and Tuscarawas (counties), and Maumee, Mohican, and Muskingum (rivers). As Aileen Moreton-Robinson alludes, such namesakes *could* and *should* indicate the omnipresence of Indigenous people, communities, and nations, but instead they are "perceived as evidence of ownership" by white possessors who believe they *rightfully* possess Indigenous territories, memories, histories, and identities.[30] The traces of Indianness strategically spattered across the state of Ohio, the so-called heart of it all, merely nod to the region's original peoples, who once lived along Lake Erie and the banks of the Cuyahoga

River, who settled in the valley stretching southward from a city called Cleveland to a city known as Akron.

This region, known as the Cuyahoga Valley, encompasses much of the area called home by the Indigenous and Indigenous-identified people whose stories comprise this book. Their stories, remembered here, often are eclipsed by stories of white settlers, whose physical and ideological possession of the NE Ohio region is undeniable. The region, for instance, is home to the Cuyahoga River, infamously called the "burning river" because it caught on fire *thirteen times* between 1868 and 1969. For thousands of years before white settlers arrived in the valley in the late seventeenth century, the Cuyahoga River was a crucial waterway. It enabled Indigenous people to travel by canoe from Lake Erie to a point where they could portage[31] eight miles on land through what is now Akron and eventually "connect to the Tuscarawas watershed, the Ohio River, and the Mississippi River."[32] The "portage path" is well known to residents of Summit County (of which Akron is the county seat) as a major thoroughfare marked by a "life-sized, metal-clad, concrete statue of an 'Indian Brave'" known locally as "Unk." As John Tully, Australian historian and author of *Crooked Deals and Broken Treaties: How American Indians Were Displaced by White Settlers in the Cuyahoga Valley*,[33] laments, Unk and three arrowhead statues[34] erected along the portage path in 2003 "are the city's only monuments to the Indigenous peoples of the Cuyahoga Valley." These commemorative monuments cleverly manipulate onlookers' memories—imbuing a nostalgic sense of the valley's Indian *past* while denying an Indian *present* or *future*. Such skillful "memory politics"[35] are deployed by white settlers whose dominant position in society enables them to amplify and disseminate constructed *settler* memories and "official" *settler* histories that overwrite what Tully calls "a dark story of dispossession, genocide, and ecological devastation" in Ohio's Cuyahoga Valley.[36]

The valley's burning Cuyahoga River is emblematic of both Indigenous peoples' dispossession and the disastrous consequences of white possession. When the last fire occurred in June 1969, the river purportedly "bubbled and produced methane" and "smelled like a septic tank." The Cuyahoga River was so polluted with industrial waste that a spark from a train crossing over it by bridge caused the river to erupt in "smoke and flames, some as high as five-story buildings." The fire was short-lived[37] but caused fifty thousand dollars in damage to two bridges and irreparable harm to Cleveland's reputation. According to journalist J. Mark Souther[38] of *Belt Magazine*, a publication "for the Rust Belt and greater Midwest," the 1969 fire inspired national ridicule and cemented Cleveland's derisive nickname, "the Mistake on the Lake."[39] Previously sloganized as the "Best Location in the Nation,"[40] Cleveland emerged from the tumultuous 1960s with fifty thousand fewer manufacturing jobs, 14 percent fewer people, increasing racial turmoil, "a river billowing smoke," and "a dying lake" (i.e., Lake Erie). The sardonic nickname undoubtedly conjures images of the burning Cuyahoga River for outsiders, Souther notes, but was frequently applied by insiders to Cleveland Municipal Stadium, a "large, poorly proportioned, underutilized, and aging" stadium located next to the water.

This so-called mistake by the lake invokes another peculiar manifestation of white possession and memory politics in Northeast Ohio—the "Indians" imagery associated with Cleveland's Major League Baseball (MLB) team for over a century. The team adopted its "Indians" name in 1915. Soon thereafter, the baseball franchise fabricated an origin myth, claiming that its new moniker commemorated the team's first Indigenous baseball player, Louis Sockalexis (Penobscot). Sociologist Ellen Staurowsky's research, however, reveals the fault lines in this beloved and oft-recited "Cleveland story."[41] In fact, Sockalexis played fewer than three seasons and, due to his racialized ethnic identity, was incessantly taunted in media and by fans. His tragic story ends in alcoholism, early death, and the exploitation of his memory by a baseball franchise that profited from his Indianness. To boost sales and team spirit, the franchise began using a caricatured "Indian" logo in 1947. In the 1950s, the logo, slightly revised, acquired the nickname "Chief Wahoo."[42]

Clevelanders' aversive feelings toward Cleveland Municipal Stadium did not affect their devotion to the baseball team that played there, or their adoration for the team's red-faced "Chief Wahoo" mascot. After the 1993 season, when the team prepared for its move from Cleveland Municipal Stadium to its new home, Jacobs Field, a small but vocal group of local people, led by local Indigenous people, argued that the "Indians" name and "Chief Wahoo" mascot should be abandoned along with Cleveland's brick-and-mortar "mistake." The Cleveland baseball franchise considered retiring Wahoo, but decided to retain the mascot, "swayed at least in part by a grass-roots campaign of fans calling them-selves 'Save Our Chief.'"[43] The campaign collected over ten thousand signatures in support of their cause—the retention of *their* chief, *their* cherished Indian possession.

Almost three decades later, the Cleveland team finally removed Wahoo from uniforms and stadium signage (2019) and initiated a name change (2020). This change, motivated by the team's "increasing focus on racial equality and social responsibility," provoked wildly varying responses from fans, who expressed emotions ranging from surprise, relief, and elation to confusion, disappointment, and anger. The team did not formally apologize for its role in the oppression of Indigenous peoples. Rather, it issued numerous statements to placate aggrieved fans, assuring them that team owner Paul Dolan "understand[s] the historic impact and importance of this decision" and that "Indians will always be part of our history." "Like many of you," Dolan said, "I grew up with this name and have many great memories of past Indians teams."[44]

In a statement clearly deflecting culpability for past injustice, the franchise indicated that it only *recently* became aware of "the negative impact our team name was having on local Native Americans and other underserved, underrepresented groups across Cleveland."[45] The team, however, has known that local Indigenous people disapproved of its ico-nography since 1972 *at least*. In that year, the Cleveland Indian Center, under the directorship of Russell Means (Oglala Lakota), brought a $9 million group libel lawsuit against the Cleveland MLB team. The law-suit accused the team of promoting imagery that was "racist, degrading, and demeaning" to Indigenous peoples. The case was settled privately in 1983, but the Indigenous community's struggles to eradicate the team's defamatory imagery continued.

In fact, these struggles will continue long after the team's transi-tion from "Indians" to "Guardians." Simply changing the team's name does not expunge fraudulent memories of Indianness promulgated by the team for over one hundred years. The team's version of Indian-ness, replete with baseball-related stories, memories, and histories, will continue to be recognized and celebrated aspects of Northeast Ohio's shared local culture. (Continued acknowledgment of these stories, memories, and histories is endorsed by the Cleveland MLB franchise.) The stories, memories, and histories of local and global Indigenous peoples are not. The dominance of the former and absence of the latter will continue to shape the way regional residents perceive Indigenous peoples well into the future. Fans of the baseball team and NE Ohioans more broadly comprise a "mnemonic community" or "thought community," meaning that their recollections, interpretations, and identities have been *collectively* shaped by Native-themed symbols, sites, and practices.[46] Thought communities are powerful agents of socialization that influence members' thoughts, habits, perceptions, and values. NE Ohioans have been socialized to value caricatured Indianness and disregard Indigenous peoples.

The baseball franchise and its retired iconography are not solely to blame for Indigenous peoples' invisibility in the NE Ohio region. The MLB team is merely one of innumerable entities responsible for erasing Indigenous stories and replacing them with fabricated myths. Across the United States and much of the world, people fail to recognize their localities' Indigenous pasts, presents, and futures. This erasure of Indigenous peoples and their stories is not an accident. It results from white people telling and retelling *their* versions of history and reality, which begin and end with *whiteness*.

Remembering Northeast Ohio's Indigenous Peoples

This brief history of Northeast Ohio begins and ends with Indigenous peoples. It acknowledges the Indigenous peoples whose lands were stolen and whose stories were overwritten by violently possessive settlers. It also acknowledges the Indigenous peoples whose contemporary presence is ignored and/or contested by ignorant (and violently possessive) settlers. It is a small, wholly inadequate attempt to counteract processes of colonial unknowing in NE Ohio, the appropriated territory in which I, a settler-trespasser-scholar, engaged in this research.

Of the region's many past, present, and future Indigenous peoples and communities, Ohioans are most captivated by peoples now referred to as "Mound Builders." Named for the massive, almost perfectly geometric earthworks they left behind, the (so-called) Mound Builders inhabited Ohio between 1000 BC and 700 AD.[47] Their extraordinary land sculptures and mysterious disappearance provide some Ohio residents with a "feel-good" Indigenous backstory that affirms white-settler innocence. Other Ohioans, in contrast, cannot square lessons learned about "primitive" and "uncivilized" Indigenous peoples with ideas regarding Indigenous civilization and technical expertise—like that required to build the elaborate earthen structures that remain part of Ohio's landscape. These Ohioans insist that "some mysterious lost race of white people, giants, or aliens" built the earthworks instead.[48] (Apparently, sophisticated *aliens* provide some NE Ohioans with a better ontological fit than sophisticated Natives.) The lesser-known Erie, or "Cat" people,[49] who lived in villages along Lake Erie and the Cuyahoga River valley for approximately 650 years (ca. 1000–1650 AD), are less celebrated and less debated than the Mound Builders. The Erie's long Ohio tenure is believed to have ended when their Iroquois enemies—interested in extending their own territory into the profitable hunting grounds of the lower Great Lakes region—attacked and defeated them with firearms obtained from the Dutch (ca. 1650).

More contemporary Indigenous residents of NE Ohio are nearly completely erased from historical memory.[50] Their stories of migration, adaptation, and, ultimately, pan-Indian resistance to white possession and Indigenous *dis*possession, however, provide an insightful backdrop to the struggles of Indigenous people living in Northeast Ohio today. "Pan-Indian" refers to the unification and collaboration of Indians *across* tribal affiliation. It denotes an expansion of group boundaries to include Indians who are ethnically and/or nationally distinct from one another. Despite their different identities, languages, spiritual practices, and political structures, pan-Indian groups engage in actions deemed beneficial to the collective. Throughout history, Indigenous peoples have found ways to collaborate and collectively make positive change in their communities, wherever those communities are located. In two different historical moments—the mid-eighteenth and mid-twentieth centuries—ethnically and/or nationally distinct Indigenous people came to Ohio and came *together* to resist colonization. In both instances, Northeast Ohio became an epicenter for organized pan-Indian resistance to white definition and white domination.

In the mid-eighteenth century, numerous Indigenous communities moved to "the Ohio country" to avoid French and British colonists invading their homelands in the East. Shawnee, Wyandot, Seneca, Cayuga, Oneida, Odawa, Onondaga, Mohawk, Lenape, Mohican, Abenaki, and Ojibwe villagers made Ohio their home. Historian Richard White[51] suggests that Ohio became a "middle ground," meaning a place between cultures, peoples, empires, and villages, a place of accommodation and cultural exchange between Indians and whites. This "middle ground," a historical era during which European and Indigenous communities "asserted a separate identity, but also claimed a common humanity," however, is overshadowed by historical accounts that distort differences between "the settler" and "the Indigenous other" to justify the former's domination.[52] According to White, this "middle ground" eroded when the French were defeated by the British in the Seven Years War (1756–1763) and ceded all territories west of the Appalachians and east of the Mississippi to the British without (apparently) a thought about their lack of title to these lands. France's secession set in motion decades of pan-Indian resistance to colonial usurpation of the Great Lakes region. Polyglot Indian villagers in Northeast Ohio's Cuyahoga Valley both participated in and led numerous efforts to push the British back east of Appalachia.[53] For instance, the (relatively) well-known Chief Pontiac (Odawa), who grew up about twenty-three miles south of Cleveland near the present town of Boston, Ohio, mobilized and commanded a confederation of regional tribes and villages against the British in what is now (misleadingly) called "Pontiac's War" (1763). Though deemed a military stalemate, Pontiac's confederation demonstrated the utility of pan-Indian organizing.

Pan-Indian efforts, however, could not prevent the formation of a new American republic that eventually colonized the North American continent. An oft-forgotten part of Ohio's history is the state's centrality to the birth of white supremacy and the US nation. The Revolutionary War, in fact, was the result of contestation between colonists and the British Crown over Indigenous peoples' rights to the Great Lakes region. After Pontiac's War, King George III tried to avoid more bloody battles by preventing British colonists from settling in Indian territories west of the Appalachians, but his efforts only strengthened colonists' determination to confiscate Indian lands. Before long the (new) American colonies seceded from Britain, justifying their revolution with accusations that King George cared more about protecting the "merciless

Indian Savages" than his own British people. When the Treaty of Paris (1783) ended the Revolutionary War, the Cuyahoga Valley was home to "the [second] largest aboriginal population to the square mile" of all areas eventually ceded by the British to the United States.[54] Ohio tribes continued to resist colonial encroachment until their defeat in the Battle of Fallen Timbers (1794) near Toledo, Ohio.

Pockets of Indian communities still lived in NE Ohio when Ohio became a state in 1803, but Britain's defeat by the United States in the War of 1812 ultimately led to "unimpeded white settlement" of the Cuyahoga Valley.[55] Northeast Ohio's pan-Indian communities disbanded and scattered across and beyond the Midwest—from Michigan and Wisconsin to Canada and Texas. Records indicate that Seneca children attended schools in Peninsula, located just outside Akron, Ohio, until 1890, but that is when the evidentiary paper trail of Seneca people in Ohio ends. Tully (author of *Crooked Deals and Broken Treaties*) ruminates on why these Seneca left and where they might have gone, but does not consider the possibility that they remained, unenumerated, in the Cuyahoga Valley. Census data reveal that only forty-two Indians were enumerated in the entire state of Ohio at the turn of the twentieth century.[56] Two Indians were enumerated in Cleveland; none were enumerated in Akron.

In the second historical moment, the mid-twentieth century, approximately five thousand Indigenous people from ninety-five different Indian nations made their homes, at least temporarily, in Northeast Ohio. Their relocations were attempts to escape the (US-created) impoverished conditions of their tribal homelands. Many relocators participated in the federal government's Indian Relocation Program. Some followed family members and friends who participated in the program, and others simply followed the tide of urban migration sweeping the nation. All Indigenous migrants to Northeast Ohio hoped to improve their families' circumstances and increase opportunities available to their children.

> An Urban Indian belongs to the city, and cities belong to the earth. Everything here is formed in relation to every other living and nonliving thing from the earth. All our relations.
> —Tommy Orange (Cheyenne and Arapaho), *There, There*

Operation (Urban) Relocation

As author and historian Philip J. Deloria (Standing Rock Sioux Tribe) observes in a book of essays called *Indians in Unexpected Places*, Indians participating in contemporary society—such as Indians living in urban environments—are disorienting to white people who "remember" Indians from past eras. Settler memories and histories construct Indianness as something embedded in the past and *diminished* over time, creating false memories of Indians as primitive, anachronistic, and inauthentic in modernity. Settler memories and histories also racialize and colonize *space*, locating "'authentic' Native places, bodies, and sets of relationships" on Indian reservations.[57] The contrariness of these ideas is explained by Eve Tuck (Unangax̂), professor of critical race and Indigenous studies, and her frequent collaborator, Professor K. Wayne Yang: "Everything within a settler colonial society strains to destroy or assimilate the Native in order to disappear them from the land—this is how a society can have multiple simultaneous and conflicting messages about Indigenous peoples, such as all Indians are dead, located in faraway reservations, that contemporary Indigenous people are less Indigenous than prior generations, and that all Americans are 'a little bit Indian.'"[58] These "simultaneous and conflicting messages" impact Indigenous people's perceptions of self and others' perceptions of Indigenous peoples.

Colonial conceptions of space dichotomize "rez"[59] and "non-rez" environments, but *all* land is Indigenous land.[60] US Indigenous people began to reclaim urbanized Indigenous spaces more than a century ago. In search of employment opportunities, Indians followed the same rural-to-urban and southern-to-northern migratory paths of other impoverished, marginalized, and racialized groups in the United States. Few scholars engaged with these earliest Indigenous city dwellers, but the scant work in this area affirms that strategies central to urban Indian organizing then—maintaining tribal ties and simultaneously expanding ethnic boundaries to include "all [Indigenous] relations"—remain important today.[61]

The number of American Indian urban migrants to US cities increased rapidly during and after World War II.[62] More than forty thousand Indians left reservations to work in war-related industries and twenty-five thousand more served in the US armed forces.[63] The federal government's Indian Relocation Program encouraged tens of thousands more to leave their homes in pursuit of material advantages unavailable on reservations. Convinced that the US government should get out of "the Indian business," Bureau of Indian Affairs (BIA) commissioner Dillon S. Myer launched Operation Relocation in 1952. This new program aligned with terminationist policies initiated in the 1940s to phase out federal support for Indian tribes. These policies, which blatantly disregarded US treaty obligations, included withdrawing federal recognition from Indian nations and transferring responsibility for Indian education, agriculture, and health to state governments. Now Myer planned to transplant reservation-based Indians to urban environments by relocating "voluntary" migrants.

Under Myer's direction, the BIA established relocation recruitment offices on Indian reservations across the United States. Indians willing to move to cities were promised educational and occupational opportunities. For a defined period of time, the government also agreed to pay for relocators' transportation, housing, and everyday necessities like groceries and bus tickets. Promotional materials portrayed happy urban Indian families in "imagined landscapes"[64]—"contented Indian men working at good jobs" and "women standing next to big appliances like televisions and refrigerators."[65] These (vacant) promises enticed more than thirty thousand individuals and families to participate in Indian Relocation.[66] So many Indians applied for relocation in the 1950s, in fact, that the BIA could not afford to process all the applications.[67]

Many Indian relocators had already experienced steady work in white-dominated environments. US military veterans, for instance, comprised 55 percent of Indian Relocation participants between 1953 and 1956.[68] For this reason, some scholars suggest that Indian Relocation was less a "rupture in Indian history" and more a "continuation of economic and migratory trends already in effect."[69] Suggesting that urbanized Indians were duped or victimized by ill-advised government policies, these scholars argue, fails to capture the fact that Indians began "reimagining" Indian Country long before the federal government devised the Indian Relocation Program.[70] While much truth exists in this framing of Indian relocation, it is also necessary to highlight the government's manipulative role in intensifying Indigenous people's urban migrations. Operation Relocation ultimately was designed to relieve the US government of its obligations to Indians. It was touted as an opportunity for Indians to achieve financial independence, but the bottom line was that it was cheaper to move Indians to cities than rehabilitate reservation economies. The federal government imagined that relocation money—nearly $15 million between 1953 and 1960—was money well spent. Indian Relocation became a "panacea for all Indian problems," and economic-development projects on Indian reservations abruptly halted.[71]

Ultimately, the BIA's urban relocation initiative was ill conceived and underfunded. The program was promoted when many US cities, including Cleveland, were experiencing financial decline due to the post–World War II loss of manufacturing jobs. Moreover, upon relocating, Indians found themselves in substandard living conditions with insufficient monetary assistance. The scant jobs available were low level and gender segregated.[72] Many Indians returned home, but the exact numbers are debated. The BIA reports high success rates, but research suggests that relocators were poorly tracked.[73] Many relocators returned home and many more wanted to but did not have the requisite resources.

Despite federal-level failings, many relocated Indians survived and thrived in cities. Ned Blackhawk, member of the Te-Moak tribe of Western Shoshone and Yale University professor, suggests that their stories and experiences are marginalized, however, because people tend to assume that urban living is "incompatible" with authentic Indian lifestyles.[74] Authors of scholarly works and fictionalized accounts, Blackhawk argues, perpetuate "bleak, seemingly hopeless portrayals" of urban Indian victims who must escape the "foreign, unfamiliar world" of cities and return to traditional communities to reanimate their lives. Rather than perpetuating "bleak monolithic portrayals," Blackhawk makes the case for "culturally sensitive and historically contextualized understandings" of urban Indian lives. Historian Douglas K. Miller also advocates for more complicated retellings of Indian urban relocation. Overemphasizing a "victimization narrative," Miller argues, "wrests agency away from active participants who courageously confronted difficult decisions for themselves and their families."[75] These decisions enabled many urban Indian families to attain upward socioeconomic mobility. Relative to reservation Indians, relocated Indians had more education, lower unemployment rates, and increased average family incomes.[76]

Moreover, urban Indians were proactive in their attempts to organize and support other Indians living in reservation and urban environments. Urban Indians advocated for resource development on reservations so Indians could *choose* where to live. The lack of opportunities on reservations, they maintained, made urban relocation coercive.[77] They petitioned the BIA for better housing, health care, and employment assistance and established social and political organizations to address areas of need that the BIA neglected. Urban Indian organizations not only provided necessities like food, health care, and return travel expenses, but they also established space in cities for Indians to come together to share and compare stories with Indigenous people experiencing similar struggles and successes. After World War II, urban pan-Indian social institutions continued to foster "complex and multi-layered identities"[78] that respected tribal distinctions while celebrating Indigenous peoples' commonalities. Rather than succumb to the assimilationist intentions of the Indian Relocation program, many relocated Indians creatively adapted to their new circumstances.

Stories That Make Me

I first became acquainted with *relocated* Indigenous people in Northeast Ohio in 2006. I had recently concluded one year of service with the AmeriCorps*VISTA (Volunteer in Service to America) national service program. My position title was "service-learning coordinator" at a community center in Tó Naneesdizí, Dinétah (aka, Tuba City, Navajo Nation). My time in Dinétah is an important part of my backstory, and therefore necessary to describe in order to contextualize ideas presented in this book. Situating knowledge is an important Indigenous project because belief in knowledge *as relational* is central to Indigenous paradigms.[79] Author of *Research Is Ceremony*, Shawn Wilson (Opaskwayak Cree), states, "Our systems of knowledge are built on the relationships we have, not just with people or objects, but relationships we have with the cosmos, with ideas, concepts, and everything around us."[80] Wilson urges scholars to consider the relationships between ourselves and "the ideas and concepts we are explaining" because "*relationships are more important than reality*."[81]

I italicize Wilson's words because this idea, which defies and invalidates Western systems of knowledge production, is crucial. Western paradigms often insist on objectivity, which I conceptualize as a vacuum-sealed void research scientists enter in attempts to situate themselves outside "reality." Ideally, the void does not allow any irrelevant stories or memories or peoples or knowledges to enter so research scientists can reveal Truths that (presumably) cannot be discovered outside the void, where reality is messy. The truth of the matter, however, is that all the stories, memories, peoples, and knowledges that perpetually shape research scientists are already in that void, which is not really a void at all, but rather a bubble filled with all the stuff the research scientists are pretending not to notice. This understanding of how to conduct research would be laughable if it did not dominate knowledge production and impact every aspect of our lives.

Contrary to this problematic Euro model of research, Indigenous paradigms implore us to understand and interrogate our relationships to our (multiform) realities to reveal kernels of truths that exist in the world. Research, from this perspective, is a relationship-building process[82] because it necessitates that we examine our relatedness to peoples and cultures and ideas and every other thing that exists within and outside a research endeavor. My research is informed by this Indigenous approach to inquiry, but I write from the perspective of a white-settler-trespasser-woman still working to understand the full extent to which my settler-colonial socialization has altered and impaired my relationships to all the things (peoples, cultures, ideas) that matter when I tell stories told to me by Indigenous and Indigenous-identified people. Though I *intend* to relay the stories in holistic, contextualized ways that capture how individuals relate to their (perceived) realities, *intention*, or commitment to accomplishing something, does not always result in the consequence intended. For this reason, everyone reading the stories I am sharing needs to know who I am so they can reflect on where I am situated in relationship to them and how they are situated in relationship to me and my ideas.

I have already described the broader context of NE Ohio, the (colonized) place where my earliest memories and perspectives were shaped. In my childhood this space taught me that modern "Indians" played baseball and long-ago Indians were evocative characters in stories about long ago. Growing up, I spent more time thinking about the non-Native "Indians" baseball team than about Indigenous people. My brother and I both played ball and we collected baseball cards and followed the Cleveland baseball team (despite their seeming inability to compete for the pennant). My mother has childhood pictures of me wearing Wahoo t-shirts, hats, earrings. Pictures of me at the ball game, beaming from the bleacher seats at Old Municipal Stadium. It is difficult to describe the emotions I feel when I see or think about these photographs of me, decked out in Wahoo paraphernalia, smiling earnestly at the camera: embarrassment, sadness, shame, frustration, anger, perhaps all these things at once. But I do not feel surprise, because it is not surprising that my parents taught me and my brother to root for the home team. They grew up rooting for the home team, too. (Almost) everyone around us did.

My white, working-class parents, after all, only knew the stories they had been told. The vast majority of those stories had nothing to do with Indigenous peoples and the few that did were wrong. Almost all the stories circulating in this environment about people who were not white were lies. My parents grew up and raised me and my brother in a small Northeast Ohio town called Louisville,[83] a probable sundown town according to a database created by the late sociologist James W. Loewen, best known for his book *Lies My Teacher Told Me*. A sundown town, importantly, is "not just a place where something racist happened. It is an entire community that for decades was 'all white' on purpose." The name "sundown town" comes from signs, strategically placed at municipal boundaries, warning members of a specific racialized group to stay away. *Which* racialized group was warned away was context dependent. Black people were deemed most threatening and least welcome in Louisville. Census data draw a vivid picture of this phenomenon. Between 1930 and 1990, *three* black people were enumerated in Louisville, Ohio.[84] By 2000, twenty-eight black people were enumerated in Louisville, Ohio, but I had graduated from high school and moved away by then. In hindsight, I think I somehow understood that something was missing from my existence in this whitewashed space. Perhaps my love of books and stories played a role. Stories opened my eyes to the existence of people, things, ideas, and ideologies I never encountered in Louisville.

Since baseball players were the only "Indians" that penetrated my consciousness as a child, it was not until college that I became aware of American Indians as a racialized and subordinated group in the United States. (It was not until *years* later that I became aware, really aware, of American Indians as citizens of sovereign nations.) As an undergraduate student in anthropology, I completed several courses in Native studies, and when I decided to serve in the AmeriCorps*VISTA program after graduation, I applied to several positions in Native nations. I received a VISTA assignment on the Navajo reservation, and in November 2002, I packed up my car, bid farewell to my family and friends, and made the long drive from Ohio to Tuba City, Arizona, located in the Western Agency of the Navajo Nation. The three-day road trip gave me ample time to imagine future possibilities. At no point during my travels did I entertain notions that paralleled realities I encountered on the reservation.

The most surprising thing I learned after arriving in Tuba City was the thing that probably should not have surprised me at all. I discovered that my VISTA position, as regional coordinator for the Center for Service Learning Opportunities in Education (CSLOE, now defunct), was not sponsored by a local organization. It was not even sponsored by a Diné organization. It was sponsored by some well-meaning white liberals (read: paternalistic white folks) who ran an Albuquerque-based nonprofit focused on expanding access to service-learning opportunities to impoverished youth. I was in my twenties and apparently was not savvy enough to notice the red flags: I was not recruited by a Diné person. I was not interviewed by a Diné person. In fact, I did not speak with a single Diné person prior to arriving in the Southwest. Further, I did not have a degree in education or a background in teaching. Yet, upon arriving in the Southwest, I learned that my role was to educate predominantly Diné and Hopi educators about education—that is, I was to teach them how to "culturally appropriately" educate the predominantly Diné and Hopi students in their classrooms.

When the white people in Albuquerque explained these responsibilities to me, I must have looked bewildered or dismayed. They confidently assured me that service learning was culturally appropriate because Indigenous peoples traditionally believed in service and learned by doing. My job was merely to remind them. Perhaps the zaniest part of this whole story is that I actually tried to do what the white people in Albuquerque told me to do—contact school administrators, attend PTA meetings, schedule talks and workshops and meetings with anyone willing to listen. I tried to carry out this nonsensical work plan for about three months. That is when I realized I could do something useful instead. I spent the rest of my VISTA year assisting the (Diné) youth coordinator at the Tuba City Community Center with projects he believed were important for Tuba City's young people. Some of these projects were more successful than others, but *all* of them were rooted in Diné perspectives and attuned to Diné youths' needs.

My VISTA year, during which I did not fulfill the designated duties of my VISTA position, was a pivotal moment in my life. The experience taught me about deeply embedded (and federally supported) paternalism toward US Indigenous peoples. I also learned how to support Indigenous people in work defined by Indigenous people as necessary and relevant to Indigenous people. When I returned to Ohio and started graduate work in sociology, I hoped to support the work of Indigenous people living in Northeast Ohio. My experiences in Tuba City provided me with some insight into the sacred relationship between Indigenous people and *place*, and I wanted to learn how to assist Indigenous people's efforts to maintain Indigenous identities and cultural practices in *urban* space. I also wanted to support Indigenous people's efforts to resist colonial definition in NE Ohio, where caricatured Indianness dominated the local landscape.

I thought graduate school would deepen my knowledge base and assist me in developing skills necessary to interrogate inequalities in US society. To some extent, it did. I learned valuable information about racialization and institutionalized racial/ethnic discrimination, and I gained insights into the experiences and struggles of different racialized groups in US society, most notably, black people, (distantly) followed by Hispanic people, and (even more distantly) followed by Asian people. Not a single reading assigned in a single class offered in my department discussed Indigenous peoples, historically or contemporaneously. The absence of Indigenous peoples from the curriculum implied that they were sociologically insignificant. I insisted, nevertheless, on focusing on the experiences of local Indigenous people in my sociological investigations, and faculty in my department did not discourage me. They did not know any stories about Indigenous people, so they encouraged me to apply sociological stories pertaining to other racialized groups *to* Indigenous people.

It took me a while, a long while, to (first) realize and (second) understand why this strategy does not work. Some parts of some race and ethnicity theories certainly apply to Indigenous peoples' experiences, but the pivotal lesson I finally learned (though many scholars knew it for many years) is that the experiences of Indigenous peoples only *seemed* superfluous to (mainstream) US sociology because the white settler–dominated discipline mirrored and bolstered colonial unknowing in its dismissal of Indigenous peoples and their experiences. Though I gained knowledge and skills in graduate school, I lost other things, like my ability to think outside a settler-oriented, settler-constructed box that reproduced settler privilege and Indigenous oppression.

I am profoundly grateful to the scholars (several of whom anonymously reviewed my work) who reoriented my thinking, introduced me to invaluable Indigenous studies literatures, and ultimately taught me that Indigenous peoples' experiences in settler-colonial society *deepen* sociological insights into the experiences of other racial and ethnic groups, rather than the other way around. In the next chapter, I more thoroughly discuss the necessity of understanding how difference, inequality, and injustice in the United States and across the globe are *rooted* in settler-colonial projects and processes. Shedding light on these processes necessitates interrogations of whiteness—not only whiteness and its ramifications in the "broader society" (which so many white settler scholars like to imagine exists only *outside* ourselves) but also whiteness in our own knowledge seeking and knowledge production. I am continuously surprised and disarmed by my acquiescence to processes of colonial unknowing *while knowing* but not quite comprehending how sociological paradigms erased Indigenous peoples from memory and experience and theory and analysis. Now I better understand the errors in my thinking, the whiteness in my understandings, but I also understand that my learning and unlearning are lifelong processes.

I am committed to *unsettling* the spaces in which I trespass. I hope this book helps other sociologists and social scientists break out of the settler-constructed box hindering our collective understandings of social injustices in contemporary settler-colonial societies. Additionally, I have changed what and how and whose work I teach. Students seem appreciative of these changes, and they frequently comment on how little they knew and how much more they want to know *now* about Indigenous peoples. In both undergraduate and graduate courses, students are enthusiastic about interrogating the settler-constructed stories to which we all are exposed. They are committed to understanding how these stories shape us and make us and influence every aspect of our mental, emotional, physical, and material existences. That students eagerly take this plunge with me—investigating, discovering, remaking stories, and remapping terrains traversed over time—fills my heart with joy and hope. I am just barely beginning to imagine what our disciplines, communities, families, and nations can achieve if we teach more truths, if we truly educate people and impart deeper understanding, if we create different rhythms and patterns of thought and behavior, if we make different values by telling different stories.

Stories That Make This Book

Storytelling is another important Indigenous project. In her book *Decolonizing Methodologies*, Linda Tuhiwai Smith (Ngāti Awa and Ngāti Porou, Māori) states, "Storytelling, oral histories, the perspectives of elders and of women have become an integral part of all indigenous research. Each individual story is powerful. But the point about stories is not that they simply tell a story, or tell a story simply. These new stories contribute to a collective story in which every indigenous person has a place."[85] I take this statement to mean: individual stories are powerful but how they exist *in relation to* the collective is what makes each individual story especially meaningful. It took many years and many revisions for me to figure out how to tell the stories in this book, how to reveal each story's relationship to the collective. I grappled with how to tell so many unique yet interrelated stories in ways capable of revealing relationships in settler-colonial, white-supremacist society, in ways capable of exposing how deeply some people's lives are impacted by other people's relationships with ideas.

I needed to maintain accountability to the people who shared their stories with me, while also ensuring that "every Indigenous person has a place." As Wilson states, gaining knowledge should not be an "abstract pursuit," but rather, humans desiring knowledge should also be committed to fulfilling their "end of the research relationship." In the beginning, I never imagined it would take over a decade to bring this book to fruition, but now I know I needed this time to fulfill my end of the research relationship. I was not ready to share these stories prior to my (ongoing) interrogations of whiteness. I needed this time to more deeply engage with the stories of Indigenous and Indigenous-identified people and to converse with and reflect on my relationships with the ideas in this book. I believe the stories offer more insight now that they are "bookended" (quite literally) and interspersed with understandings gleaned from sociological *and* Indigenous studies literatures.

No stories, including the stories in the book, are static. Stories live and breathe and co-create meanings and identities and other crucial and consequential aspects of our realities. I am aware, however, of the potential harms caused by words set to paper, especially regarding Indigenous peoples, who often are portrayed in static, anachronistic ways, as if their communities and cultures were completely erased by settler colonialism. I am simultaneously aware of the violence in silence, the ruthless erasures of empty space and unwritten words and unknown, uncommemorated lives. In reflecting on my accountability to the people who told me their stories, I entertained numerous mental wrestling bouts between these two ideas—permanence and absence. Rather than give credence to this false dichotomy, I tried to attain balance while writing this book. I labored to exclude ideas and conversations potentially harmful to Indigenous people to whom I am accountable.

Further, not only are the ideas and conversations presented in the book impermanent because *change* is the only constant in all our lives, but the truths they convey are my versions of truths. I am the storyteller and the accounts in the book inevitably are grounded in *my* white-settler-trespasser-woman experiences. I cannot and do not speak for anyone but myself, and I ask readers to recognize that whatever insights might be gleaned from reading the book are "just a small part of things." I borrow these words from Bly, an Indigenous woman whose stories occupy pages in this book. In describing how Indigenous perspectives differ from white/settler perspectives, Bly (Sioux) said, "Spiritually speaking, we're only the size . . . of a mustard seed. That's the way you're supposed to think of yourself. . . . You're supposed to think of yourself as being little, little, just barely a small part of the whole world. . . . You're supposed to feel like you're just a small part of things." Each of us is "just a small part of things," yet how we relate to each other is everything.

Indians "off the Reservation"

When I began this project, my goal was to connect and work with NE Ohio Indigenous people on issues they defined as problematic. I was already participating in Native-led protests against the Cleveland MLB team's "Indians" mascotry, so I had some, albeit limited, understanding of two interrelated struggles local Indigenous people faced: (1) invisibility, which was complicated by (2) the inundation of NE Ohio space with caricatured, racialized Indianness. In time, I learned that caricatured Indianness is a problem that extends beyond the Cleveland baseball franchise into urban pan-Indian community spaces (unjustly) shared with people with tenuous Indian-identity claims. These struggles steal time, energy, and resources away from urban Indigenous people's primary concerns, which center on sustaining crucial relationships between Indigenous peoples and perspectives across time and space. This book is my effort to expose continuing impacts of settler-colonial structures and stories on urban Indigenous people's lives. My goal is to improve understandings of Indigenous people's realities in ways that increase settlers' accountability to Indigenous peoples and communities.

While the Cleveland MLB team's Indian mascotry foregrounds fictionalized Indianness in NE Ohio, Ohio's lack of Indian nations and reservations supports the illusion that "real" Indians live elsewhere. The presumed absence of Indians fits many Ohioans' understandings of where US Indigenous people live, e.g., in the past or on distant Indian reservations. In fact, approximately 75 percent of *enumerated* Indians— people who identify as American Indian or Alaska Native (AIAN) on the US Census—live off the reservation.[86] This book draws attention to this facet of contemporary indigeneity. When "off the reservation" first entered the US lexicon, it referred to Indians who were literally and *illegally* off the reservation. In the nineteenth century, being "Indian" and "off the reservation" was an offense punishable by death.[87] Federal authorities forcefully removed Indians—portrayed as godless enemies to civilization—from their homelands to remote reservations where they were expected to *stay* out of the way. People continue to use "off the reservation" today to mean "to break with one's party or group," "to engage in disruptive activity outside of normal bounds,"[88] or, as the Urban Dictionary defines it, (simply) "crazy." People using this phrase are ignorant of or ambivalent about its original meaning because the brutalities it evokes have been excised from settler-constructed histories. The current connotation inevitably reinforces settler-colonial notions about the "normal bounds" of Indianness. It dichotomizes space and constrains Indianness by distinguishing between "Indian" and "non-Indian" spaces.

According to Mishuana Goeman (Tonawanda Band of Seneca), professor of American Indian and gender studies, this spatial dichotomy became a "marker of 'Indian' identity" during Indian Relocation.[89] Indian Relocation is the federal program that brought Berta, the Lakota woman quoted at the start of this chapter, and her family to Cleveland. For most of her life, Berta resided in Cleveland, but when I asked Berta if she identified as an urban Indian, she responded, "I don't know. I always think, I *am* an urban Indian, but I don't want nobody calling me that, you know. Like, I always say, I'm not an urban Indian, I'm just an Indian. But I am an urban Indian, even though I know a lot of my culture and my ways of life. . . . So I'd rather be just an Indian, you know, even though I am an urban Indian." Throughout her life, Berta learned that Indians like herself, Indians who know their cultures and ways of life, cannot exist, cannot *be* Indian, in urban spaces. Yet Berta *was* Indian and she wanted people around her to recognize that. Berta's comments seem to indicate irreconcilable tensions between her experiences as an urban Indigenous woman and settler-colonial conceptions of space, but greater familiarity with Berta's stories, shared throughout the book, reveals the deep-rootedness of Berta's indigeneity *across* the spaces she occupies. This part of Berta's story, which Berta shared with other Indigenous residents of NE Ohio, is central to this book.

Berta remained connected to her tribal homeland, her family, her clan. She remembered stories passed on to her, and she passed stories on to her children and grandchildren. Such "continuous, ongoing storytelling," Goeman asserts, sustains Indigenous peoples, communities, and belief systems.[90] In *Mark My Words: Native Women Mapping Our Nations*, Goeman examines the published works of Native women poets and authors to elucidate how these Native women writers (re)map settler terrains. Such "(re)mapping is not just about regaining that which was lost and returning to an original and pure point in history," Goeman states, but rather, "understanding the processes that have defined our current spatialities in order to sustain vibrant Native futures."[91] The works of Native women authors, Goeman maintains, illustrate how "imaginative geographies" that resist settler-colonial constructions of space can provide Indigenous peoples and communities with new possibilities. Centering place-based knowledge and Indigenous stories empowers Indigenous peoples to develop and practice what Goeman calls "living traditions." Living traditions are perspectives and practices that emerge organically over time to account for the shifting needs of Indigenous communities impacted by still-enduring structures of settler colonialism. They are powerful means by which Indigenous peoples decolonize space *and* time. Struggles to "defy colonial categories," Goeman concludes, are not contained within particular spaces but rather are contained within Indigenous *stories* that bind "fragile, complex, and important relationships to each other."[92]

Collective Memories and Urban (Pan)Indianness in Northeast Ohio

This project elucidates how "continuous ongoing storytelling" sustains Indigenous memories, perspectives, and identities in an urban setting. It also explores the unique impacts of settler-colonial policies and remembrances on the day-to-day experiences of Indigenous residents of NE Ohio. It is an excavation of multilayered memories, stories, and histories that accumulate to form collective memories, sometimes called "cultural memories." *Collective memories* are recollections resulting from the "collectively shared experience and learning processes" of social groups.[93] Like all memories, they take shape at every level of society and are "susceptible to forgetting, distorting, forging, manipulating, and silencing."[94] At the structural level, governments and institutions have powerfully *imposed* upon entire populations memories "intended to homogenize . . . belief systems, to create national identity and unity, and to foster commonly shared interpretations of history."[95] In settler nations like the United States, the imposition of retooled histories disregarding US imperialism and colonialism reproduces and perpetuates colonial unknowing.

At the interactional level, collective memories are shared by members of smaller groups, or "mnemonic communities," composed of family and friendship networks or groups of people who occupy similar categories, comprise cohorts, and/or belong to certain organizations.[96] These memories, too, are filtered and distorted as they are repeatedly (but not precisely) recalled and reinterpreted in the specific contexts of people's lives. In family settings, for instance, people "remember" things they never experienced because they recall stories shared with them by parents, grandparents, siblings, aunts, uncles, cousins, etc. These shared memories become part of an individual's personal biography, and in turn, "an indispensable part of [their] social identity."[97] In other group settings, such as within cohorts or organizational settings, group members "celebrate and cultivate" collective memories as persons with similar *specific* experiences—for instance, American Indians who relocated from Indian reservations to metropolitan areas in the mid-twentieth century. In such cases, group members' experiences are "authentic and true from their point of view," but also partial and nongeneralizable.[98] Successful socialization in mnemonic communities creates jointly remembered memories—even when members do not jointly experience the remembered events. In a sense, an individual's "personal biography" fuses with "the history of the groups or communities to which [they] belong."[99] *Personalized* manifestations of a mnemonic community's *collective* memories, sociologist Eviatar Zerubavel warns, should not be confounded with a person's particularized remembrances.[100]

The organized communities to which Indigenous people in Northeast Ohio belong are *pan-Indian*, so this project also explores the effects of pan-Indianness on urban indigeneity. "Indian" is a label imposed on diverse Indigenous populations that vary across national and cultural dimensions. A multiplicity of Indigenous people's stories, memories, histories, identities, customs, spiritual beliefs, and political practices exists, yet processes of colonial unknowing amalgamate this diversity into a homogenized "Indian" indistinguishable from other Indians. Because Indigenous peoples are often haphazardly lumped into one undifferentiated group in US politics and popular culture, pan-Indianness is sometimes seen in a negative light. Only pan-Indian communities are viable in NE Ohio, however, due to the absence of federally recognized Indian nations as well as the pathways that brought Indigenous and Indigenous-identified people with different national and ethnic affiliations to the state. Despite drawbacks associated with homogenized Indianness, early scholarship about urban Indigenous people lauded pan-Indian organizations for providing support structures contributing to the well-being of *all* Indians, regardless of their national or ethnic identities. Moreover, the successes of the Red Power movement (discussed in the next chapter) illustrate the utility of pan-Indian collaborations for building and centralizing political power among previously differentiated groups. This project looks at whether and/or how two urban pan-Indian communities foster "complex and multilayered identities" among Northeast Ohio Indians (and Indian-identified people) who vary in regard to national and ethnic affiliation *and* with respect to how they became both "urban" and "Indian."

Two Pan-Indian Communities, Two Pathways to Urban Indian Identities

Two distinct pan-Indian (–identified) communities in Northeast Ohio—with meeting hubs located approximately forty miles apart—are central to this book. These "communities" are not specific geographic areas (e.g., neighborhoods or municipalities) with concentrated populations of Indigenous residents and businesses. Like other urban Indian communities, both communities are dispersed residentially, diverse socioeconomically, multicultural, and multigenerational.[101] Both communities sponsor tax-exempt 501c3 organizations to serve Indigenous, Indigenous-identified, and non-Indigenous members who live in or just beyond the vast Cuyahoga Valley region. I refer to these organizations as the "relocator" and "reclaimer"[102] communities because they provide regular meeting space and social, emotional, and material supports to their respective members, who, with a few exceptions, differ across two pathways to urban Indigenous identities–*relocation* and *reclamation*. Whereas members of the relocator community arrived in NE Ohio by means of relocation from Indian nations, members of the reclaimer community were already Ohio residents when they began working to reclaim Indigenous identities and practices. Relocators' and reclaimers' experiences differ in important ways, and their respective communities attempt to address the unique needs of the specific population served. Across community groups, many relocators and reclaimers are acquaintances who politely mingle at public events like powwows, but community crossover is rare. Following a description of each community's participants, I briefly explain my entrée into the field and data-collection efforts. I conclude this introductory chapter with a rough sketch of the remaining chapters of the book.

Relocator Community: Relocation Pathway

Elder members of the relocator community primarily arrived in Cleveland as youthful participants in the Indian Relocation Program (ca. 1956–1973). Elder relocators predominantly identify as "full-blood" Indians. They were initially socialized on Indian reservations to which they return occasionally for visits with family and friends. Though some relocators married other (relocated) Indians, many relocators married interracially and have multiracial families. A majority of relocator elders are enrolled in federally recognized Indian nations, but the percentage enrolled decreases with each successive generation. Despite many relocators possessing phenotypic traits associated with Indigenous people—e.g., dark hair, brown skin—relocators say they are rarely recognized as such. Instead, they are mistakenly categorized as Latinx or Asian by Ohio residents oblivious to the presence of Indigenous people in the region.

Relocator community elders and their multitribal, multiracial families, now four generations strong, remain a relatively close-knit (multiracial) pan-Indian community. Community members are like "family off the reservation," according to relocators, some of whom have known each other for half a century. For decades, the relocator community has sponsored activities like harvest dinners and powwows to immerse their children, grandchildren, and great-grandchildren in Indigenous (pan-Indian) culture and foster pride in their Indian identities. Continuity as Indigenous peoples is the community's first priority, followed by the eradication of stereotypical "Indian" imagery, which relocator adults see as particularly harmful to the self-esteem of Indigenous youth.

Reclaimer Community: Reclamation Pathway

Many members of this community are "mixed-blood" Indians primarily socialized into white/settler sociocultural norms in families with muted, hidden, and/or contested Indian pasts. Reclaimers are extremely diverse with respect to their distance from and knowledge of the long-standing Indigenous communities they claim. Their claims range from nebulous and unsubstantiated to genealogically traced, documented, and approved by tribal nations in which they are now enrolled. (Tribally enrolled reclaimers comprise a small minority of NE Ohio reclaimers.) Still other reclaimers, like the community's executive director, grew up identifying as Indian and can trace roots back to specific Indian territories, but remain unenrolled. Reclaimers are mostly disconnected from Indian reservations, but a few reclaimers have reservation-based adoptive kin who instruct them in "Indian ways." Reclaimers with phenotypic traits (stereotypically) associated with Indigenous people are exceptions to the general rule, and as a result, many reclaimers bemoan the "whitened" complexions that prevent people from recognizing them as Indians. Further, reclaimers are fully aware that some people, including other Indians (i.e., many relocators), discount their Indian identities. This reality is a consistent source of tension in some reclaimers' lives.

Almost all reclaimer community members choose Indian identities from a number of "ethnic options,"[103] but their investments in their identities vary drastically. Whereas a portion of reclaimers have symbolic Indian identities they admittedly assume or conceal as a matter of convenience, other reclaimers alter the patterns of their lives in efforts to learn and live according to "Indian ways." Because the community exists to support members of the latter group *and* "promote cultural awareness," it does not turn anyone away. As the director explained, "policing" Indianness would derail the organization's mission to serve dislocated and/or undocumented urban Indigenous people. Ousting ignorant individuals, despite their offensiveness, would undermine the community's mission to disrupt settler-constructed fantasies about Indigenous peoples. To accomplish its mission, the community assists people trying to connect with tribal nations of origin, hosts monthly meetings with educational keynote speakers, and sponsors workshops, powwows, and other activities that encourage members' participation in (pan-)Indian practices like crafting, drumming, and dancing. The community's most engaged members are deeply appreciative of the encouragement and assistance they receive from other reclaimers who understand their histories of dislocation and their struggles to fully inhabit their Indigenous identities.

Data Collection

I spent approximately two and a half years "in the field," meaning that I participated in the lives and community-based activities of relocator and reclaimer community members during this time frame. My entrée into the relocator community was through my initial acquaintance with a prominent relocator elder named Berta, whom I met in 2006. Berta (Lakota) led protests against Cleveland's Major League Baseball (MLB) franchise and its "Indians" imagery, and as a protest participant, I was invited to attend other relocator community events. By the time I initiated field observations for this research project in February 2008, I was familiar to many relocator community members, who knew me as a white woman, volunteer, and graduate student. That I did not claim Indigenous ancestry was crucial to my acceptance by the group. I continued to attend protests against the Cleveland MLB team and began attending the community's monthly administrative meetings (also run by Berta), fundraising events, powwow planning meetings and powwows, powwow dance classes for youth, and a number of formal and informal gatherings, including Easter egg hunts, back-to-school barbeques, harvest dinners, winter holiday parties, and spur-of-the-moment potlucks. I collected data in the relocator community until August 2010.

In July 2009, a little over one year into my data-collection efforts, a member of the relocator community—one who crossed the relocator-reclaimer divide because his job involved outreach to local Indigenous people—introduced me to the executive director of the reclaimer pan-Indian community. I participated in and observed this second community organization from July 2009 to August 2010. I gained entrée somewhat effortlessly, in large part because white people, like myself, are welcome participants in reclaimer community events. Community members not only welcomed me, but several individuals volunteered to teach me "Indian ways" so I could participate more fully. I politely declined, but such offers were aligned with the community's interest in sharing Indian perspectives and practices with anyone interested in learning about them. In this community, I attended monthly community meetings, drum practices, and crafting nights, in addition to the annual community powwow. Between June 2009 and August 2010, I also observed a number of Ohio pan-Indian powwows, events with Indigenous speakers, and multicultural fairs with Indigenous people present. Relocators and reclaimers often attended these events as well.

I also conducted formal interviews with Indian and Indian-identified residents of NE Ohio. Of these respondents, thirteen participated in the relocator community and eighteen participated in the reclaimer community. Interviews lasted between one and four hours and were conducted at locations selected by interview respondents, frequently their homes, but occasionally coffee shops and/or workplaces. During interviews, I participated in conversational dialogue with respondents and also encouraged respondents to discuss any relevant topics, whether or not I inquired about them. I digitally recorded and transcribed the interviews, which covered six broad topical areas, including early racial/ethnic/Indigenous experiences; family influences on racial/ethnic/Indigenous identity; current lifestyle and Native community practices; feelings about and identification with Indigenous people, communities, and nations; societal perceptions of US Indigenous peoples; and experiences with prejudice and/or discrimination.

Data Analysis

Throughout the data-collection process and for many years to follow, I analyzed the observational and interview data I collected. I wrote descriptive, analytic memos that enabled me to document and reflect on emergent themes and patterns in the data.[104] My early memos and reflections of my experiences were categorically sorted across three spaces—relocator community events, reclaimer community events, and (unaffiliated) powwows, multicultural fairs, and other Ohio events featuring Native people and/or highlighting Native issues. Over time, I progressively incorporated comparative analyses into my memo writing, specifically comparing and contrasting relocators' and reclaimers' unique community formations and identity experiences. Though I transcribed the interviews, I also listened to each interview numerous times to avoid missing verbal cues and other conversational nuances. Coding the data enabled me to develop themes able to elucidate patterns and relationships discussed throughout the book.

Identity Conundrums and Identity Contestation

Throughout the book I use generalizations to describe either reloca-tors or reclaimers, *but with a crucial caveat*: the relocator and reclaimer categories are convenient but crude designations. Similar historical circumstances draw participants to either the relocator or reclaimer com-munity, but more arbitrary criteria (e.g., county of residence) are also factors. Participants' stories, memories, histories, and experiences diverge and converge both within and across each community's fuzzy boundar-ies. This fluidity elucidates the quandary of urban Indian identities.

The interconnections between social (interpersonal) and structural identities, collective memories, and "official" settler histories make In-digenous identities messy and intensely meaningful at the same time. Individuals' social identities, or senses of self, develop in interactions with others. Identities are fundamentally relational because they shift and change over time as individuals negotiate their in-group and out-group statuses in an infinite number of possible social groupings. Each social group—whether comprised at the interactional or structural level—is a mnemonic community with collective memories elucidating a shared past that differentiates them from other groups. This "active past," com-posed of serial reinterpretations of group members' (imperfect) recollec-tions, forms group members' identities.[105] The grandchildren of Indians who participated in the Indian Relocation Program, for instance, "re-member" this aspect of their histories because their grandparents and parents shared stories of relocation with them. Because memory is "a central . . . medium through which identities are constituted,"[106] this collective memory is integral to all family members' Indian identities—whether or not they directly experienced relocation. Memories of relo-cation, in other words, differentiate *relocated* Indian families from *other* Indian families who continue to live or never lived on Indian reservations.

The external validation of individuals' identities within familial and other intimate contexts does not guarantee external validation in other social realms. In social interactions, people negotiate definitions of *self* and *other* through assessments of "fit" into a range of socially recogniz-able categorical identities.[107] These categorical appraisals are *contextually variable* because people's assessments of "fit" depend on their exposure to information embedded in (constructed) memories, stories, and histo-ries. In the United States, white settler society is inundated with images that construct Indians as prehistoric and unsophisticated, and therefore, absent from modern metropolitan society.[108] These durable images, em-bedded in US residents' shared memories, stories, and histories, create ignorance about and ambivalence and even hostility toward urban In-digenous people who do not conform to expectations.

Contestation, however, is "at the center of both memory and iden-tity,"[109] and US Indigenous peoples resist settler society by creating countermemories that challenge settler discourses. This "memory work" is simultaneously "identity work" that resists negative labels and asserts Indigenous definitions of indigeneity.[110] When Indigenous people *col-lectively* fight for their stories and reinterpretations of the past, collective memories[111] and collective identities[112] emerge. Effective collective mo-bilization, which can occur at the structural and/or interactional levels, is dependent on *boundary work* that establishes meaningful distinctions between in-group and out-group members.[113] At the structural level, the successes of the Red Power Movement elucidate the benefits of US In-digenous peoples organizing across tribal affiliations to construct shared, pan-Indian memories and identities. This *expansion* of the boundaries of Indianness—i.e., the creation of a boundary distinguishing between *all* "Indians" and *all* "non-Indians"—enabled US Indigenous peoples to claim more political power. At the interactional level, members of dif-ferent Indigenous and Indigenous-identified groups—such as members of the relocator and reclaimer communities in NE Ohio—may choose to highlight *dissimilarities* between groups' collective memories, sto-ries, and histories. The distinctive boundary-making strategies of the relocator and reclaimer communities amplify differences between each community's members. Importantly, in NE Ohio and beyond, *who* is included in group categories is never fixed and boundary work is never complete because "the boundaries of difference are continually reposi-tioned in relation to different points of reference."[114]

Central to this book is elucidation of how numerous *axes* or *intersec-tions* of Indian identities create unique reference points that shift group boundaries and create different collective memories, identities, and mobilization strategies. In this chapter, urban residence is highlighted as one intersection of Indian identity. That this book is about Indigenous and Indigenous-identified residents of Northeast Ohio is important because unique urban environments have local power structures that differently construct memories, stories, and histories that, in turn, differently impact Indian identity experiences. How many Indians live in a place, how long Indians lived in that place, why Indians live there, and whether they have faraway or nearby reservation homes to which they sometimes return also contribute to shifting narratives in ways that matter for Indian collectivities, collective memories, and identities. Finally, pathway to urban Indian identities—relocation or reclamation—is an important intersection explored throughout the book because it enables deeper understanding of the damaging consequences of settler-constructed histories for contemporary Indigenous peoples, families, communities, and societies. In the next chapter, I delve into three more intersections of Indian identity that impact experiences of indigeneity in NE Ohio and beyond: nation, race, and ethnicity.

Book Outline

The book proceeds as follows. Chapter 1 explores three critical intersections of Indian identities, including nation, race, and ethnicity. It outlines various reasons for intense contestation over who rightfully claims Indian identities in an era of Indian ethnic reclamation. It also elucidates shortcomings of conceptual approaches to indigeneity in Indigenous studies and sociological scholarship. Whereas the former's focus on cultural continuity diminishes the complexity of contemporaneous indigeneity, the latter's focus on race and racialization dismisses the continuity of settler-colonial structures in US society. Combining these foci is necessary to understand the experiences of Indigenous people in NE Ohio.

Chapters 2 and 3 highlight three stories of relocation and three stories of reclamation, respectively. These stories elucidate the experiences and perspectives of people who are habitually invisibilized: Indians off the reservation. The specific stories represent a range of experiences of the NE Ohio region's Indian and Indian-identified residents. They reveal the vagaries of different routes to urban Indian identities and provide insights into how reservation-based Indians became urban and how urban NE Ohio residents became Indian and/or Indian-identified.

Chapters 4 and 5 show how different routes to urban Indian identities result in different experiences of urban Indian identity. Chapter 4 explores what it means to *be* Indian to first-generation relocators, who refer to earlier, reservation-based experiences of poverty and discrimination when describing their Indigenous identities and perspectives. The same chapter delves into reclaimer adults' experiences of *becoming* Indian, a phenomenon spurred by intuitive feelings and assisted by Indigenous mentors. Spirituality, important to both relocators and reclaimers, is also discussed in chapter 4. Chapter 5 looks at how NE Ohio Indians learn to *act* Indian across the reclamation and relocation pathways to urban Indian identities. Reclaimers commit themselves to learning specific Indigenous practices and passing them on to their children. Relocators, on the other hand, have more fluid understandings of how Indians should act and focus on passing Indigenous values on to their children. The impact of Indian stereotypes on young relocators' identity development is also explored. Finally, chapter 5 discusses the importance of powwows as critical sites for socializing urban Indian children.

Chapters 6 and 7 look at how two pan-Indian communities in Northeast Ohio collectively negotiate the distinct troubles members experience as either relocators or reclaimers. Chapter 6 explores relocators' resistance to false memories and images of Indianness propagated by the Cleveland MLB team and white/settler "pretendians" who claim Indianness. Many relocators accuse reclaimers of being "wannabe" Indians whose actions harm Indigenous people living in the region. Reclaimers, in contrast, maintain that invalidation of their Indian identities by the people around them, including other Indians and family members, complicates their lives. Chapter 7 elucidates the strategic boundary work engaged by Northeast Ohio's urban, pan-Indian communities. The creation of community "comfort zones" by expanding (reclaimers) or contracting (relocators) group boundaries—meaning, regulating who has access and/or is welcome to participate in the respective communities—is discussed, as well as how these different strategies create unique problems.

The conclusion highlights key findings from the book and concludes with a few suggestions for honoring the stories, memories, histories, and realities of US Indigenous peoples.

1

Toward a More "Sophisticated" Sociology of Complex Urban Indian Identities

Nation, race, and ethnicity are differently emphasized by Indigenous and Indigenous-identified people living in Northeast Ohio. These categorical identities, constructed to delineate boundaries between human populations, are also differently prioritized by Indigenous studies and sociology scholars. As with all social constructs, their interpretations and implications shift and change as people and societies negotiate their meanings. Deceptively distinct yet irrevocably entangled, these categories overlap and intersect to produce complicated Indian identities. These categories remain significant to Indigenous people today, but their settler-colonial origins also make them contentious. Accordingly, understanding their historical roots is necessary to appreciating the stories, memories, and histories that culminate in complex collective urban Indian identities.

Nationhood

Native nationhood (peoplehood, tribal sovereignty) is a "critical site of identity and struggle for Indian people,"[1] and therefore a focal point of much academic and political discourse on Indian affairs. Federally recognized Indian tribes are *sovereign* political entities operating (not entirely) independently of the US government due to hundreds of "treaties" purportedly negotiated between the United States and tribal nations between 1778 and 1871. I use scare quotes to indicate the suspect nature of what Donna Akers (Choctaw) calls "sham treaties"[2] almost exclusively "procured through corrupt and dishonorable practices sanctioned by the highest levels of US government."[3] US treaty making, Akers cogently explains, "was clearly a major tool of conquest wherein no behavior was too low, no tactic too dishonorable, as long as the goals of cheating the Indigenous peoples out of their lands and wealth and the infliction of abject poverty and subjugation were achieved."[4]

Following this "treaty period," the Supreme Court of the United States (SCOTUS) issued numerous rulings to clarify the complicated relationship between the United States and Indian nations, which are neither states nor foreign countries. By declaring the United States the overriding sovereign and giving Congress "plenary" or *absolute* power over Indian nations, SCOTUS profoundly limited Indian nations' autonomy. Though immune to state authority, tribes are "domestic dependent nations"[5] lacking powers to develop militaries, mint currencies, or enter into government-to-government relations with foreign entities. This unique status, also referred to as "quasi" or "permeated" sovereignty, stems from Native nations' "precontact existence as free and independent peoples Indigenous to the continent."[6] This status also explains the dual citizenship of members of *federally recognized* Indian nations, who are citizens of their tribal nations *and* the United States.

Native nationhood is a priority issue for Indigenous people because sovereignty empowers Indian nations to maintain their stories, memories, histories, and territories. Importantly, sovereign Indian nations also have the power to determine their own membership boundaries, delimiting in-group from out-group members through established citizenship criteria. The various metrics used to establish tribal citizenship in different Indian nations are contested, due (at least in part) to deep entanglements between US efforts to *racialize* Indigenous peoples and Indigenous nations' efforts to exert and protect their sovereignty in the context of ongoing settler-state colonialism. Before exploring some of these variations, it is important to understand the conflation of Indigenous peoples' national and racial identifications in US settler society.

Essentialist notions of "race" are central to the organization of groups of people into hierarchies in settler-colonial societies. "Racialization" refers to social and political processes used to create otherwise arbitrary boundaries around groups to justify their subjugation.[7] These arbitrary boundaries are constructed on the basis of meaningless "racial" characteristics like skin color, hair texture, and face shape, and are believed (wrongly) to influence the abilities and preferences of racialized group members. The racialization of US Indigenous peoples, deeply rooted in the colonial formations of the US settler state, continues in the twenty-first century. Racializing images and stories still depict Indigenous peoples as less intelligent, less civilized, and less *human* than white settler populations. They also create erroneous understandings of Indigenous peoples as homogeneous *across tribal citizenship groups*, leading most US residents to think of Indians as a singular "race" of people. In fact, people subsumed under the label "American Indian" are citizens of different tribal nations, hail from different geographic regions, speak different languages, have different spiritual beliefs, and practice different cultural customs. American Indians are tribal citizens *first* because they are members of self-determining Native nations.[8] Race-based identification is a secondary meaning system imposed by a US settler-colonial state intentionally obfuscating and reimagining Indigenous peoples' histories to disguise the sovereign status of Native nations. In the next section on racialized understandings of Indigenous identities, I more thoroughly discuss how US racializing projects continue to blur boundaries between nation and race.

Race

The US government consistently has deployed racializing ideas about Indians to justify settler appropriation of Indigenous lands. Through intentional manipulation of Indigenous representations, for instance, President Andrew Jackson convinced Congress to pass the Indian Removal Act (1830). This act enabled Jackson to remove eastern Indian nations from their homelands to reservations west of the Mississippi River. Jackson couched Indian Removal as an act of US benevolence (rather than US expansionism) by claiming that childlike Indians needed federal protection from land-hungry white settlers. The devastating facts of Indian Removal clearly elucidate the outrageous sophistry of this paternalistic claim. Though (ill-begotten) treaties ratified at this time detailed how Indian homelands would be allocated to whites, they did not describe how Indians would be removed or treated during their migrations to western reservations.[9] This and other aspects of Indian Removal—such as the passionate appeals of many US Congress members who argued on behalf of Indigenous peoples' rights to remain on their homelands—are carefully shrouded in settler-constructed histories of this era.

Government authorities were more interested in saving money than saving Indians, and as a result, removal was chaotic and deadly. Thousands of Indigenous men, women, and children died from hunger, thirst, disease, and exposure to the elements during forced westward migrations. The Cherokee "Trail of Tears" is the best known of these forced migrations, but it is only one of many migration stories. The US government ratified nearly seventy removal "treaties," many *despite* the protestations of tribal leaders,[10] and approximately fifty thousand Indians were forcibly removed to territories west of the Mississippi during Jackson's presidency.[11] Though neglected in most historical accounts of Indian Removal, countless Indians refused to leave their homelands.[12] For instance, as many as four thousand Choctaw Indians remained in the Southeast after removal.[13] Members of the Eastern Band of Cherokee claim direct descendancy from Cherokee Indians who defied removal—those "who were able to hold on to the land, hide in the mountains, or eventually return to Western North Carolina."[14] Because the Eastern Band of Cherokee is a federally recognized Indian nation, tribal members' collective stories and memories of hiding are accepted as legitimate.[15] Similar stories divulged by unrecognized groups or individuals, however, are less well received. This phenomenon provides a backstory for some people (re)claiming Indian identities in Northeast Ohio.

After removal, the United States again broke promises to protect Indian lands from white encroachment. Federal authorities commenced the "allotment period" of US-Indian relations (1887–1934), which enabled the United States to appropriate ninety million more acres of land from approximately one hundred thousand Indians.[16] This land grab was accomplished by partitioning Indian lands into individual agricultural plots divvied out to Indians who met arbitrary and fluctuating criteria. Federal officials made the remaining lands available to whites. The Dawes Act of 1887, which kick-started the allotment period, was much more than a land grab, however. It disrupted Indigenous lifeways and implemented a new strategy for racializing Indians.

The Dawes Act institutionalized the notion of Indianness as something innate or inherent within the *blood* of Indian people. Indians could not receive their individual agricultural plots until their names and blood quanta were recorded on census rolls, also called base rolls and, in one particular case, the Dawes Rolls. Blood quantum presumably measures an Indian's biological ancestry and is reported as a proportion. If an Indian has only Indian ancestors, for instance, their proportion, or "degree of Indian blood," is four-fourths. They are considered "full-blood" Indian. Indians with any degree of blood that is *not* Indian are frequently called "mixed-blood" Indians. Their supposed mix of blood is calculated according to what is *believed* to be their biological inheritance based on everything known about their ancestors, starting with an ancestor listed on a base roll. An Indian whose only non-Indian ancestor is a grandparent, for instance, is considered three-fourths Indian. If this Indian with three-fourths blood quantum has children with an Indian with one-eighth blood quantum, their children are deemed to have seven-sixteenths blood quantum. As scholar Kim Tallbear (Sisseton Wahpeton Oyate) asserts, it is critical to remember that these "fractions on paper" have nothing to do with the actual "physiological substance" of blood.[17]

This utterly complex and thoroughly essentializing measure of Indianness was instigated by a US government that benefited from reducing the number of Indians who qualified for the few protections and entitlements guaranteed by treaties. As Eva Garroutte (Cherokee) notes in *Real Indians: Identity and the Survival of Native America*, "The ultimate and explicit federal intention was to use the blood quantum standard as a means to liquidate tribal lands and to eliminate government trust responsibility to tribes, along with entitlement programs, treaty rights, and reservations. Through intermarriage and application of a biological definition of identity, Indians would eventually become citizens indistinguishable from all other citizens."[18]

Mixed Meanings, Mixed-Bloods

Despite the complexity and colonial roots of blood quantum, many Native nations continue to use blood quantum criteria to determine citizenship. In a comparison of 2018 tribal citizenship boundaries,[19] Desi Rodriguez-Lonebear (Northern Cheyenne and Chicana) discovered that approximately 59 percent of recognized Indian nations in her sample of 286 (of 347) federally recognized Indian nations in the contiguous forty-eight states still use blood quantum.[20] How tribes use blood quantum varies,[21] but the most common threshold for citizenship, one-quarter blood, is used by 40 percent of Indian nations in Rodriguez-Lonebear's sample. This research, which provides a much-needed update to prior work in this area,[22] indicates increasing variation in citizenship criteria across Native nations, overall declines in the use of blood quantum, and correlations between citizenship criteria and structural features of tribal nations (i.e., geography, size, governance capability, and gaming operations). Tribal nations in the western United States, for instance, are more likely to use blood quantum–based citizenship criteria than tribal nations in other regions of the country.

Whether and how Indian nations use blood quantum is highly contested. Some scholars suggest that blood quantum criteria evince colonial race thinking that contradicts traditional modes of tribal incorporation and diminishes Indigenous populations.[23] They maintain that blood quantum computations lack validity because the starting point for calculating someone's degree of Indian blood is often a base roll created by US government officials during the allotment era.[24] Moreover, the federal government *still* has trouble obtaining accurate counts of the US Indigenous population, so base rolls compiled at the turn of the twentieth century are unquestionably imprecise. Federal agents no doubt failed to document the names and blood quanta of countless Indians, including those who refused to comply with federal dictates and intentionally avoided enumeration. People (re)claiming Indigenous identities sometimes reference this phenomenon to support their identity claims.

Interestingly, Eva Garroutte (Cherokee) reports that thousands of white people with "homesteading ambitions" in Oklahoma bribed enumerators to place their names on Indian census rolls. The descendants of these "five-dollar Indians" potentially retain access to Indian identities and entitlements.[25] Even nonexistent people are listed on federal rolls; in an amusing case of inaccurate documentation, Lakota Indians seeking additional rations exploited the census system by getting back in line "to be enumerated a second time using fictitious and rather imaginative names." Translated from Lakota, these colorful (albeit crude) names included "Dirty Prick," "Bad Cunt," and "Shit Head." Census takers were oblivious to the Indians' shenanigans.[26]

Other scholars insist that more nuanced analyses are needed to understand the intricacies of blood-based boundary making. Kim Tallbear (Sisseton Wahpeton Oyate), author of *Native American DNA: Tribal Be-*

longing and the False Promise of Genetic Science,[27] argues that Native nations reliant on blood-based citizenship metrics are not passive victims of colonial race thinking. To the contrary, Tallbear and numerous others[28] point out that Native people have always referenced blood as symbolic of belongingness in tribal communities. Some blood talk within tribal communities may be biologically deterministic, Tallbear acknowledges, but "the counting of relatives and establishing a genealogical connection to them is also clearly at play in our blood talk." Tallbear continues:

> The language of blood and blood fractions . . . is shorthand for what we know is a far more complicated story of our lineages. When I cite those fractions, I think of my grandparents and great-grandparents. I remember their names and their parents' and grandparents' names. I remember how, through both dispossession and restricted choices, they came to be on the particular reservations now denoted in my blood-quantum fractions. These are relatives whose stories have been passed down to me, sometimes from their own mouths. I am not alone in Indian Country in this practice of accounting.[29]

Tallbear admits that blood-based boundaries are imperfect. Blood quantum calculations are bureaucratically messy, expensive, and imprecise. Yet, so-called decolonized metrics like cultural competence, according to Tallbear, displace understandings of US Indigenous peoples as citizens of sovereign Indian nations *first*. Culture, she argues, is *not* a proxy for citizenship.

More than blood symbolism keeps Indigenous nations tied to blood quantum citizenship metrics, however. The passage of the Indian Reorganization Act (IRA) in 1934 (also called the Wheeler-Howard Act) initiated the coerced reorganization of Indigenous nations. Native nations received federal subsidies to establish governments and adopt governing styles that mimicked US/settler political regimes. IRA policies redefined reservation lands as tribal homelands and required tribes to enumerate their populations and establish membership criteria.[30] The federal government, unsurprisingly, coerced numerous tribal nations into modifying their proposed criteria and implementing relatively exclusive citizenship standards that fit settler assumptions and US priorities regarding Indians.[31]

The federal government maintained the right to determine whether or not to *recognize* the sovereignty of tribal nations. Currently, more than 570 Indian nations have federal recognition. This number steadily increases as tribes successfully negotiate the federal-recognition process. This process requires proof of "tribes' status as distinct political communities with ties to precontact aboriginal peoples."[32] These ties, described as "race" in *United States v. Montoya* (1901) and "lineage" in *United States v. Sandoval* (1913), recognize Indigenous peoples' historical connections to territories now claimed by the United States. Proof of descent, or *ancestry*, therefore, is foundational to tribal sovereignty as it is defined by the US settler state. Ancestry (which can be documented) is not the same as race (which is socially constructed), but racialized understandings of indigeneity continue to impact Indigenous peoples' sovereignty in myriad ways. In the paragraphs below, I provide specific examples regarding (1) the determination of citizenship criteria on the Flathead Reservation, and (2) the defense of sovereign rights affirmed by the Indian Child Welfare Act (ICWA) in US courts, to elucidate tensions between national and racial identities caused by the continuing racialization of Indigenous peoples in US settler society. Innumerable examples exist, but I chose these instances due to their comprehensibility.

With respect to citizenship criteria, anthropologist Theresa O'Nell offers a straightforward analysis of the impacts of colonization and racialization on the Flathead Nation's tribal enrollment policies.[33] The Confederated Salish and Kootenai tribes of the Flathead Reservation in Montana constitute a federally recognized tribe. When O'Nell conducted fieldwork on the reservation in the late twentieth century, the population was predominantly white, with non-Indians outnumbering tribal members five to one.[34] This imbalance resulted from the US Congress's passage of the 1904 Flathead Allotment Act, which, despite strong opposition from the tribe, reorganized Flathead communal lands into individual allotments. The so-called land surplus was awarded to white homesteaders through a lottery.

Over time, high rates of intermarriage between tribal members and white people compromised previously rigid divisions between the reservation's Indian and white populations—though segregation ensured better access to resources (like jobs) to whites. Federal officials argued that Flathead Indians "were already 'white,'" and therefore, no longer a *distinct* political community warranting sovereignty. Exclusive enrollment policies like blood quantum requirements did not align with Flathead values, but the nation needed to defend itself against federal threats of termination by constructing "a more purely 'Indian' membership" in terms dictated by whites/settlers. Flathead enrollment polices have since oscillated "between poles of exclusivity and inclusivity that reflect the waxing and waning of the threat of legal annihilation . . . posed by the federal government." Today Flathead enrollment policies remain rather exclusive, with one-quarter blood quantum and lineal descent necessary for enrollment for people born after May 4, 1960. "Even though the era of overtly terminationist policy may have come to an end," O'Nell explains, "the historical weight of treaty violations, betrayal, and racism is never far from [Flathead] consciousness."

The next example, regarding challenges to the Indian Child Welfare Act (ICWA), also elucidates continuing encroachments on Indigenous peoples' sovereign rights due to racialized understandings of indigeneity.[35] The ICWA, passed in 1978, sets minimum standards for handling cases of child abuse, neglect, or adoption involving Native children. It was created in response to "alarmingly high" numbers of Native children being placed in non-Native foster and adoptive families. In addition to protecting "the best interest of Indian children," the act also aims to "promote the stability and security of Indian tribes and families." In short, the ICWA protects Native nations from being divested of members necessary to tribal survival.

Opponents of the ICWA argue that requirements for tribal citizenship (broadly), e.g., lineage and blood quantum, are *race*-based, making tribal members *racial* rather than *political* actors. In turn, they argue that ICWA protections are unconstitutional because they violate the Equal Protection Clause of the Fourteenth Amendment, which protects against racial and other forms of discrimination. Because Indian children are racially defined, ICWA opponents argue, their ineligibility for adoption by non-Indians is racially discriminatory. Under the ICWA, however, Indian children are treated differently not on the basis of race but rather *on the basis of eligibility for tribal membership*, over which tribal nations have sole authority. Nonetheless, numerous courts, including SCOTUS, have crafted exceptions to ICWA, suggesting that a child's ancestry is too "remote" (despite *descent* being the only tribal citizenship requirement in this case) or that a child's parents are too "assimilated" (despite the fact that culture is not synonymous with citizenship) to qualify for ICWA protections. As legal scholar Sarah Krakoff shrewdly observes, these exceptions "replicate the very circumstance the Act aimed to redress: that of non-Indians, and state courts in particular, passing judgment on the validity of Native identity and culture."[36] Krakoff concludes that "equal protection" attacks on the ICWA result from understandings of tribes as *racial* rather than *national* groups, and thereby exemplify "the eliminationist structure of racism against Native peoples."[37]

The racialization of indigeneity and regulation of Indigenous identities by the US settler state continue to obfuscate and complicate Indigenous people's experiences as citizens of tribal nations. Federal control over Indianness disrupted traditional organizational structures and ways of relating within and among Indigenous communities. Further, the US settler state continues to exert political and economic power over (semi)sovereign tribal nations, which perpetually "wrestle" with "the reality of ongoing colonial encroachment," and thereby, realize the need to "assert some sort of boundary" distinguishing tribal citizens from whites/settlers.[38] Native nations fear losing "the last vestiges of Native distinctiveness, the last defense against the colonizing culture,"[39] and consequently are compelled to utilize what scholar Gayatri Spivak calls "strategic essentialism"—"the useful yet semimournful position of the unavoidable usefulness of something that is dangerous."[40] Importantly, however, Indigenous peoples continuously resist colonial definition, as Rodriguez-Lonebear's work, which demonstrates increasing variation in tribal citizenship metrics and decreasing utilization of blood quantum, elucidates.

Ethnicity

The entanglements between Indian nationhood and Indian race already produce complicated Indian identities. *Ethnicity*, another intersection of Indianness, muddles matters further. Through a dynamic, ever-evolving process, ethnic identities are both internally crafted by stories, memories, and histories and externally constructed by social, economic, and political processes. The Indian Reorganization Act, for example, reorganized Indigenous communities into tribal political units that are now central to Indigenous peoples' (social) *ethnic* identities. As a result,

Indigenous peoples' national and ethnic identities frequently overlap. This overlap does not exist for white/settler Americans, whose national identities as US citizens are generally unrelated to the myriad ethnicities they claim.

Many US Americans' conflated understandings of race and ethnicity, in fact, parallel earlier (mid-twentieth century) sociological and anthropological treatments of the ethnicity concept, which conflated it with race and thought of it as culture. The concept was primarily applied to the incorporation (assimilation) of white European immigrants into US society. As a result, sociologists Michael Omi and Howard Winant suggest that these earlier "ethnicity theories of race" "regard[ed] racial status as more voluntary and consequently less imposed, less 'ascribed.'" Many white/settler Americans, in turn, reduced race-and-ethnicity "to something like a preference, something variable and chosen," like a cultural orientation or lifestyle adaptation. This understanding of race-as-ethnicity ignores consequential "corporeal markers of identity," like skin color, and "downplay[s] questions of descent, kinship, and ancestry."[41] This reductive perspective fell out of favor with 1960s-era social scientists trying to understand the distinct struggles of *racially* defined, colonized groups, like black, Latinx, and Indigenous peoples.

The earlier interpretation of the ethnicity concept did not lose its power, however, because it was adopted by neoconservatives, who use it to defend individualism, colorblindness, and multiculturalism.[42] It also remains entrenched in whitestream US culture, and therefore provides some insight into exponential increases in the number of people who previously identified as white but later claimed Indian ethnic identities. For many continuously identified Indigenous people, claims to indigeneity unanchored in long-standing Indigenous communities are nonsensical because, from their perspectives, Indigenous identities are always grounded in *relationships* to kinfolk, clans, community members, tribal nations, and environments.[43] Claiming to be part of a community that does not *also* claim you does not cohere with deeply engrained Indigenous perspectives and practices. Yet, the number of people claiming American Indian and Alaska Native (AIAN) identities rose exponentially in the last half-century—a phenomenon driven by the identity claims of people *without* connections to long-standing Indigenous communities.[44]

In *American Indian Ethnic Renewal: Red Power and the Resurgence of Identity and Culture*, sociologist Joane Nagel (1996) documents wild demographic shifts in the enumerated American Indian and Alaska Native population in the twentieth century. Historians and epidemiologists estimate that anywhere from ten million to more than one hundred million people lived on the American continents prior to European contact.[45] Disease, slavery, war, starvation, forced relocation, and other brutal settler-colonial actions reduced the Indigenous population to less than a quarter-million people by the end of the nineteenth century. In the 1930s, the population of Indigenous people in the United States began to increase—somewhat slowly at first, then quite rapidly. The AIAN population increased 46 percent between 1950 and 1960 (from 357,499 to 523,591),[46] another 51 percent between 1960 and 1970 (from 523,591 to 792,730), and a whopping 72 percent between 1970 and 1980 (from 792,730 to more than 1.3 million), before nearly doubling *again* between 1980 and 1990 (from one to two million people). Traditional explanations of population growth—like immigration, declining morbidity, and increased birth rates—cannot account for these high rates of change. The only feasible explanation, then, is identity change—specifically, people previously identified as non-Indian shifting their self-definitions and ethnic identifications to Indian.[47]

Nagel and others partially attribute these AIAN demographic shifts to the popularity of the American Indian Movement (AIM) and other Red Power groups. AIM, founded in Minneapolis, Minnesota, in 1968, became a hub for progressive urban Indian activists who organized across tribal differences. They focused on commonalities in their stories, memories, and histories to strategically resist their oppression in the US settler state. By raising urban Indigenous people's consciousness of their collective identities and shared concerns, AIM helped foster the growth of pan-Indian communities in cities across the United States. In addition to creating new pan-Indian institutions and practices by borrowing and blending Indigenous and urban cultural forms, pan-ethnic community organizing enabled urban Indigenous people to amass the political power needed to call attention to their stories, assert counter-memories, and demand action on Indigenous issues.[48] A critical legacy of the Red Power movement was increased funding from the federal government for social services, educational programs, and health clinics in Indigenous communities.

Though initially focused on the plight of urban Indigenous people, in time the Red Power movement focused on tribal nations' concerns. In addition to drawing national attention to Indigenous peoples' sovereignty struggles, the movement's shift in emphasis increased urban Indians' awareness of the importance of *tribal* membership and political participation. Many relocated urban Indians who previously were separated from kin and culture found their way back to urban Indian communities. Participating in pan-ethnic Indigenous communities, in turn, supported community members' reconnections to their tribal nations of origin.[49]

Despite the benefits of pan-Indian mobilization, critics alleged that Red Power activism misrepresented Indigenous peoples and their needs. Some traditionalists on Indian reservations, for instance, accused movement members of being "too urban to speak and act on the behalf of Indian people."[50] Others suggested that Red Power activists were not "real Indians" and their tactics did not represent "the Indian way."[51] Such accusations were rooted in fears that "city raised Indians," who did not behave or think in "distinctly Indian" ways, endangered Indigenous peoples' distinctiveness and ultimately threatened tribal sovereignty.[52]

One outcome of publicity garnered by Red Power activism was reinvigoration of the Indigenous identities of urban Indians somewhat recently removed from Indigenous families still living in (explicitly) Indigenous territories. Another outcome was the enchantment of (previously) non-Indigenous-identified people with Indianness. Red Power movement activism peaked in the 1960s and 1970s, but the enumerated AIAN population *continued* to grow, doubling *again* between 1990 and 2000 (from two to four million people) and steadily increasing well into the twenty-first century.[53] Identity change remains the primary explanation, but more recent demographic data reveal important distinctions between newly identified ("new") and previously identified ("old") Indians. Old Indians are more likely to report a single ancestry and tribal affiliation. They are also more likely to speak an Indigenous language and live in a rural area, in an Indian household, in a state with historically high numbers of AIAN.[54] Using linked data from Census 2000, Census 2010, and the 2006–2010 American Community Survey, demographers Carolyn Liebler, Renuka Bhaskar, and Sonya Porter demonstrate that old Indians also identify as Indians *consistently* over time, distinguishing them from other people who have *ever* claimed AIAN identities on the census. Their research shows that American Indians enumerated in one decade are not the same people enumerated in previous or future decades; rather, people consistently join and leave the AIAN group. The AIAN population is constantly "churning," in other words, and people who have ever identified as AIAN are more likely to engage in racial switching than members of other racial groups.[55]

Contested Indians and Access to Critical Resources

Who are these "new" Indians and why do their identities matter? That depends on who you ask. In a study of Indian reclaimers in the US South, sociologist Kathleen Fitzgerald[56] suggests that Indian identity reclamation by phenotypically white people with Indian ancestries positively impacts Indigenous communities by increasing their visibility and contesting racial stereotypes.[57] Moreover, Fitzgerald maintains that reclaimers' blurring of racial boundaries challenges racialized power structures. On the other end of the spectrum is Michael Lambert, a Cherokee anthropologist, who insists that claiming Indian identity "on any basis other than sovereignty" is antithetical to Indian causes.[58] To Lambert, anyone identifying as Indian who is not recognized as a member of a sovereign Indian nation is both illegitimate and damaging to "real" Indians addressing "real" Indian concerns like sovereignty.

Circe Sturm,[59] a Choctaw-descended sociologist who studied what she calls "race shifting" with respect to Cherokee identities, maintains that the *context* of Indian ethnic reclamation affects the *extent* to which Indian identification matters. Sturm states that her "citizen Cherokee"[60] friends are not particularly alarmed by *individuals* opting for Indian identities, but they believe self-identified *groups* of Indians "asserting tribal status and seeking federal or state recognition" are concerning.[61] Federal recognition is difficult to attain, but requirements for state recognition are less stringent, and the number of state-recognized tribes is growing.[62] The existence of more state tribes, Sturm notes, creates competition for federally recognized tribes trying to access state and federal resources. Additionally, state recognition affords legal rights otherwise unavailable to (federally) *un*recognized people, such as the right to sell wares under the Indian Arts and Crafts Act, passed in 1990 to protect recognized Indigenous people from being undercut by non-Indigenous vendors selling inauthentic goods.

As Indigenous studies scholars clearly articulate, perpetual claims to Indigenous lands, resources, and identities by white people are undergirded by "white possessive logics" of US settler colonialism.[63] Indigenous rights and entitlements, reserved for recognized members of sovereign Indian nations *on the basis of sovereignty*, are too frequently claimed by "ethnic frauds" and "pretendians" whose whiteness already grants them structural benefits in US society. Sturm provides examples of threats to the assets and well-being of Cherokee peoples, but this phenomenon impacts sovereign Indian nations across the United States. Investigative journalists at the *Los Angeles Times*, for instance, tracked contracts awarded by the Small Business Administration (SBA) to American Indian–owned businesses.[64] As minority-owned businesses, Indian businesses are exempt from contract limits imposed on other companies. The *Times* investigation shows, however, that American Indian companies owned by people with "unsubstantiated claims" to Indianness (i.e., persons not enrolled in federally recognized tribes) secured hundreds of millions of dollars in federal contracts in twenty-seven states.

Two state-recognized tribes in Alabama—the Echota Cherokee Tribe and the Ma-Chis Lower Creek Indian Tribe—were awarded a combined $500 million in minority SBA contracts. At the time of this writing, the BIA (Bureau of Indian Affairs) had not ruled on the Echota Tribe's federal standing (though the Cherokee Nation was adamantly opposed), but it denied federal recognition to the Ma-Chis Tribe due to scant evidence of indigeneity. According to the BIA's experts, it is possible that approximately one-quarter of Ma-Chis tribal members have "a 1900-era ancestor who was possibly the great-great-granddaughter of a woman 'said to be' the sister of a half-Creek man." Such tenuous ties to Indigenous ancestry may seem insignificant, but the case of the Ma-Chis tribe underscores important issues regarding claims to Indigenous identities, evidence of indigeneity, and who can legitimately possess Indigenous identities and resources.

Deeply entangled threats to sovereignty and resources are the overriding concerns of tribal governments. Ethnographic studies conducted with new Indians in the United States and Canada, however, indicate that *emotional* and *symbolic* capital, rather than material gain, is the primary driver and reward of Indian identity reclamation.[65] Even among new Cherokee groups working to obtain state and/or federal recognition, Sturm finds that many "born again Cherokees" feel so enriched by their new identities that they "spread the Cherokee gospel" to bring even more new Cherokees into the fold. By claiming *indigeneity* in a *settler* society, states Sturm, these new Indians access both community and feelings of moral and cultural superiority: "Once settlers, now they are Indigenous. Once socially alienated, now they are part of a tribal collective. Once spiritually unmoored, now they have new moral convictions. And once culturally empty, now they are fulfilled."[66] Recent Indigenous studies scholarship more explicitly links "race shifting" to settler logics of *elimination*, suggesting that white people (i.e., settlers) claiming Indianness is the ultimate conclusion to centuries of physical, cultural, and representational annihilation. Like Sturm's scholarship, work in this area documents the social and emotional benefits derived by white people convinced that their tenuous and/or unsubstantiated claims to Indigenous ancestry entitle them to Indigenous identities and Indigenous resources.

Authenticating Indigenous identities, however, is complicated by colonial projects that violently, bureaucratically, and representationally disappeared Indigenous peoples. These projects simultaneously degraded or dissolved ties binding unknown numbers of Indigenous people to Indigenous identities. That people falsely claim Indian identities is a fact. Yet some people were dispossessed of their indigeneity by colonial projects that intentionally severed Indigenous people from their communities. Centuries of settler-colonial projects—like Indian removal, Indian boarding schools, and Indian relocation—purposefully purged Indigenous people of their identities and perspectives. These projects *also* encouraged white settlers to possess the identities of Indigenous peoples whose authentic realities are shrouded by mythical stories and romantic images of Indianness. As a result, murky boundaries sometimes blur distinctions between "possessive" settlers and (Indigenous) people working to repossess legitimate forms of indigeneity.

Studying Indigeneity: "A Sophisticated Indigenous Studies Discipline"

Colonization, racialization, and ethnic appropriation have mystified, in many ways, the *substance* of indigeneity. Métis scholar Chris Andersen[67] calls it the "density" of Indigenous peoples. Specifically, Andersen uses "density" to describe the complexity of indigeneity produced by centuries of interactions between Indigenous peoples, cultures, and communities and settler-colonial society. According to Andersen, this density, comprised of the numerous subject positions of Indigenous peoples in contemporary society, is overlooked by Indigenous studies scholarship that too often constructs indigeneity in terms of cultural continuity. Māori scholar Brendon Hokowhitu[68] agrees that focusing on continuity, or sovereign Indian communities with continuous, tribally specific knowledge, reifies notions of authenticity that locate Indigenous people in a mythological "pure-past" and limit conceptions of indigeneity in the *present*.

The logics of colonialism, Andersen, Hokowhitu, and Moreton-Robinson assert, are built into the settler-constructed stories and systems that continue to impact Indigenous lives. These logics make critical examinations of race and racialization necessary to understanding experiences of indigeneity in contemporary settler societies. Indigenous people learn and to some extent *remember* the same settler-constructed memories and histories imposed on all US citizens—and, as Andersen articulates, "the cultural power of nation-states do [*sic*] not merely oppress, but seduce as well." Indigenous studies scholars, therefore, must not assume that "legitimate Indigenous communities" always act in accordance with Indigenous (rather than colonial) values. Andersen also warns against assuming who or what comprises a "legitimate" Indigenous community. Both assumptions ignore power relations in colonial societies. Neither Indigenous studies scholars nor Indigenous people can step outside the power of whiteness, these scholars argue, so whiteness must be engaged and problematized. "A sophisticated Indigenous studies discipline," Andersen maintains, "must focus on Indigenous communities *as a critique of colonial society*."[69] He and Moreton-Robinson suggest investigating "how Indigenous people know whiteness"[70] and "how racialization works to produce Indigeneity through whiteness"[71] to deconstruct settler histories and reconstruct the stories of Indigenous peoples.

Using Lessons from Indigenous Studies to Develop a "Sophisticated" Sociology Discipline

Aside from compartmentalized areas of sociological interest, like the "churning" AIAN population, US sociology has largely overlooked US Indigenous peoples.[72] In an undercited article, Dwanna L. McKay (formerly Robertson),[73] sociologist and citizen of the Muscogee (Creek) Nation, takes contemporary sociology race scholarship to task for this neglect. McKay critiques three oft-cited theories—racial formation, white racial framing, and color-blind racism—for their failure to incorporate the experiences of Indigenous peoples. Michael Omi and Howard Winant's *racial formation theory*, for instance, explains how political, economic, and social processes construct race in ways that impact racialized groups' access to critical resources. Such racializing processes (e.g., blood quantum metrics) profoundly impact US Indigenous populations. As McKay points out, however, the original book-length explication of racial formation theory,[74] cited more than thirteen thousand times, mentions American Indians on only two pages and in three end notes. The third edition, published in 2015, mentions American Indians on only thirteen pages and in only two end notes.

Joseph "Joe" Feagin, another prominent race theorist, criticizes racial formation theory for failing to explain the *persistence* of US racism. In response, Feagin theorizes that a rationalizing *white racial frame*, composed of stereotypes, interpretive concepts, images, emotions, and inclinations to act in discriminatory ways, interacts with racial hierarchies and material oppression to systematically and perpetually oppress people of color.[75] Feagin recognizes that "anti-Indian ideas and imagery became part of the developing white racial frame,"[76] but then reveals a "black exceptionalism" bias: "While [Native Americans] have been the recurring targets of extreme white brutality and recurring genocide," Feagin asserts, "[they] have not played as central a role in the *internal* socio-racial reality of the colonies or the United States as have African Americans."[77] Feagin's perception of Indigenous peoples' *less* central role aligns with a century of sociological scholarship that *decenters* Indigenous peoples' experiences. Further, Feagin seems to embrace a white racial *framing* of history—one that disregards settler colonialism, yet relies on settler-constructed "rules of remembrance."

Eduardo Bonilla-Silva also purports to deal with limitations of *racial formation theory* with his *racialized social systems* approach. Racialized practices that reinforce, perpetuate, and legitimize white supremacy, Bonilla-Silva asserts, are normal, dynamic, rational, historical, *and* contemporary. They are sometimes overt, but more often covert in the post-civil rights era. In articulating *color-blind racism theory*, Bonilla-Silva suggests that "publicly racist terminology" is peripheral to the reproduction of white racial privilege because contemporary social norms (generally) forbid blatant racism. McKay argues that this conceptualization of "color-blind" racism, a leading theoretical orientation in sociological race research, does not apply to Indigenous peoples who still experience overt forms of racism. US norms that prohibit minstrelsy but socialize US children to "play Indian" at Thanksgiving illustrate McKay's point: socially normative racism against Indigenous peoples is *not* deemed "right or reasonable" when applied to other racialized groups. Color-blind racism theory, McKay submits, invisibilizes Indigenous peoples *and* "the overt racism they experience . . . because it is not seen as racism."[78] McKay suggests that knowledge production grounded in these theoretical frameworks ultimately contributes to *legitimized racism* against Indigenous peoples. Legitimized racism is "multilayered, intersectional, and dynamic [systemic] racism" that is normalized and internalized and therefore legitimized such that it is "simultaneously overt and invisible within social norms and social institutions."[79]

As McKay beautifully elucidates, the exclusion of Indigenous peoples from sociological race scholarship prevents holistic understandings of racial formations and racialized oppression in the United States. When sociologists include Indigenous people, they frequently focus on settler-constructed notions of race and racialization as *the* defining features of indigeneity. Doing so ignores the *density* of Indigenous peoples and literally "[re]produce[s] Indigeneity *through whiteness*."[80] Sociologists should investigate this phenomenon, but instead contribute to it. Importantly, sociologists cannot simply add Indigenous peoples to studies undergirded by our most celebrated theoretical frameworks. A "sophisticated" sociology discipline (to borrow Andersen's language) must attend to Indigenous peoples *as well as* Indigenous sovereignty and settler colonialism, the origin or initiation point of racial categorization, racialization, and racism.

I suggest that Indigenous invisibility is *anchored* in sociology due to disciplinary disregard for *settler colonialism*. This "alternative starting point" can produce "more historically and structurally grounded" analyses of US inequalities, but much sociology scholarship continues to ignore or gives a perfunctory nod to settler colonialism as the foundation of systemic racism in the United States. Feagin's *Racist America: Roots, Current Realities, and Future Reparations* (2014) contains zero mentions of settler colonialism. Omi and Winant's third (and significantly revised) edition of *Racial Formation in the United States* (2015) contains only two mentions. Interestingly, in a 2015 reflection of his previous work, Bonilla-Silva suggests that race theory should "begin at the beginning."[81] He proposes rooting theories about race in "the experiences of the first peoples who experienced racialization," specifically, peoples of Latin America and the Caribbean. This idea, while exceedingly important, parallels and complements decades of settler-colonial studies scholarship that Bonilla-Silva fails to acknowledge.

The depth of sociological neglect also is revealed in historical works, like Robert "Bob" Blauner's *Racial Oppression in America* (1972).[82] Blauner is partially exempt from this critique because the publication of his book co-occurred with the emergence of settler-colonial studies (ca. 1970s).[83] Still, his exclusion of Indigenous peoples, who are mentioned but not theorized, in a book *about* colonialism is telling. Blauner interrogates *internal* colonialism as a variation of a global "colonial complex," but fails to recognize Indigenous peoples' oppression as the root of this complex on US soil. Blauner instead asserts that "systems of colonialism . . . *most central to the modern era*" have subjugated "nonwhite Asian, African, and Latin American peoples" (emphasis added).[84]

Sociologists have much work to do to rectify our disciplinary contributions to colonial unknowing. We have invested too much time and energy on theories of race relations reliant on settler-constructed timelines. For over a century, sociologists used the enslavement of African peoples as a starting point for exploring systemic racism in the United States, causing the discipline to reify dominant understandings of historical "relevance" that disregard much of Indigenous peoples' histories and, in turn, obscure their current and future realities. But change is on the horizon. Settler colonialism is finally making its way into sociological discourse. For the first time in 115 years, the American Sociological Association has a section, Indigenous People and Native Nations, devoted to scholarship in "Indigenous sociology."[85] Sociologists (outside Indigenous studies) are finally drawing attention to the discipline's "possessive investment in white sociology"[86] and exploring "ways in which white supremacy structures how we *do* sociology."[87] How we *have done* sociology has been in accord with settler-colonial processes of Indigenous *erasure*. Thanks to the works of Indigenous sociologists and their academic allies, however, more sophisticated and informed sociologies promise to shape our collective future.

Elucidating the "Complexity of Racism" Undergirded by US Settler Colonialism

This research, which centers the stories and struggles of Indigenous and Indigenous-identified people participating in urban pan-Indian (-identified) communities, illuminates the continuing structure of settler colonialism and the reproduction of white supremacy. Indigenous people continue to face discrimination in interactions with the federal government and *every other social institution* that comprises the US social structure. Many of these institutional abuses, including forced removals and relocations, forced assimilation, forced sterilization, and cultural and corporate exploitation, are discussed throughout the book by Indigenous people impacted by them. These abuses—set in motion by unrelenting forces of settler colonialism—have contributed to the bottom-rung status of AIAN people on nearly every indicator of economic, occupational, educational, physical, and social well-being.

Statistics are difficult to compile due to small AIAN population size, geographic dispersion, inconsistent racial classification, and/or racial misclassification, so the information presented here is a broad overview meant only to indicate the predicament of contemporary AIAN who are *not* well served by US institutions. More American Indians, for instance, live in poverty (28 percent) than members of any other racial/ethnic group in the United States.[88] Reservations have the highest unemployment rates in the nation, with some tribes reporting rates as high as 85 percent.[89] Though the AIAN population has seen a 10 percent increase in high school graduation rates since 2005, high school dropout rates for Indian youth are still double the national average.[90] A UCLA study found that fewer than half of American Indian students living in seven states with the largest American Indian populations graduate from high school.[91] Moreover, AIAN college graduation rates are only about half the national average.[92]

American Indians also have poor health outcomes. They have significantly higher death rates and lower life expectancies than other racial/ ethnic groups. They suffer higher rates of diabetes, asthma, tuberculosis, and liver disease. They also suffer from high levels of depression, alcoholism, posttraumatic stress disorder, and suicide. AIANs die from alcohol-related deaths at 6.6 times[93] and suicide deaths at 1.7 times[94] the rate of the total US population. When opioid addiction and overdose deaths were front-page news across the country, that AIAN death rates exceeded national rates was rarely reported.[95] Moreover, American Indians living on reservations experience extremely high rates of crime victimization, including aggravated assault rates that are double the national average.[96] Approximately 84 percent of AIAN women have experienced violence in their lifetimes, including experiences of sexual violence (56 percent), physical violence by an intimate partner (56 percent), stalking (49 percent), and psychological aggression by an intimate partner (66 percent).[97] American Indians—men and women—are more likely than other racial groups to experience violence at the hands of an interracial perpetrator. According to data collected by the Centers for Disease Control between 1999 and 2015, American Indians were more likely than other racial groups to be killed by law enforcement officers.[98]

Rather than reporting the critical issues impacting Indigenous peoples and communities, US sociocultural institutions largely ignore or provide consistent *mis*information about them. This misrepresentation of Indigenous peoples and Indigenous issues has specific impacts on urban Indians—Indians "off the reservation" whose stories do not cohere with disorienting misinformation broadcast throughout US society.

The Density of Indianness in NE Ohio

My research addresses the complexities of urban indigeneity in Northeast Ohio, a contextual sphere with its own disorienting stories about Indianness. Ohio's small American Indian/Alaskan Native population (less than .3 percent)[99] and lack of federally recognized Indian nations contribute to AIAN invisibility and uniquely orient Indigenous people's identities. Each intersection of Indigenous identity outlined above—national, racial, and ethnic—remains critical to experiences of indigeneity in this metropolitan region, but matters of sovereignty sometimes (necessarily) take a back seat to everyday problems experienced by NE Ohio Indians. Members of tribal nations, for instance, find it challenging to traverse the hundreds of miles separating them from "home," making it difficult to participate in tribal politics, access tribal resources, and attend tribal ceremonies. Maintaining Indian ethnic identities and passing cultural traditions to the next generations are prioritized by NE Ohio Indians, but also utterly complicated by their dislocations from tribal communities. Additionally, both relocators and reclaimers are immersed in a white-washed urban setting that not only obscures Indigenous sovereignty but also thoroughly inscribes racial meanings on indigeneity. For decades, racialization reared its *literal* head in NE Ohio in the guise of Chief Wahoo. Indians who endure daily acts of racial discrimination in NE Ohio are repeatedly reminded of their subordinated *racial* status, and thereby, understand their racial categorization as foundational to their oppression. For these reasons, whether Indigenous participants in this research prioritized ethnic, racial, or national categories of identification frequently depended on the month, week, day, or moment.

Sovereignty was not highlighted in stories NE Ohio Indigenous people shared with me, but settler colonialism plays a prominent role in the identity processes described in this book. Its ongoing structure so thoroughly hides Indigenous histories and distorts Indigenous realities that the authenticity of contemporary urban Indians is constantly questioned. Relocators and reclaimers alike talked about negotiating unrealistic expectations of Indianness. Despite their efforts to retain and/or reclaim Indigenous identities and practices, they were continually scrutinized for not looking or acting Indian *enough*. To varying degrees, they also internalized these expectations, leading them to scrutinize each other.

Anthropologist Theresa O'Nell's work with peoples of the Flathead Reservation in Montana provides some insight into this phenomenon. According to O'Nell, there was some consensus regarding who was "really Indian" among the Flathead peoples—and *no living Indian* measured up. O'Nell uses the heuristic of "the empty center" to describe local rhetoric surrounding Indigenous identities threatened by erasure. She conceptualizes Indian identity as a set of concentric circles, with the innermost ring filled by "really Indians" and the outermost ring filled by not-really-Indians and "the intervening circles representing successive gradations of being Indian." The empty center, O'Nell admits, is not *really* empty because it is filled with "really Indians" from generations past—people who practiced "real Indian ways," spoke the Salish language, "knew who all their relatives were," and always lived on the reservation.

This static image, however, does not account for the situatedness of Indigenous identities in time, so, O'Nell suggests, "It is more useful to imagine a moving picture made up of a series of telescoping images, in which the individuals closest to the empty center in earlier generations are continually moving into the empty center as new individuals in succeeding generations are moving into the circle immediately surrounding the empty center."[100] The "telescoping images" elucidate processes of settler-colonial erasure that invalidate the identities of contemporary Indigenous peoples. Representational erasure via caricatured, anachronistic Indianness creates the illusion that only individuals from "earlier generations" are "really Indians." Individuals from current generations can never measure up *because they exist in the present*. Whether someone is "more" or "less" Indian also varies across space due to fluctuating contextualized definitions of Indianness. Settler-constructed definitions of Indianness in the United States deem reservation Indians "more" Indian than urban Indians, for instance. Among urban Indians, Indians who *ever* lived on reservations are deemed "more" Indian than Indians who *never* lived on reservations, and so on and so forth.

In NE Ohio, the Indian identity claims of *all* Indians are suspect, but the identity claims of reclaimer community members are *more* suspect than relocators' claims because reclaimers occupy circles some distance from "the empty center." Some reclaimers, in fact, arguably are situated far beyond the boundaries of the telescoping circles. Because reclaimers predominantly are *unclaimed* by tribal nations, many Indigenous people, including some relocator community members, suggest that they are white pretendians, i.e., "race shifters," intent on coopting Indigenous identities for social and emotional (and occasionally material) gain. Reclaimers' claims, thus, are believed to be manufactured by and irrevocably entangled with settler logics of Indigenous possession and Indigenous elimination.

Rather than dismissing this possibility outright or accepting it uncritically, I elucidate how the racialized landscape of settler colonialism interferes with all memories—those of Indigenous and non-Indigenous folks—and blurs boundaries between authentic and fraudulent indigeneity. This project also provides insight into the *density* of Indianness. It reveals how Indigenous and Indigenous-identified people in NE Ohio engage, problematize, reinforce, and/or *resist* the power of whiteness in this colonized space. My analysis shows that relocators and reclaimers develop distinctive understandings of what it means to *be* and *act* Indian in this contextual sphere. Relocators' and reclaimers' different stories, memories, and histories lead them to engage contrary strategies for creating collective identities and negotiating ethnic boundaries at the community level. Their respective communities—shaped by members' stories and formulated to meet the needs of relocators *or* reclaimers— ultimately reify relocators' and reclaimers' dissimilarities and contribute to tensions between members of the two community groups.

Belongingness in Indigenous communities and unanchored claims to Indigenous identities are issues just as politically fraught in NE Ohio as they are elsewhere. Yet, the cogency and truthiness of stories of Indigenous ancestry vary *across* the relocator and reclaimer communities, and individuals' stories of relocation and reclamation do not neatly correspond with individuals' tribal citizenship or noncitizenship status. The relocation/reclamation divide, thus, is somewhat useful but also somewhat arbitrary and merely intended to provide a lens for investigating different understandings and experiences of racialized urban Indian identities.

NE Ohio is awash with impersonations and impersonators of Indianness. In lieu of arbitrating the validity of people's identity claims (which is beyond the purview of this research), I contextualize research participants' identities with backstories. In recognition of tribal sovereignty and the rights of Indian nations to determine their membership, I distinguish tribally enrolled from nonenrolled relocators and reclaimers by stating the tribal affiliations of the former and indicating that the latter are Indian-identified or tribally identified. Importantly, I also engage this strategy at Kurt's behest. Kurt, the executive director of the NE Ohio reclaimer community organization, is an unenrolled, Choctaw-identified man. His "only piece of advice" regarding my research was to differentiate between enrolled and unenrolled Indians. "Because if anybody goes out here identifying as such and they're not really enrolled with that tribe or connected with that tribe," Kurt warned, "it can cause you some problems down the road." Kurt knows because he knows a lot of Indians. And he has identified as one his entire life.

2

Stories of Relocation

Berta looked positively vibrant. She was wearing a southwestern-style jacket in dark, earthy tones, black pants, and long, beaded earrings. Her salt-and-pepper hair framed her face, the short, choppy layers clinging to her broad forehead and curling around her ears. The front layers gave way to a skinny ponytail only visible when she turned her head. She was the invited guest lecturer at an American Indian Speaker Series event held in the (not so) "great room" of a small liberal arts college. She seemed right at home in the old, musty library, leaning on the back of a burgundy antique parlor chair, casually scanning the crowd of twenty or so people who had gathered to hear her tell her stories. Whenever Berta's eyes landed on mine, she raised her eyebrows and half smiled in acknowledgment even as she continued to talk to the audience, casually and conversationally, without notecards or props. Within minutes of introducing herself, she declared her allegiance to the American Indian Movement (AIM). AIM had had an indelible impact on her life, she explained—not only because she had come of age during the movement's "heyday" in the 1960s. She also came from a "family of politicians." Her grandmother taught her everything she needed to know about social movement politics. Her mother led the initial resistance against Cleveland's Wahoo mascot. And now, four decades later, Berta was honored to lead this same struggle for the rights and dignity of American Indian people. Throughout the evening, Berta sprinkled her storytelling with tales of relocation—the experiences that prompted the college's original request for her to speak. Berta's political savvy, however, impelled her to turn the spotlight on other things, activist things. From her perspective, these were the things that mattered most.

* * *

Just eight months prior to Berta's American Indian Speaker Series lecture, members of the urban, pan-Indian community in which Berta had come of age held a potluck in her honor. Berta's friends organized the potluck because they wanted to "gift" her with food and love and money to offset her medical expenses. She had just started dialysis treatments for her failing kidneys. "At least I am starting to feel better," Berta said. "Only two treatments so far, but I have more energy," she assured her friends, who crowded around her. She had not been feeling well for some time now, but was surprised to find out she was *so* sick. Still, she smiled and nodded and reassured her friends that she was going to be alright. Her friends could see, however, that her color was not right and her usual zeal was missing. For the first time in all the years they had known her, Berta seemed tired, old. But everyone was together now, and that meant Berta would laugh—the solemnity of the occasion notwithstanding. Humor was what had *always* kept them going. It was as much a part of being Indian as eating fry bread. Berta's potluck had both.

Shortly after we finished eating, a short, pudgy woman in a purple, oversized Haskell Indian Nations t-shirt stood on top of a chair and whisper-screamed "*Hush!*" until everyone at the potluck was silent. "This young man wants to sing an honor song for Berta," she said, nodding toward a man wearing Wrangler jeans and a light blue work shirt, sleeves rolled up to reveal a faded dreamcatcher tattoo. He stood silently for a moment, and then, eyes cast downward, started singing, slowly and melodiously. He shifted his weight from one foot to the other, keeping the beat of his song, while his voice—soft and quiet, then loud and forceful—swirled around the room. The house was almost perfectly still. Several women wept silently, only emitting quiet little sniffles, and Berta used a wadded-up tissue to dab the corners of her eyes. When the song ended, this man, who had offered up a little piece of his soul, suddenly seemed quite bashful. He spoke softly. "This honor song," he said, "is for Berta, a strong and wonderful woman who is such a positive influence for my daughter, a guide for her." He quickly raised his eyes to meet Berta's, then cast them downward again. "I know my daughter will grow up to be a strong woman, too," he said hoarsely, "because she will follow in her grandmother's footsteps." The silently weeping women now cried openly and unabashedly.

The room was steeped in heaviness—until June, a feisty, round-faced Navajo woman, shouted, "You better hope she doesn't follow in Berta's footsteps!" Now the room erupted with laughter. The weeping women giggled while wiping tears from their eyes. When the room quieted, June got everyone's attention again. "We wanted to have something for Berta," June said softly, "because she is on hard times." She thanked everyone for coming even though the potluck was hastily planned. June looked toward Berta, and with great sincerity, said, "We want you to be happy and healthy, Berta." June and Berta exchanged knowing nods. Suddenly June's eyes lit up. She leaned forward in her seat, as if to tell a secret, and then, with a quick look around to ensure she had everyone's attention, June shrieked, "So we can keep talking about you!" Again, laughter shook the room.

* * *

By the time I sat down with Berta and her husband, Greg, for a formal interview two years later, I was familiar with many of their stories. We had spent a lot of time together over the previous four years—at anti-Wahoo protests, conferences, barbeques, dance classes, powwows, and potlucks. I had spent entire afternoons selling fry bread and Indian tacos with the couple at one fundraising event after another. Berta was always in a storytelling mood, and she told stories with panache. I never tired of her funny, spunky anecdotes. Greg seemed never to tire of them either. He always looked so excited just before the punchline, even if he had heard the story dozens of times. Occasionally he jumped in, adding a little tidbit that Berta overlooked—or one that she denied. Conversations with the couple always flowed this way, with Berta taking the lead and Greg playing the role of loyal sidekick. Our interview was no different.

Berta explained that her existence has always been defined by a syncretic blend of Indian ways and white ways. "It was all mixed together with us," Berta said. Her paternal grandfather, for instance, was a Lakota medicine man and an Episcopalian minister, so Berta grew up with traditional spirituality and Christian religion. She learned to "speak Indian" first, and then learned English as a second language. She lived on an Indian reservation early in life, and then she lived in Ohio—a state devoid of Indian nations. Berta strongly identifies with her Indian heritage, but she also knows how to maneuver within a society dominated by whites. She has been doing it for sixty years.

In some areas of Berta's life, her Indian and white ways commingle somewhat harmoniously. Her "very traditional grandparents," for instance, were "powwow people," and even though Berta lives far from the powwows her grandparents attended, she is able to attend Ohio-area intertribal powwows throughout the summer months. She often sits at a vending booth, selling beaded jewelry and handmade dream catchers to Indians who are at the powwow to dance and whites who are at the powwow to experience (and purchase pieces of) Indian culture. Berta has Indian and white friends. She has even informally "adopted" some white people into her family.

Some areas of Berta's life, however, are less than perfectly blended. Neither Berta nor her siblings speak their Indigenous language. They learned the language as children, but lost it when they were school aged. Berta explained, "That's our first language. English is a second language for us, but um, as we got older and got into the school system, my one sister—this is how it started: my one sister got into first grade and she couldn't speak English so they failed her. That was bad, for my parents, you know, so after that they quit speaking the language [at home]." Because they wanted their children to be successful in an English-speaking world, Berta's parents enforced an English-only policy in their home. Berta and her siblings retained only enough of their language to communicate with non-English-speaking family members. Berta had an uncle, for instance, "who only spoke Indian. He never spoke English at all," Berta explained, "never said no words in English, and so we had to know the language, but we didn't speak it fluently." Berta blames her and her siblings' language loss on the government-run boarding school they attended: "They wouldn't let us have life, liberty, and the freedom of speech—even though they taught it!"

The intentional disruption of Indigenous peoples' lifeways by white settlers is central to any discussion of language loss, which is common in both urban and reservation-based Indian communities. An estimated three to five hundred Indigenous languages existed in North America prior to European contact. More than two hundred of those languages are still spoken by *someone*, but only thirty-four of the remaining languages are being passed on to Indigenous youth as a primary or first language. The others, spoken only by elders, may disappear with the people currently keeping them alive. A team of well-reputed Indigenous linguistics studies scholars, Teresa McCarty, Eunice Romero-Little (Cochiti Pueblo), and Ofelia Zepeda (Tohono O'odham), blame language loss on a "genocidal and linguicidal past" in conjunction with "the modern influences of English media, technology, and schooling."[1] Such loss has detrimental consequences for the identities of Indigenous children, these scholars state, because language identifies a people: "who [they] are, where [they] come from, and where [they] are going."

That no Indigenous person interviewed for this project spoke an Indigenous language illustrates the universality of language loss for urban Indians. For Indians like Berta, who attended Indian boarding schools, language loss was just part of growing up Indian in the United States. After all, Indian boarding schools like the one she and her siblings attended did what they could to separate Indian children from Indian culture. That process began with separation from their Indian families and ended, at least in theory, with total assimilation. "They didn't teach us any of our customs, like the dances or the artwork that we [Lakota] did," Berta said. "They kept it from us." Berta is grateful that her grandparents "were real strong in the culture," because that helped her retain some knowledge of her traditional ways. "Against all odds, I guess you would say, we still survived," Berta said.

Berta lived on the reservation until she was thirteen years old. Her parents picked her up from boarding school and drove her, along with six siblings, from South Dakota to Ohio. Berta and her family started their new lives as enrollees in the federal government's Indian Relocation Program in 1965. The BIA's Relocation Services first opened their Cleveland office in 1952. Altogether, five thousand Indians were processed through that office, which was tasked with connecting Cleveland's newcomers with housing, jobs, and training programs.[2] In the end, Ohio was not a particularly popular relocation destination, perhaps due to its distance from many reservations. Yet, Berta's parents chose Ohio, or possibly were persuaded to relocate there by BIA agents intent on meeting quotas, due to the educational and occupational opportunities presumably available. In the decade prior, NE Ohio schools were nationally ranked and the region was brimming with factories that provided middle-class incomes to entry-level workers.

Despite her tender age, Berta remembers this frightening and exciting period of her life. She recalls the loneliness she and her siblings felt in the big city, and compares it to their previous life on the reservation. "We grew up in extended families," said Berta, "with our grandparents, our uncles, cousins, so that's how we grew up, you know? So when we moved here, we lived by ourselves. . . . We missed the closeness of the extended family." She and her siblings also found the city itself to be quite intimidating. Berta remembers staying inside the family's tiny apartment for months after their arrival. Eventually, however, she and her siblings learned to navigate big city bus lines, and they enrolled in big city schools. In school, Berta and her siblings discovered that they were not the only students experiencing a period of adjustment. "It was hard for people to adjust to us, too," Berta said. The racialization of Indigenous peoples was so total and eclipsing that Berta's classmates *and* teachers were discomfited by the presence of "primitive" Natives in *their* settler-constructed reality. Berta believes her brashness enabled her to deflect the abuses she experienced as a result of Indian stereotypes.

Racializing and dehumanizing stereotypes of Indianness existed across the country. Morris Udall, a US representative from Arizona, articulated the problem quite clearly in 1977: "These stereotypes arise of a [willful] 'knowledge vacuum'" rooted in "the anti-Indian bigotry that has existed from the days of the earliest white settlers."[3] For centuries Indians were portrayed as the "bad guys," and this depiction remains fixed in the American psyche. As Donald Fixico (Shawnee, Sac and Fox, Creek, and Seminole), distinguished professor of history at Arizona State University and author of *The Urban Indian Experience in America*, points out, urban Indians are consistently blamed for failing to adjust to urban life, but their biggest obstacle remains the alienating attitudes of non-Indians. Indian inclusion, Fixico argues, cannot happen without a more informed public, and yet the public remains uninformed.[4]

For relocated Indians like Berta, only the presence of thousands of other Indigenous people seeking a better life made the city a livable space. Berta remembers how living in Cleveland's Indian "projects," memorably described by her little brother as a place where the houses "all stuck together," enriched her life: "So when I moved here is when I first found out we had other [Indian] nations. I knew about Apaches because we watched them on TV, but I never knew about Navajos, Choctaws, Chickasaws, Seminoles. . . . There was a real good educational experience for us to see all the different nations and learn some of their culture from them. They formed an Indian Center . . . so that's how we kept our culture going—through each other, from meeting all the other people." For Berta's family, Indians at the Indian Center made them feel a little more at home in the Cleveland environment. The Indian Center sponsored softball and bowling leagues, dance classes, picnics, and other "stuff that kept the Native community together." Other relocated Indians were "like family off the reservation," Berta said.

Across the country, urban Indian Centers like the one in Cleveland were bringing urban Indian people together. An estimated forty Indian-managed urban Indian Centers were operating in the United States by the end of the 1960s.[5] In January 1975, Congress extended funding for anti-poverty programs covered under the 1964 Economic Opportunity Act. The act enabled the provision of funding for fifty-eight urban Indian Centers. Then, in 1977, HUD's Office of Native American Programs provided a total of $5 million to sixty urban Indian Centers across the country. "Since the 1970s," Fixico states, "virtually every large urban area has operated an Indian center, or at least an Indian organization providing some type of job-related services and/or counseling to the Native American community."[6] Still, an estimated 50 percent of sponsored Indian relocators returned to their home reservations within five years.[7]

Berta's parents, on the other hand, made it in the city. By the time they decided to return home, Berta was in her mid- to late twenties. She was an integral part of the bustling Cleveland American Indian Center and an active member of AIM. These activities, along with her traditional family back on the reservation, nurtured an intense pride in her Indian identity. "I grew up during that Russell Means time," Berta explained, "so I was really politically aware of my roots, of my people." Once a leader of the American Indian Movement, Russell Means (Oglala Lakota) is also known for his performances in movies like *The Last of the Mohicans* (1992) and Disney's *Pocahontas* (1995). Berta met Russell Means in 1968 when he relocated to Cleveland, only three years after her family's arrival.

Russell Means described his life in Cleveland in his autobiography, *Where White Men Fear to Tread*.[8] According to Means, the BIA did not adequately provide for his family's needs—or the needs of any relocated family, for that matter. He describes the seedy apartment, located in "the meanest section of the red-light district," that the BIA originally provided for him, his wife, and his children.[9] Means reports that the BIA provided his family a meager spending allowance and little to no assistance with his job search. He sought out and found some other Indians in Cleveland, but desired an Indian hangout that was *not* Club 77, one of a few bars where relocated Indians tended to congregate. Means, after all, had hoped that relocating to Cleveland would curb his problematic drinking and save his marriage.

Means was entirely dissatisfied with his relocation experience until he got involved in the Minneapolis-based American Indian Movement. "AIM," said Means, "crystallized thoughts and feelings and desires long buried within my psyche. . . . No longer would I be content to 'work within the system,'" Means declared. "Never again would I seek personal approval from white society on white terms. Instead . . . I would get in the white man's face until he gave me and my people our just due." Means recruited other relocated Indians—Berta's mother among them—to help him establish the Cleveland American Indian Center in 1970. When Means left Cleveland in 1973, the Indian Center offered twenty-six different programs that assisted Indians with everything from applying for Social Security benefits and food stamps to learning job skills, maintaining cultural traditions, and procuring medical and legal assistance. The center worked with Cleveland schools to revise its American Indian curriculum and even initiated a "reverse relocation" program that helped pay the way for American Indian families to return permanently to their home reservations.

Berta grew up in this environment—a stable, urban, pan-Indian community that looked to the American Indian Movement for strength and leadership. Participating in local pan-Indian activism inspired by national movements for social change had an indelible influence on Berta's personal politics. She describes her young self as "very militant minded." "I used to have pictures up on my walls of Indian Power, Huey Newton, Cesar Chavez," Berta said. "All the militant fighters, you know? I really liked their philosophies . . . about community empowerment and stuff like that."

* * *

Greg grew up on a Lakota reservation across the state line and just a few hours north of Berta's hometown. His family was not particularly political, and they were not militant at all. In fact, they had a tradition of military service. Greg's grandfather, father, and uncle all served. Greg's family is not exceptional in this regard. For more than two hundred years, the US military has depended on the service of American Indians and Alaska Natives (AIAN), who serve at higher rates per capita than other racial or ethnic groups. Indians served long before being granted the rights of US citizenship, and they have served in every war, from the Revolutionary War to the Gulf Wars. Research indicates that the strong draw of American Indians to the military results from several factors, including warrior cultural traditions and family military involvement.[10] The Navy is the most common military branch in which AIANs serve, followed by the Marines.[11]

Greg never really considered military service his destiny or his duty, but he ended up in the Marines anyways. He describes his enlistment as an impulse decision. The year was 1970. The war in Vietnam continued to drag on. And Greg was graduating from high school. Like many of his high school friends, he had applied to several different colleges. As their college acceptance letters rolled in, he received nothing. "They were all ready to go, and I'm waiting," Greg said. Even forty years later, he could not hide the exasperation in his voice. He continued,

> I still didn't get mine in May, the month I was graduating. . . . And the day I graduated, I still didn't get nothing, you know, so . . . in June, I went and signed up for the military, the Marines. My dad was proud because he was in the Army, he was a paratrooper, and he said, "Okay son, if that's what you want." But I did it on impulse. And um, I don't regret it. But my mom didn't want me going in. . . . Of course, I was thinking about [the military as an option] before that, but [pause] when it came right down to it, I didn't have a choice. . . . I graduated May 28th, and by June 8th I was inducted.

Greg was lucky, though. "I was on my way to Vietnam when we went to a station battalion in Okinawa for the last dropping-off point. In Okinawa, I got my orders changed—to stay in Okinawa with the Thirteenth Battalion, instead of going off to Vietnam." According to Greg, it was "a blessing in disguise." He fondly remembers his time in Okinawa. "We used to frequent a lot of bars off that base," he said, "and the Japanese people would try to guess what nationality I was, you know? And they would guess *everything*!" he said, laughing. "'Hawaiian?

Chinese? Japanese?' 'No. . . . I'm Indian, American Indian.'" Inevitably, his inquisitors raised their hands to the backs of their heads and splayed their fingers to create makeshift "feathers." "Oh, you mean *this* kind of Indian?" they asked. "And I said, yeah, yeah—that kind!" Greg chuckled. When Greg completed his tour of duty, he decided to try his luck in Ohio.

* * *

Berta's political activism kept her busy, but on Friday nights she could be found hanging out with friends at a local bowling alley. She enjoyed participating in the Indian Center bowling league and admits that a young Lakota man named Greg was a large part of the draw. Greg, a relocator from North Dakota, came to Ohio to attend an electronics trade school. "We used to go bowling together," said Berta, "and then slowly we just started dating." Even now, it seems an implausible coupling. While Berta was participating in the AIM takeover of the BIA building in Washington, DC, Greg was dutifully serving his country in the Marines. Berta's family had a habit of saying that Indians in the military were "sellouts." Greg's family, on the other hand, was proud of its military service.

After thirty-five years of marriage, Berta and Greg are like two peas in a pod, but their different backgrounds created some tensions early in their relationship. "It was hard at first," Berta said about their earliest years together, "because my way was different from his." Berta looked over at Greg for confirmation. A smile slowly stretched across her face. "He says I was real militant," she said as she placed her hand on his knee. The couple exchanged a look, smiled knowingly at each other, and gently nodded their heads in agreement. "You only fly the flag upside-down when a nation's in distress!" Greg exclaimed. "And she used to carry it wrong all the time, you know?" he said, feigning indignation. With mocking disapproval, he shook his head from side to side. "I wasn't trying to be disrespectful to the flag," Berta said, playing along. "It was just that *our people* were in distress." AIM, in fact, adopted the upside-down flag as a symbol of their struggle in 1970. Even at the time of its adoption, the symbol was controversial. "White people protested, of course, and a lot of our Indian people protested, too," AIM leader Dennis Banks relayed—but, he added, "This was the international distress signal for people in trouble, and no one could deny that Indians were in bad trouble and needed help."[12] Berta's account of the flag's symbolism corresponded with AIM's. Her eyes twinkled as she looked toward Greg and patted his knee. Both of them giggled. Almost gleefully, Berta proclaimed, "I don't know how we made it all these years!"

They not only made it but also managed to raise a big, beautiful family. When Berta and Greg decided to have children, they traded in their urban apartment for a tiny home on Berta's reservation. They remained on the reservation until their oldest children, "the twins," turned ten. The decision to move back to the city was a painful one. "But the [reservation] economy was so bad," Berta recalled, "that we just, you know, we couldn't make it." With the unemployment rate at more than 80 percent, just getting by was a challenge. As Berta said, "It was really hard to live a full life that you really wanted." So Berta and Greg and their three boys re-relocated to Cleveland.

Susan

Susan is a thoughtful, attentive Dakota woman with warm, golden-brown skin and expressive, almond-shaped eyes. She was nineteen years old when she enrolled in the federal government's Indian Relocation Program. She learned about the program after completing one dissatisfying year of college in her North Dakota hometown. "My guidance counselor signed me up to be a social worker, which, I really didn't want to be!" Susan explained. "I think back then, they made all the girls, or women, go into social work. . . . And they were pushing the relocation program," she remembered, "saying you could travel to these cities, go to school, and make big bucks!" Susan laughs as she recalls how thrilling it all sounded at the time. "I thought, okay, I'll try it because there's nothing, *nothing* in North Dakota except for farming."

Government agents told Susan about different relocation cities that offered different training programs. "I could go anywhere I wanted to go, actually," Susan said, "but I picked Ohio." Even now, she seems a bit mystified by this choice. "[Cleveland] is not the greatest city to live in," she said. Throughout our acquaintance (and prior to the Cleveland MLB team's name change), Susan enjoyed calling Cleveland the "mistake by the lake," a little dig against the Rust Belt city appreciated by opponents of the team's "Indians" name and "Chief Wahoo" mascot. Susan, who was generally soft-spoken, became intensely animated when the conversation turned to "Chief Wahoo's" long tenure as a regional embarrassment. Susan described a protest sign she had made the previous baseball season. "It said, 'Cleveland is number one'—that would get people's attention—it said, 'number one in poverty, number one in obesity, and most racist.'" Susan chuckled. "You know, due to the MLB team," she explained. At the time of our interview (2010), Susan already had protested the team's "Indians" imagery for nearly two decades—ever since she heard Vernon Bellecourt of the American Indian Movement address the mascot issue in a talk at Oberlin College in 1992.

Despite her misgivings now, Susan was excited to move to Cleveland in 1965. Her parents were not particularly enthusiastic about her decision, but they did not discourage her from going either. "So they put me on a train [and] I came by myself," said Susan. BIA workers met Susan at the train station in Cleveland, took her to an apartment, and introduced her to her new roommates. Susan was delighted initially to share an apartment with several "girls from different reservations and nations," but they did not remain her roommates for long. As with many relocators, their longings for home prompted their returns to reservations. Susan persevered, but remembers feeling terribly homesick. Her parents, like most Indians on her reservation at the time, did not have a telephone, and Susan did not have enough money to visit. "They [the BIA] didn't give you money to travel," Susan explained. "They only gave you money for rent and food. So I didn't go home for a long time." BIA workers helped Susan enroll in medical secretary classes and taught her basic urban survival skills. "They showed us [how] you take the bus, go down there, go to classes," Susan remembered, "and then, you know, you could shop for groceries and clothes and all that."

Susan adapted to her new life in the city. She learned to appreciate the sights, the sounds, the throngs of people. She enjoyed her medical secretary classes at the business school. "I did learn quite a bit there," she said. Susan was still enrolled in the courses when she met her future husband, Luis. Originally from Puerto Rico, Luis's family migrated from the island to Cleveland, Ohio, when Luis was only five years old. "He had a hard time," Susan said. "They put him in school speaking no English whatsoever. He had to learn a complete different culture." Susan believes her and Luis's shared experiences of displacement—though Susan migrated at a different stage in her life—solidified the bond between them. In fact, it was the common thread linking Susan to nearly all her new (urban) relations. When she and Luis met, her friendship circle, comprised of young, relocated Native women like herself, had already combined with his friendship circle, comprised of young Puerto Rican men. "There was a whole group of us that would hang out, go to the same places, dance, and that," Susan remembered. Susan and Luis were not the only people to pair off, either. "Actually, two of my friends," said Susan, "married Hispanic, Puerto Rican."

Luis's family filled some of the void left by the absence of Susan's own. They were warm and welcoming and Susan enjoyed their company. Her mother-in-law babysat the children when Susan, due to financial need, returned to the workforce part-time. She was able to use her medical secretarial skills working as an intake receptionist in a hospital emergency room. Susan is still grateful to her mother-in-law for helping her and Luis out. "Yeah, I was close to his family," Susan said a bit wistfully. Before long, however, they were absent from Susan's life, too. Luis's whole family moved back to Puerto Rico when his and Susan's children were still quite young. Of their five children, only the eldest two daughters remember their Puerto Rican grandmother.

None of Susan's children remember their Indian grandparents. They never met them. "I never took them home," Susan confessed, "because number one, we couldn't afford it with all of them." "I don't know," Susan said, seeming uncertain of the decisions she has made, "I just never took them back." After her parents and brother passed away and one of her sisters moved out of state, Susan said, "I thought, there's really nothing there for them to see! We did have relatives," Susan explained, "but most of the elder relatives had passed on and I really didn't know my cousins well." Eventually, however, she and Luis changed their minds and visited her reservation with the children in tow. "I think when they were almost out of high school," Susan said. "To them it was like culture shock," she continued. "They had never been on a reservation. I think they never realized it was so much poverty."

Susan admits that she did not put a lot of effort into socializing her children to be Indian. They always *knew* they were half-Indian, half–Puerto Rican, but they were estranged from both sides of the family. Furthermore, they do not speak Spanish or Dakota. "They don't know my language," Susan said ruefully, "because I don't. I forgot my language, too." Susan is saddened by and ashamed of her language loss. She relayed that her sister occasionally "says something in Sioux" during phone conversations, and "I'm like, I just feel so dumb, but I don't know what [she] said! I know words, like phrases and that," Susan explained, "but that's it. A whole conversation in Sioux is hard."

Susan was in second grade when she was diagnosed with tuberculosis and sent away to a sanitarium. "That's probably," said Susan, "when I lost my language." Her brow furrows beneath her wiry black and silver bob as she recalls this childhood experience. "I just remember a lot of medication and rest," she said. "And my mother and father never came to visit." She remembers being hopeful at first, thinking her parents would arrive any day to take her home. But the days turned into weeks and the weeks turned into months, and eventually Susan felt abandoned and alone. She finished second grade and started third grade, and still, she received neither visits nor letters from her family. Finally, ten months after arriving at the sanitarium, Susan was well enough to go home. "In those ten months," Susan explained, "I didn't speak with anyone Native. . . . And then, after I went home," she continued, "I never spoke that much Sioux. I could understand it, you know, but I really didn't speak it. It was like—now I'm white!" Discomfited by this thought, Susan giggled nervously. "I was pale and skinny," she explained. She remembers her sisters teasing her about her short haircut, too.

Unfortunately, Susan's sanitarium experiences are not unique. For centuries, tuberculosis threatened the lives and well-being of Indigenous people across the North American continent. Scholars debate whether or not the disease affected Indigenous peoples prior to European contact, but the devastating impacts of the disease on Indigenous populations postcontact are evident. It was a leading cause of death on many reservations (US) and reserves (Canada) and was especially devastating among the Dakota, where it often accounted for half of all deaths annually in the late nineteenth and early twentieth centuries.[13] Government officials and medical experts offered various explanations for the excessive mortality rates among Indigenous populations. Some insisted that Indians' "hereditary inferiority," either physically or culturally, was to blame and their "extinction" was inevitable. Others believed the deaths were a temporary contingency of Indians' transition from "primitive" to "civilized" lives. More thoughtful analysts identified the reservation system, and relatedly, the terrible living conditions imposed on Indigenous peoples by US colonial authorities as the most likely reasons for Indians' inordinately high infection and mortality rates. Whereas some regional governments "seemed content to allow natural selection to solve the tuberculosis problem," others recognized the impact of socioeconomic disparities on Indigenous peoples' health.[14] Resolving these disparities, however, was not a priority.

Prior to the utilization of streptomycin (first used on a human patient in 1949), no therapies, aside from "extended rest and sunshine," were available to treat tuberculosis patients.[15] It is unlikely that Susan received the precious antibiotic, as she was diagnosed in the early 1950s and treated at Sioux Sanitarium, a facility for "scrofulous" Indians in Rapid City, North Dakota.[16] Formerly the Rapid City Indian School, the sanitarium, in operation from 1939 into the 1960s, primarily served the role of isolating infected persons from healthy persons.[17] Susan's sanitarium memories are fuzzy, but the memories she has are echoed by other Indigenous people whose lives were impacted by the TB epidemic that ravaged poor communities, both Indigenous and non-Indigenous, in the first half of the twentieth century.

In research conducted in a Canadian First Nations reserve community that had high infection rates, Jessica Moffatt, Maria Mayan, and Richard Long learned that TB patients, much like Susan, experienced repressive isolation from their communities and cultures, including an inability to engage in culture-based health and healing practices, and confusion about why they were removed from their families.[18] Left to interact with predominantly white medical staff, many Indigenous sanitarium patients reported language loss. Additionally, former sanitarium patients said they were ostracized and treated like "outsiders" when they returned to reservation communities. Their language loss made it difficult for them to communicate with family members, and their pale skin made them seem "white," as Susan noted. Further, many tuberculosis patients reported living in fear of the virus *and* the medical care system for many years following their traumatizing experiences at sanitariums. Lisa Stevenson's thoughtful research, which explores Western medical strategies for treating (past) tuberculosis and (present) suicide among Inuit peoples in Nunavut, Canada, further elucidates the harms of what she calls "colonial care."[19] Despite caregivers' humanitarian intentions, Stevenson suggests that healthcare workers' inabilities to understand their patients' cultures, coupled with a "bio-political approach" to care— one that erases patients' identities and measures success by the absence of death—potentially *exacerbate* the harmful effects of tuberculosis (and suicide) in Indigenous communities.

Susan was not the only member of her family to experience the social and physical ravages of tuberculosis. Her older sister, also diagnosed with TB as a child, was sent to the "white" sanitarium in Custer, South Dakota, for treatment. This facility was purportedly nicer and pro- vided better care, but Susan is suspicious of health workers' treatment of Indigenous patients. "She was there a long time, I don't know how many years," Susan said. "Seems like she was gone forever!" Moreover, Susan worries about her sister's stay at the "white" facility and wonders whether it resulted in the loss of her reproductive rights. "When she got out and got married, she never had children," Susan said softly. "I'm thinking," she continued, "was she one of those [girls] they sterilized at the time, without her knowing?" Susan sighed and shrugged her shoul- ders. "I never really talked to her about it before she passed on," she said quietly, "but she never had children." Susan will likely never know if her sister could not or simply opted not to have children, but she is aware of the forced sterilization of US Indigenous girls and women that occurred under the auspices of "treatment" for other ailments. She, like other sanitarium survivors, remains distrustful of the US medical/colo- nial care system.

The sanitarium was not Susan's only negative experience with medi- cal/colonial care on the reservation. She still feels upset when she recalls the poor and inadequate health care provided Indians in her home- town. Specifically, she remembers the long waits to be seen by a medical practitioner. When her family visited the Indian hospital, they always "prepared to spend the whole day there." "We used to take water and bread," Susan remembered, "and sit there and wait and wait and wait and wait—and then they have lunch, so they close the doors! So you have to sit there and wait *again for care*," Susan said exasperatedly. "And if they couldn't see you that day, you went home without care. It was so bad!" Some people suggest that reservation-based health care improved after responsibility for care was transferred from the BIA to the Public Health Service in 1955. The Indian Health Service (IHS) was created at this time.[20] From Susan's perspective, however, nothing changed in her hometown. She described what happened when her sister sought IHS care for her son, Susan's nephew, in the 1980s: "She took him, they waited all day for care, and then when he went in there to see the doctor, they had his father's, his *deceased* father's, health chart. They didn't even have his health chart!" Susan said indignantly. "So they said, 'We can't see you today.'" Susan threw her hands up in disgust. "I thought, this is the eighties! Why can't they get it right?!'"

Susan had many unpleasant memories of her early life on the reservation. In addition to the trauma she endured at the sanitarium, and general loathing she developed for reservation-based healthcare systems, she also remembers blatant racism and debilitating poverty. These experiences of oppression, discussed in more detail in chapter 5, continue to shape Susan's perceptions of Indianness and life on Indian reservations. She does not *love* Ohio, but she prefers it to the reservation. "I met my husband," Susan said, "and I stayed in Ohio ever since. I thought—I'm never going back to North Dakota if I can help it!" The mere thought of returning to the reservation after experiencing life in the city makes Susan laugh out loud—almost fifty years later.

Gertrude

Gertrude (Cayuga) was seventy-two years young when I spoke to her, and she looked even younger. The clear, smooth, shiny skin of her olive-toned face was framed by tidy, short brown hair. She seemed perpetually happy or amused, the corners of her lips frequently turned up into a soft, radiant smile. Gertrude was warm, witty, and incredibly *nice*. She seemed to scan her words for meanness and negativity before saying them aloud. She rarely said anything derisive or discouraging. Words like "wannabe," for instance, were not in her vocabulary. She did not believe in judging others—including "white" people claiming Indian blood. "I mean, who's to say?" Gertrude asked me, her lips beginning to curl into her customary half-smile. "I mean, you can't judge," she said. "You can't be the judge and jury and say you're not!" She rolled back into the couch and slapped her hand on her knee, her grin stretching to occupy even more territory on her round face. "Yeah," Gertrude said, "there's a lot of people that don't look Indian." She learned this truth in "Indian school." "I went to school with [sisters who had] blonde hair, blue eyes, and they were three-quarter Mohawks," Gertrude explained. "I couldn't believe it," she said, shaking her head. "But you know, [the sisters] showed proof! Otherwise they wouldn't be in the Indian school!"

Gertrude was born on the Tuscarora Indian Reservation in Niagara County, New York. Her mother died two years after she was born and her father was an alcoholic, so Gertrude and her siblings were immediately placed in state custody. "Right from the graveyard we were taken," Gertrude relayed. "Of course, my brothers told me the stories, you know, because I was young and I don't remember. . . . Just, I remember being very unhappy and sad a lot when I was little," Gertrude said, "and I never knew why." Now, at age seventy-two, Gertrude has had plenty of time to reflect on why she spent her childhood in such a depressed state. Like other Indian wards of New York State, Gertrude and her brothers grew up at Thomas Indian School, originally the Thomas Asylum for Orphaned and Destitute Indian Children. It was the first orphanage for American Indian children in the United States.

Indian boarding schools like Thomas earned their reputation for being (perhaps the most) destructive agents of forced assimilation. Taking Indian children by coercion or force was outlawed by the federal Indian Bureau in 1917, but enrollments remained high. Schools like Thomas filled the void left by disillusioned Indian communities still reeling from nineteenth-century displacements.[21] The cultural and spiritual practices that might have spurred recovery were forbidden by US federal law. Families "suffering from death, disease, divorce, and destitution" were compelled to send children they could no longer care for to schools like Thomas, which were underfunded and overwhelmed with admittance requests. Ultimately, children like Gertrude were caught up in the political, cultural, spiritual, and social turmoil caused by settler-colonial processes set in motion more than a century earlier.

The "sharpest and most painful" memories shared by survivors of the Thomas Indian School "involve their separations from their families."[22] Gertrude is unable to conjure up an image of her mother, but she acutely recalls being separated from her siblings. The boarding school "had very strict rules about girls on this side and boys on this side," Gertrude relayed. "They had a line and that was it, you know? You wasn't allowed to cross that line. . . . We weren't allowed to even associate with siblings." Not only were girls kept separate from boys, but younger children were separated from older children, so even siblings of the same sex were split apart. Thomas's strict segregation policies may have been for protective purposes, but for many boarding school students, the policies "acted to sever their last ties to their families."[23]

Along with her inexplicable sense of sadness, Gertrude remembers the school's austere, anti-Indian environment:

> When you went to that school they cut your hair off really short, and bangs. Everybody looked alike. All the girls looked alike. We looked like the little girl on the tomato soup can. We all wore the same kind of outfits. And you wouldn't believe, back then they had the stockings that we used to put rubber bands [on] and then roll them down. And we all wore the same kind of shoes and it was like a uniform. . . . And I guess it was because there was no fence around the place or bars or anything like that, I guess this way they could tell if you were theirs or not.

Children at the school were not allowed to "talk Indian" or dance. "They wanted us to be white," Gertrude said, "and that wasn't right, back then, you know." Gertrude also remembers marching. "Everything was marching," she said. She marched to eat, marched to classes, marched to bed. "It was like the service, like military," she explained. In fact, one of her brothers—with whom she eventually developed a relationship—told her that it was easy for him to transition into military life after graduation. "When my brother went in the service, he said those guys would cry around because they had to march so much, [but] that was nothing to him," Gertrude said with a sense of amusement and pride. "He was used to it!"

Graduating from Indian school seldom brought Indian children relief. Graduates who did not join the military or enter the domestic labor force frequently sought enrollment in another Indian school. Siblings, who were isolated from each other in boarding school, tended to become *more* rather than less estranged after graduation. Gertrude, however, refused to accept this fate. She could not get into Haskell Indian Nations University in Lawrence, Kansas, the Indian school her youngest brother enrolled in, but she managed to gain admittance to Chilocco

Indian School, which was about four hundred miles south in Newkirk, Oklahoma. Not surprisingly, the same family upheavals that led students to Thomas also led them to Chilocco, so Gertrude found herself surrounded by familiar faces. In addition, Indian boarding schools like Chilocco were frequently the only schools open to Indian children. If schools existed near Indian children's hometowns, they tended to serve white children only.

Chilocco was founded for the same purpose as the infamous Carlisle Indian School in Pennsylvania (ca. 1880)—to assimilate Indian children into "American" culture by subjecting them to severe conditions, hard labor, harsh discipline, and Christian teachings—but Gertrude has fond memories of her time there. Of course, her primary point of reference was Thomas, which was state run and therefore unfettered by federal regulations aimed at improving the conditions of Indian children's lives. (Whether these federal regulations were enforced is another story.) "It [Chilocco] was totally different," Gertrude said. "I mean, they were very strict where I come from [in New York] and then all of a sudden you're let loose, you know. . . . Here you are on [Chilocco] campus and you can eat with the boys and you can hold hands and you can kiss," she continued. "And we didn't have to march. I liked that!" At Chilocco, Gertrude was finally introduced to Indian cultures and customs. Students participated in Indian dance groups and were encouraged to speak Indian languages. "It was a *real* Indian school, you know?" Gertrude said.

Despite her pleasant memories, Gertrude fell in love with an Indian boy and dropped out of school to follow him to nearby Ponca City. "Big mistake!" she exclaimed as she smacked her hand against a table for emphasis. "All I was looking for," Gertrude reflected, "was somebody to love me, I think." She was silent for a moment, then asserted, "I *know* it was because I never had that. I never had that love before because they [i.e., boarding school matrons] don't have time to put you up on their lap or even give you a hug, say 'Oh, I love you.' It wasn't like that, you know. It was just too many kids. I'm not saying they couldn't have done it, but they didn't do it. But anyway, so there I was, somebody tells me they love me, I believed it, you know." Gertrude learned a *lot* about being Indian in Ponca City. She described her new family as "very traditional." Her father-in-law was a central figure in the Native American Church, sometimes called Peyote Religion. "He was over all the peyote in Oklahoma,"

Gertrude explained. She continued, "A lot of people think that peyote is bad . . . something to get high on. But the American Indian people used peyote for, not Christian beliefs, but I'd say spiritual beliefs. I've seen people really been sick and they would go into the teepee, the men would go into the teepee and pray. That's all they do, is pray." Indians came from all over Oklahoma to engage in ceremonial peyote use inside the teepee situated on Gertrude's in-laws' land.

Gertrude learned about Indian traditions in Ponca City, and she also learned about Indian hardships. Her new family lived in poverty. They had eighty acres of land, but it was undeveloped. The house had electricity, but no running water. "It was rough, I tell ya," Gertrude said. She remembers hauling water from a nearby farm. "And I remember being pregnant, still hauling that water—in those big milk cans!" Gertrude exclaimed. Gertrude also experienced blatant racism for the first time in Ponca City. "Whites did not like the Indians," she said. "They were very prejudiced in that town." She continued, "I mean, you could go into a restaurant, and you would have to go way in the back, like black people. . . . And there were some places that had 'No Indians Allowed' [signs]. And I'll always remember that. It was that time, that era, [when] it was like that, you know. So I wanted to go back to New York."

Gertrude had never experienced such hostility. The constant barrage of messages she received—constant reminders that she was not wanted—wore on her. It was "a time in my life when I didn't want to be Indian," Gertrude said, "when I went through the prejudice thing." She believes that whites' prejudicial attitudes toward Indians were based on the actions of only a few—the Indians who "would go and drink and stagger" at the downtown bars. "They label all the Indians like that," Gertrude explained. "It's not good to label people by bad ones, you know. There's good and bad in everything, in *everything*." Gertrude gravely nodded her head. "But some people are like that. They label you right away."

Gertrude knew one thing for sure. She did not want to stay in Ponca City. "I knew there was a better side of life than that." She and her husband decided to join his siblings, who had relocated to Cleveland. The young couple easily procured housing in the same Italian neighborhood where her siblings-in-law lived, a popular, BIA-supported location for urban Indian transplants. She and her husband were quickly absorbed into the vibrant scene. They enjoyed dancing with other young Indian couples. "We used to go all over and dance," Gertrude reminisced. "I remember, we even danced downtown at a Christmas parade. That was a long time ago. And I've danced at Indians [baseball] games," Gertrude confessed. "Back then," she said, "they didn't care about the Wahoo sign." Gertrude, admittedly, still is not personally offended by the baseball team's Indian mascotry. "Now why should I, years ago, go and dance down there *in the stadium*, you know, and they paid us for it, and then turn around and say something like [the mascot is racist]?" she asked incredulously. "I respect the Natives that go down there [to protest]," she continued. "If that's what they believe in, I respect that. But that's not my belief, so I don't go down there, you know?"

Over time, Gertrude's quality of life in the city deteriorated due to her husband's drinking. "It got so that every time we'd go somewhere, there was drinking involved," Gertrude explained, "and when that started, my ex-husband just couldn't handle himself." Gertrude's husband was not alone. For many relocated Indians, drinking became a "survival mechanism" that helped them deal with the pressures of mainstream society and reaffirmed their sense of belonging in the world.[24] Unfortunately, social drinking was not just the cure for loneliness; for Indians like Gertrude's ex-husband, it caused turmoil. Part of the problem, according to Fixico, is that drinking became linked to urban Indians' sense of group identity, and the desire to *fit in somewhere* made it difficult for Indians to stop drinking even when it wreaked havoc on their lives.

As Gertrude's husband drank more and more heavily, their relationship became more and more violent. "And every weekend, every weekend he was drinking," she said. When he drank too much, he beat her, and over time the beatings became more and more severe. On several occasions, Gertrude needed to be hospitalized. "One time," she said gravely, "they didn't even think I was gonna live." Gertrude knew she had to leave the man with whom she had spent the previous fourteen years. "I just had it, you know?" she said softly. "When I got that divorce, I said I'd never marry again," Gertrude said. "Especially an Indian. Oh my god, I was hurt so bad." She was only thirty years old, but Gertrude felt as though she had been through war. She escaped with her three children and nothing else—only the clothes on their backs. Thankfully, she had a good job at Ford Motor Company. "That helped me," she said. She enjoyed the work and the pay was reliable. In addition, Ford was located in the suburbs. "So I got an apartment there and we lived there and my life changed," Gertrude said. She was reluctant to leave everything familiar behind, but she knew it was necessary. "When something isn't working right," Gertrude explained, "you have to change your whole life. You can't keep part of it. Otherwise it may drag you back down, you know, and I didn't want that." She decided to separate herself from the Indian community entirely. She needed to forsake her Indian friends to save herself. "Everybody knew everybody," said Gertrude, "so I just got out of it and started living a different kind of life."

Almost a decade later, Gertrude finally made her way back to the community. She reconnected with old Indian friends and made new Indian friends, and she cannot imagine what her life would be like without them. "I consider them real good friends," Gertrude confided. "I know that if I ever got way down, I know that I could depend on them. That's the Indian community that I know."

* * *

The stories in this chapter draw out commonalities and variations in the intergenerational experiences of Indigenous people who relocated to Northeast Ohio. Like Berta and Greg, whose stories comprise the first vignette, all relocators interviewed for this research moved to the Cleveland metropolitan area in search of "fuller" lives for themselves and their children. Whether relocators came alone, like Greg and Susan, or in partnership with loved ones, like Gertrude, everyone hoped to establish new roots and create brighter futures in Northeast Ohio. Some relocators felt *pushed out* of reservation communities that could not support their financial needs. Berta and Greg, for instance, tried raising their children on the reservation but returned to the urban environment of NE Ohio, where Greg more easily secured employment that provided a living wage. Other relocators, like Susan, were *pulled to* Ohio, enticed by educational and occupational opportunities.

However relocators described their motivations for their NE Ohio migrations, all were aware of the hardships accompanying reservation life. Relocator elders, like Berta, Greg, Susan, and Gertrude, described their reservation communities as (fiscally) impoverished and lacking critical resources. These elders also experienced racially discriminatory behaviors in schools they attended and businesses they frequented. Gertrude's story highlights discrimination against Indians in both dimensions. The hostile treatment Gertrude received from white people as an Indian boarding school student and Ponca City resident resulted in the loss of her Indian pride. Though it pains her now, Gertrude admits there were times in her life when she did not want to be Indian anymore. The scorn she received from others was too burdensome for her younger self to bear.

Like all Indigenous peoples in the United States, relocators are extremely diverse. They represent different tribal nations and cultures, they grew up in different regions of the country, and they learned and developed different strategies for maintaining their Indian identities. As migrants to Northeast Ohio, however, they share an important commonality: deep and heartfelt appreciation for the urban pan-Indian community that brings them together. This community structure not only brought Berta and Greg together but also eased their transition back into the urban environment when they could not make it on the reservation. The community also was a lifeline for Susan and Gertrude. Susan remains committed to the community despite her disengagement from Indigenous cultural traditions. Gertrude temporarily left the community when she left her abusive husband, but she could not stay away for long. Both women agree that relocator community members comprise their closest friendship circle and most dependable support network. The significance of this urban, pan-Indian community to NE Ohio relocators is an important part of relocators' stories.

3

Stories of Reclamation

Dean was born in 1934, just one decade after American Indians were granted US citizenship. In his lifetime he experienced tremendous change in the way people treat Indians. Dean delights in his ability to "fit into the crowd" now, but remembers the fierce discrimination he experienced in his younger years. "People didn't take to us like they did the white people," he said in his low, gravelly voice. "Back in them days you used to sit there like a dog. You wasn't human, in other words." He peered at me from under the brim of his baseball cap, which had the word "MARINE" etched in gold block letters. The whole time we talked his voice inflection never changed, but his eyes lit up when he was excited. He answered questions directly, without any sugarcoating.

Though born in Kentucky, Dean spent his childhood in a small West Virginia coal mining town, surrounded by poor white folks who either farmed or mined coal like his father. Despite the poor treatment they received as Indians, Dean's father expressed deep pride in his heritage. "He'd tell you in a hurry that he was an Indian and he wouldn't try to pass himself off as nothing but an Indian. And he helped up with the Indian people, too, wherever he could," Dean said. Dean followed in his father's footsteps. When he enlisted in the Marines, just in time to serve in the Korean War, he made certain "Indian" was noted on his records. This decision had consequences, however. Dean recalled, "Well, when I first got there, the VI looked at me [and] he said, 'You an Indian?' I said, 'Yes sir.' He said, 'Well, some day you going to have to prove that you an Indian.' So I didn't get to walk on the road like the others. I had to walk on the left flank or the right flank . . . on swamps and quicksand and all that, so he told me that he gonna make a Marine out of me or kill me." Dean experienced harsher treatment than the non-Indian recruits in his Marine battalion, but he tells this story with more pride than resentment. The assumptions that Dean's superior made about Dean's "innate" soldiering abilities—based solely on his Indianness—were deeply engrained and widespread in the US military and in popular culture. American Indians' US military service began as early as the Revolutionary War, when Indians served as scouts. Indians continued to serve the US military as scouts during the War of 1812 and the Civil War, and in 1866, the US Army formalized this service by establishing the "Indian Scouts," a corps that remained active well into the twentieth century.[1] Indians' reputation for being particularly suited to military service was due to their (presumed) "natural" tracking abilities and warrior traditions. The "natural abilities" of Indians to scout, "survive in harsh battlefield conditions," and "work behind enemy lines" were even touted by Indians themselves in an early-twentieth-century publication of Indian intellectuals called *American Indian Magazine*.[2]

Dean was not the first enlisted man in his family, and he would not be the last. His grandfather, like so many Indians before him, was a scout for the US Army. Dean's grandfather was on a scouting mission, in fact, when he disappeared, leaving Dean's grandmother with multiple children to feed in Oklahoma Indian Territory. Dean's father was the eldest of these children, so to relieve his mother's burden, he left home at age seventeen and hitched a ride north with a white couple who shared both their home and their Christian teachings with him. Dean's father earned a living working in the coal mines of Kentucky and West Virginia. When he was not working, he preached the gospel. "They called him the little Indian preacher," Dean said with pride, "and he had a pretty good crowd of people that would come and listen to him." Over time, serving country, God, and Indians became a family tradition.

When Dean was released from active duty, he accepted his sister's invitation to live with her in Ohio. With a mischievous smile that caused his black eyes to disappear behind his round, ruddy cheeks, Dean said, "She wrote me and told me there's pretty girls in Ohio, so when I got out of the military, I caught the bus and come to Ohio." In Ohio, Dean worked in the ministry and sang in a gospel choir while holding a full-time factory job that provided him with money to support his family. He got involved in a local Indian Center and eventually became a board member. For the first time in Dean's life, he started "going to pow-wows . . . and learning more about the [Indian] culture." He had learned some things about being Indian from his full-blood Indian father— things like taking care of people and taking care of the earth and just basically doing things the right way, the Indian way. His father taught him respect for God and all of God's creations. And finally, Dean's father taught him to have enduring pride in his Indian heritage and to hold onto his Indian values. His father never took him to powwows, though. "Dad taught me a lot of stuff, but . . . we didn't have the money to go no place. There was eleven of us in the family . . . and it took all the money to feed us and clothe us and pay for the house."

Dean's birth certificate says he is an Indian, but he can't remember if his sons' say the same. "Back in them days, and today, they want to put the majority. What is it? European or Caucasian or something like that?" Dean said hesitantly. "They don't want to put American Indian down no more." Nevertheless, Dean raised his boys to be proud of their Indian ancestry, and Kurt, the eldest, followed a path much like his father's. He served in the military, entered the ministry, and by the time he was forty-six years old, Kurt had devoted twenty-five years of his life to working for the betterment of Indians living in NE Ohio. Kurt directed the reclaimer Indian community organization that his father, Dean, founded in 2001. Kurt is a jovial guy with black eyes that form deep crinkles in the corners when he smiles, which he is apt to do. His shiny bald head and salt-and-pepper goatee contour his friendly, handsome face. Kurt is quick to laugh and when he does, it is contagious. He is serious when he needs to be, though, and some people at the center—Dean's crew of friends, in particular—think Kurt is sometimes overly serious or stern. They do not seem to fully appreciate Kurt's work and all that it entails, the sacrifices he makes to work full-time for an Indian community too many people refuse to recognize as such. Overall, Kurt is well loved at the center, where he serves as leader, role model, and friend.

Dean's family's devotion to country, God, and Indians does not stop with Kurt. Kurt's son, Daniel, is quick to admit that he follows in *his* father's footsteps. Like Kurt, Daniel is a military veteran and an ordained minister. Daniel looks a lot like Kurt, too, with similarly dark eyes set just a little closer together, and a rounder, more boyish face. And much like his father, Daniel has always "taken an interest" in his Indian background. "I can't remember when we actually started talking about like, what we were. I just remember knowing. It's just like, I'm Native. I'm Choctaw. Forever." "I guess I've always been proud of who I am and where I come from and what it means to me, even in all aspects—spirituality, traditions," Daniel said. As early as kindergarten, Daniel understood that he was different from the other children. "I mean, there was no one like me at my school. . . . It was all white kids and me and my brothers." Daniel remembers going to powwows with his grandfather Dean, though, and by the time he was nine or ten years old the powwow scene had become a place of refuge. "I mean, that's where I met my wife and my best friends nowadays. They're all powwow people," Daniel said. "We all hang out once a week. We have a game night . . . and we have dinner. . . . I guess we have a sense of community between us, which is cool."

When Daniel entered the Navy right out of high school, he found it difficult to be so far away from everything and everyone he knew. He stayed connected to his "little Native community" during his four years of active duty, but it required a little disobedience and a whole lot of hustle. Daniel was stationed at a Navy base in the South, so he and his Ohio friends arranged to meet at powwows that split the distance between them. Daniel, however, was not permitted to travel more than 350 miles from his ship, unless he was on leave. "Oh, yeah, I was hustling," he said. "I would always hit like 375 or 400 [miles]," Daniel confessed, "and I'm like—Alright, [my car] can't break down until I'm at the 300 mark! I mean, looking back on it, it wasn't the best idea," Daniel admitted, "but it was something I needed, so it was worth it. It was worth sixteen hours straight driving, just *woosh*! Get there Saturday and leave Sunday." He pauses for a moment, remembering, and then nods. "It was worth it," he repeats, this time with a little more conviction. Even while serving in the US Navy, Daniel prioritized his commitment to his Indian family and his Indian roots.

Dean, Kurt, and Daniel represent three generations of Indian reclaimers. Their collective story—one with roots in Oklahoma Indian Territory—is not altogether uncommon. None of the men ever lived with uncertainty about their Indian heritages. They never tried to leave their Indianness behind. They did not hide it or take it underground. Dean's father left his Oklahoma home, but he took his Indian identity with him. He passed that identity on to his son Dean, who passed it on to his son Kurt, who passed it on to his son Daniel. This story—one of consistent, cross-generational identification as Indians—is true for some NE Ohio reclaimer families. They are close enough to their Indian roots to claim Indian identities with some sense of authority. Often, however, their Indian traditions were lost along the way. The following stories of reclamation—stories belonging to Cheryl, Danna, and Valerie—reveal critical distinctions in how reclaimers learn about, come to appreciate, and decide to assert their Indian identities.

Cheryl and Danna

Danna is a self-assured woman who unapologetically takes up space. Though we never met before our interview, she did not even let me finish introducing myself before asking, "So what made you decide to study Natives?" Her blunt manner caught me off guard. She did not ask the question in a friendly or conversational way. She was not making small talk. She wanted to know why she should talk to me and how much information she should provide. I had been shuffling through my bag, collecting my interview accoutrements, e.g., consent forms, interview guide, recorder, pen, but abruptly stopped to refocus my attention on her. Now that we were face to face, I could see the resemblance between Danna and her mother, Cheryl, whom I had interviewed only three days prior. They both had bronze skin and broad, friendly faces. Danna, however, had faint freckles that brought out the golden hues in her eyes. Her makeup-free face and short pixie haircut might have seemed boyish if she did not exude such bold, womanish confidence. In response to her question, I quickly touched on the pivotal experiences that led me to this topic and this moment in my life—earning a bachelor's degree in anthropology, serving as an AmeriCorps*VISTA in Dinétah (i.e., Navajoland), starting graduate school in sociology, participating in protests against the Cleveland MLB team's "Indians" imagery. Danna nodded her consent.

Like Dean, Kurt, and Daniel, Danna always knew she was American Indian. Growing up, she spent a lot of time at a local Indian Center where her mother was a board member. But the "Indian" part of her life was compartmentalized until high school. Sure, children in elementary school made fun of her mother's brown skin, calling it "dirty," but Danna just tuned them out. In high school, Danna started developing a stronger sense of herself as different from her classmates. "We're not, like, radical people or anything like that, but just [have] different beliefs," Danna explained. She continued, "My mom's always been very spiritual. Not ever religious . . . just, she feels like she owes some gratitude to na-

ture or something. That's kind of odd to say, but she feels this relationship with outside and stuff. I don't think she's mentally ill, but she's just
a little bit different about things. I don't really know how to explain it.
I can't pinpoint it, but it wasn't the same as like, the white people that
I knew or the black people that I knew." But Danna's mother, Cheryl,
did not proactively teach Danna about their Indian heritage. Cheryl did
not know much about it herself. Cheryl's mother always said they were
Indians, but Cheryl's father always said her mother "[didn't] know what
she [was] talking about." Cheryl's mother tried to tell her children stories
about their Indian past, but, Cheryl said, whispering, "My dad would
kind of, not actually beat it out of us, but beat it out of us."

Despite her father's intense denials, the lingering doubts Cheryl had
about her mother's Indianness dissipated by the time she reached adulthood. Her mother, after all, had always told Cheryl and her brothers
they were Indian, and she frequently insisted on driving the children "up
North" in Michigan for family "gatherings." "Now they call them powwows," Cheryl said. "They probably called them powwows before, but
my mom wouldn't use that word." Cheryl's Indian identity grew stronger over time. Despite being a single mother who worked full-time, she
started volunteering at an urban Indian Center and eventually served on
the center's board of directors.

The Indian Center was an important source of information and identity affirmation for Danna, too. Much of what she knows about being
Indian, Danna says, is "just stuff that I absorbed, and then I think being
around the people at the Indian Center, I learned a lot," she reflected.
Danna's mother took her to powwows, too, when she could afford it. "I
absolutely loved it. It was so much fun because everybody was Indian,"
Danna said. "And everyone kind of wanted to do the same things, you
know? Dance and have fun. And it was fun to me because I was younger,
and I didn't see the politics." To Danna and other reclaimers, "Indian
politics" describes the actions of any person or entity involved in policing the boundaries of Indianness.[3] The word is uttered disdainfully,
almost spat out, as though it leaves a bad taste in the mouth. People
who engaged in Indian politics, according to many reclaimers, falsely
believed that only Indians enrolled in federally recognized tribes were
real, legitimate Indians. Danna's awareness of Indian politics grew as
she matured and had a child of her own. The Indian Center, in fact, ul-

timately pushed her to discover and legally document her tribal origins. Danna's quest for enrollment began when the Indian Center denied her financial assistance. Danna explained,

> My son is blind in one eye and he had a lot of medical issues and I didn't have insurance, so I went to the Indian Center and I said, you know, I need help to buy him glasses. I mean, I had paid for everything else. She says, "We can't help you if you don't have a card. You have to be a registered tribal member." And I'm like—I, I've been coming here since I was one [year old]! You guys *know*! And they wouldn't help me. . . . To me, that was like . . . a stab in the back. I *am* Native. You know I am, but now I have to *prove* this to you? Like, you want to count my blood?!

In that moment, Danna determined she would work to ensure no one, ever, would be able to deny her Indianness again. "It was just kind of sad to me," she said. "My own people said that I'm not."

For Danna, the issue of enrollment had come up before. She never knew how to identify on surveys or censuses. She knew she was Indian, but "there's a lot of things where you have to have a card. And that started to really bother me," she said. "When I went into the military, it really hit me because I couldn't check Native American. I didn't have a card. . . . On all my military records," Danna lamented, "it says white." Despite having a direct link to her Indian ancestry—Danna's grandmother was tribally enrolled—Danna was not enrolled because her mother, Cheryl, had not been enrolled by *her* mother. For whatever reason, Cheryl never considered enrolling herself. Cheryl knew she was Indian, so "to her," Danna said, "it was never a big deal. She was like, 'I'm Indian. It doesn't matter.' And I'm like, to *me* it does," Danna stated exasperatedly, "because now you've told me that I'm not." The Indian Center's denial was a strong motivator for Danna to obtain a tribal identification card, and she was able to do so without much trouble. Danna already knew her grandmother belonged to a Michigan tribe, so she started with an Internet search and then started calling tribal offices in Michigan. She described the process: "You can give them somebody's name and say, 'Is this person enrolled?' And so I called like ten different [tribes] and I finally found the one where my grandmother was enrolled. So, it was just paperwork and you've got to submit birth certificates and your family tree and everything, and basically see if your family tree matches up with the family tree your relative had given. And that's about it." All of the paperwork went to an enrollment committee, which voted to approve Danna's and Cheryl's applications for tribal membership.

Danna admits that being enrolled has not drastically changed her life, but it has changed the way she thinks about Indianness—or rather, who she thinks has the right to claim an Indian identity. "See, I struggle with that. I really do," Danna said. Often, when people discover Danna is Indian, they tell her about *their* grandparent, or their great-great-grandparent, who is Indian, too. Danna explained why this response sometimes annoys her: "I had to prove that [I'm Indian]. I have to carry a card that says that I am, so I guess I get a little bit offended that now you want to be part of my group, you know? Just stay where you're at. Just do whatever you want to do and don't think that now we have this bond because your great-great-great-grandmother or whatever was Indian. I don't really, you know, I don't like that. That's just a personal thing and I know I'm probably an ass for being like that."

Danna thinks she is "probably an ass" because she generally keeps her nose out of other people's business. Being nonchalant about other people's actions aligns with her "live and let live" philosophy. "I mean, I guess anybody has the right to say that they are [Indian]," she stated. "That doesn't affect my life, so you can go ahead and keep saying that. I don't give a shit, really." But Danna reluctantly admits that it bothers her a bit, too. "Internally it makes me a little mad, but, I mean, people can say whatever they want." What really matters to Danna is that other people can't say she is *not* Indian now that she has an "Indian card." She even got her identification number tattooed on the back of her neck. Danna has complete confidence in herself as an American Indian woman. "How does [being Indian] make me feel?" she asks. "Like an overwhelming sense of pride every day I get up and I look at myself. I think I've just come to a point where I'm just proud of who I am and what I am."

Being "carded" has changed Danna's mother's perspective on the enrollment issue, too. Despite her initial disinterest in applying for tribal membership, Cheryl quickly asserts her *carded* Indian status now. When I asked how she responded to the race question on the US Census, Cheryl abruptly stated, "Native American. I do have a card and I do have a number." And when I told her I knew another woman from her tribe who lives in NE Ohio, Cheryl pointedly asked, "Oh, does she have a card that says that?" (In fact, she does.) Cheryl's enrollment changed the way she remembers her own mother, too. Over the years, Cheryl had nagging doubts about her mother's claims to Indianness. Now that she has her Indian card, she finally understands that "everything [mom] told me, it wasn't just somebody rambling on. It was true."

Valerie

At age forty-eight, Valerie is frustrated that she *still* has to convince people she is Indian. She knows she is Indian. The Indians in her family know she is Indian. Yet so many people in Valerie's life refuse to recognize this vital aspect of her identity. When I interviewed Valerie, she talked extensively about her efforts to get enrolled in a Cherokee tribe. Her devotion to this cause was rooted in her desire to finally *belong* to something, to finally belong *somewhere*.

Valerie worked at a midsized, family-owned farm, but this Saturday evening she was cleaning a large barn used by the band boosters of a local high school. She preferred working outdoors, but needed "odd jobs" like this to make ends meet. She smiled and waved with childlike enthusiasm when I entered the building. She was wearing baggy denim overalls, her light brown hair pulled back into a loose ponytail. The misfit strands created a halo effect under the bright fluorescent barn lights. We sat across from one another on a cold aluminum picnic table. Valerie took a deep breath and plunged right in, divulging intimate details of a childhood shaped by poverty, abuse, and buried Indian ancestors.

As far back as she can remember, Valerie knew she was Indian. She just did not care. Being poor seemed much more significant. Valerie thought being poor was why she never fit in at school. "Some people made fun of you or treated you differently," Valerie remembered, "because of the way you looked or the way you dressed." Valerie did not like school, but conceded that "it was better than what you were getting when you went home." Rather than a safe space or comfort zone, *home* was where Valerie and her younger brother experienced horrific abuse at the hands of a babysitter. Their father cared for them as best he could after their mother left, but steady employment was difficult to come by.

He frequently did temp work out of state, and as a result, was oblivious to the abuses his children suffered. At age sixteen, Valerie and her little brother ran away from home. They unwittingly stumbled into Dean's Indian Center one day, on a mission to find food. "Yeah, that's how I actually met Dean," Valerie said, "and then lost track [of him], because, you know, I was fifteen, sixteen and you know, got married, had a couple kids, and then my brother got killed and, don't remember too much at all for a few years."

Five years after their initial acquaintance, Valerie's and Dean's paths crossed again. "I had just divorced my first husband, had just lost my brother, lost my grandmother," Valerie explained. She had never felt more isolated or depressed in her life. Valerie was barely getting back on her feet when she met someone who invited her to a gathering at a local Indian Center. Valerie was astonished and delighted to discover that the Indian Center's "chief," as Valerie alone referred to him, was *Dean*. "It's kind of weird," Valerie reflected, "how sometimes God puts different people in your path at different times to nudge you into situations that you otherwise may have been, mmm, more reluctant to do." At the time Valerie was not searching for an Indian community, and she had little interest in digging up her family's Indian past. She was too busy dealing with everything else—isolation, abuse, poverty, loss, motherhood.

Valerie became more curious about her Indian ancestry as she attended more Indian Center meetings. She admitted as much to Dean, who encouraged her to investigate her family tree. Soon after, she attended a family reunion and discovered a shocking truth—that her great-grandfather was a full-blood Indian. Excitedly, Valerie relayed this information. "I always knew we were Native American, [but] never realized it was my great-grandfather!" she exclaimed. Valerie always assumed her closest Indian relation was further removed. "And that was the—*BOOM!*" Valerie clapped her hands together. That was the stimulus she needed to become "very diligent" about excavating her Indian roots.

When Valerie embarked on her search for her Indian past, she was not prepared for the twists and turns she would experience. "It was unbelievable!" Valerie blustered. I mean, the route they send you on and the amount of information they're asking for—it's almost as though they make it impossible to do the paper trail." When I interviewed Valerie, she had already spent five years tracking down paperwork she needed to

obtain Cherokee citizenship. She could not give up now, she insisted, because she had exhumed nearly every Indian in her past. The only document she needed was her great-grandfather's death certificate. It was the
missing link, the only thing blocking Valerie's access to the "ID number"
that, in Valerie's words, "completes who you are, where you came from,
where your family came from, what they've accomplished."

Valerie had already been denied membership in the Eastern Band of
Cherokee Indians, one of three federally recognized Cherokee tribes,
when we met for our interview. "Which didn't make sense to me!" Valerie said incredulously. She told me about traveling all the way from
Northeast Ohio to Cherokee, North Carolina, only to be rebuffed by
a BIA employee. "I mean, I'm at the Bureau of Indian Affairs," Valerie
explained, "and I can prove everything up to [great-grandfather's] death
certificate, and all she could tell me was, you know, 'I'm really sorry, but
without that information, you can't go forward.'" Valerie threw her hands
up in disgust. Valerie did not explain why she visited the Eastern Band
knowing she did not have the necessary death certificate, but acknowledged that she was "so aggravated and so frustrated" by this experience
of rejection that she almost gave up her quest for enrollment entirely.
She threw all the documents she had collected in a dresser drawer and
willed herself to abandon her dream.

But, Valerie told me, she could not let it go. She could not disregard
the experience she had while visiting Cherokee, North Carolina. "Even
though I didn't get what I initially went after," Valerie said, "I did get exactly what I was after." She explained, "When I was at the reservation, I
have to say I never felt such peace, at home, as though my inner spirit
was where it was supposed to be. . . . I loved it. I mean, I walked around
the creeks. I picked up rocks. I sat and thought and just reminisced and
did my own little smudging ceremony. I did my prayer ceremony—and
had butterflies just appear out of nowhere! Hundreds of them landed on
my hands and on my feet, as I'm sitting there going, 'Okay. What is going
on?!'" Valerie described her visit as "a very emotional, *moving experience.*"
Her memories of this experience eventually convinced her to continue her
quest. She became more determined than ever. She knew she needed to
"go all the way with this," she said passionately, "to fill the need that I have,
personally, to say that this is why I'm the way I am. This is why I have the
colored skin. This is why my hair's the way it is, my eyes are the way it is."

With a renewed sense of purpose, Valerie set her sights on obtaining enrollment in the Cherokee Nation of Oklahoma (hereafter, Cherokee Nation). She intentionally targeted the Cherokee Nation because its enrollment criterion—proof of descent with no blood quantum requirement—is the least restrictive of the three Cherokee tribes. In fact, the other nations—the United Keetoowah Band and the Eastern Band—accuse the Cherokee Nation of Oklahoma of being a "nation of racially and culturally white Indians" or "thindians" due to the tribe's lax enrollment policies.[4] Valerie did not care which tribe enrolled her. She just wanted to feel connected to something bigger than her family and herself. And she already had come so far.

Valerie explained that her genealogical odyssey, initiated five years earlier, started on a high note. She was able to locate her great-great-grandfather's name on the Dawes Rolls. Now she only had to *prove* this man listed on the rolls was, in fact, her great-great-grandfather. Valerie explained, "In order to verify who he actually is in my chain of information, I had to have my birth certificate, I had to have my father's birth certificate. . . . Then had to show on his birth certificate who his parents was, then their birth certificates and death certificates. Of course, his mother would have been the descendant of [my great-grandfather], so we had to go show on her birth certificate who her parents was and then go back and try to get their death certificates." Acquiring this documentation was anything but straightforward. Valerie, for instance, had to solve the puzzle of her grandmother's birth certificate. The birth certificate did not state her grandmother's real name. "They didn't anticipate that she was going to make it," Valerie said, "so she was actually just listed as 'baby.'" This protective mechanism for parents of seemingly moribund babies proved to be "very frustrating" for Valerie. "We had to actually go back through to where her two sisters had went to the courthouse," Valerie explained, "filed a paper stating that they were her direct sisters, this was her name, this is the day she was born, and she is not just known as baby girl." This process was time-consuming, but ultimately rewarding.

Encouraged by this experience, Valerie believed she could overcome the final obstacle in her path to Cherokee citizenship—locating her great-grandfather's death certificate. She knew it would not be easy, but at the time of our interview, she remained hopeful. She had already covered some ground. For instance, she learned that the funeral home "was no longer in business" and the cemetery records "were no longer at that facility." She talked about tracking down death certificates that had crossed the state of West Virginia: "Well, those names that they had records for were then sent to Parkersburg, but Parkersburg didn't want to be responsible for them, so they shipped them to the capital of West Virginia. So now you have to go to Charleston. Well, with all of the fraud and what-not going on, you literally have to show documentation of who you are as to why you're getting and asking for a death certificate that was done in 1954." Excitedly, Valerie said, "And it gets even worse!" She could not find the precise date of her grandfather's death. She only knew the month and year he died. In summer, Valerie asserted, she would travel to Charleston, West Virginia, and sift through every death certificate filed in July of 1954 until she found the one documenting the passing of her great-grandfather. When I saw Valerie at a reclaimer community gathering only a few weeks after she made the trip to Charleston, she tried to look upbeat as she told me the bad news—she would not now or ever become a Cherokee citizen. Not long after arriving in Charleston, Valerie learned that a courthouse fire decades earlier had turned her grandfather's death certificate to ash.

* * *

These stories highlight similarities and differences in intergenerational experiences of Indian ethnic reclamation in Northeast Ohio. Threaded through all reclaimers' stories—those presented in this chapter and others throughout the book—are perceptions of loss. Reclaimers generally regard their Indianness as something stolen from them. They understand their losses to be by-products of resistance strategies used by their kinfolk to survive in settler society. For reclaimers like Dean, Kurt, and Daniel, resistance meant stubbornly maintaining Indian identities despite the distance separating them from Indian communities and Indian traditions. For some reclaimers, their forebears' resistance to oppression meant abandoning, hiding, or downplaying Indianness by marrying white people, adopting white ways, and forsaking Indian identities. This description elucidates why Cheryl and Danna needed to reclaim Indian identities and obtain tribal enrollment—because Cheryl's mother would not or could not assert her Indianness. Furthermore, she failed to enroll Cheryl in the tribal nation in which she was enrolled. In some cases, reclaimers' relatives hid their Indian ancestry so well that reclaimers grew up with little knowledge or awareness of their Indian pasts. If they knew they were Indian, it did not impact their identities. Valerie, for instance, did not think about or prioritize her Indianness before participating as an adult in an urban pan-Indian community. Her involvement sparked her strong, albeit thwarted, desire to obtain enrollment in the Cherokee Nation.

Reclaimers also vary with regard to their degree of proximity to Indian-identified family members, which impacts their abilities and commitments to obtaining formal acknowledgment of their Indian identities. Such acknowledgment was extremely important to Valerie, especially once she discovered that her great-grandfather was a full-blood Indian. Ultimately, however, Valerie was unable to become a "citizen Cherokee." Cheryl and Danna, in contrast, did not place much emphasis on enrollment until they achieved enrollment status in a federally recognized Indian nation. Their new status prompted them to reevaluate the significance they attached to tribal membership. Additionally, Cheryl finally understood that her mother's stories about the family's Indian heritage were true. Cheryl's *father* lied to cover up his wife's Indian past. Importantly, some reclaimers, like the men in Dean's family, were ambivalent about obtaining legal recognition of their Indian status. Despite, or perhaps because of, their consistent identification as Indians over time, neither Dean, nor Kurt, nor Daniel prioritized enrollment. The subject of enrollment infrequently arose during interviews or informal conversations with these men, which is why enrollment matters are omitted from their opening vignette. All three men were committed to being Indian, practicing Indian ways, and serving other Indians in their urban Indian community. They just did not put much stock in enrollment. They knew they were Indians and, according to them, no piece of paper certifying their Indianness was going to change that fact.

Despite their differences, reclaimers come together to support one another within the structure of an urban, pan-Indian community. The current community organization, founded by Dean and directed by Dean's son, Kurt, developed in response to the need for identity affirmation and collaboration among NE Ohio residents working to reclaim Indian identities. Dean and Kurt recognized the need for a community organization that served *all* urban Indians, whether or not they were enrolled in federally recognized tribes. Reclaimer community members especially appreciate this space, which provides them with a sense of belonging in a world that frequently dismisses their Indian identity claims. Valerie's story, the final vignette in this chapter, brings this issue to light. Her response to repetitive denials of her identity claims was to (try to) become a citizen Cherokee, which she believed would silence people dubious about her Indian heritage. Danna also used enrollment as a shield against others' denials of her identity claims. Dean and Kurt, in contrast, engaged a different strategy altogether. Rather than expending energy and resources on verifying their own claims, they created an open and affirming urban pan-Indian community, structured to accommodate the specific needs of NE Ohio reclaimers.

4

Being and Becoming Indian

Relocators' and reclaimers' stories of being and becoming Indian cohere around different themes. Indianness, according to first-generation relocators who migrated to Northeast Ohio from Indian reservations, is *embedded* in their minds, bodies, and everyday realities. Though it begins with their bloodlines, families, and heritages, it encompasses the whole of their lives, their children's and grandchildren's lives, and the lives of each generation moving forward. Additionally, first-generation relocators described being Indian as a gratifying existence despite its entanglements with profound oppressions. It means lives comprised of Indigenous memories, stories, and histories experienced, expressed, retold, and understood in contexts that (for many relocators) sustain family and spirituality. Ultimately, being Indian to many Northeast Ohio relocators means *maintaining* Indian identities, families, and communities. Reclaimers, in contrast, experience Indianness in terms of being *and* becoming. Their *intuitive* Indianness, as they experience it, is innate but requires nurturance. For some reclaimers, grandparents, despite their disconnectedness from Indigenous communities, passed on memories of Indianness able to nurture Indian identities for generations to come. For other reclaimers, Indianness is an identity necessitating discovery and reclamation, sometimes through nonfamilial networks and adoptive family on and off Indian reservations. Native mentors provide reclaimers previously detached from Indian communities with memories, histories, and new understandings of Indianness.

Relocators: Rez Life, Rez Cred

To grow up poor, in poverty, and to experience a reservation—I would say that's what makes you Native. If you're born in the city, that's completely different. Even my kids, they'll never know what it's like to be poor and to be a real Indian!
—Susan (Dakota)

Susan (Dakota), whose relocation story is highlighted in chapter 2, grew up on an Indian reservation in North Dakota. Now in her sixties, she has spent more of her life in the city than on the "rez," as many relocators and reclaimers referred to reservation lands. Despite Susan's primarily urban experiences, she summons experiences from her past to answer the question, What does it mean to be Indian? Of course, it means something different to everyone who identifies as such, but for first-generation relocators like Susan, those whose early lives took shape on Indian reservations, two experiences were prominent in molding their understandings of indigeneity: discrimination and poverty.

Susan's most pronounced memories from childhood revolve around these dual oppressions. She described daily experiences of discrimination in her hometown, which was overrun with whites. "It was a farming town," said Susan, "and *we* were the minority—a small group of Indian families—even though it was a reservation." Although the whites had encroached on Indian lands, they believed they were too good to associate with Indian people. "Growing up in a town like that, a white town on the reservation, you still kept separate," Susan explained. Except for her siblings, Susan's classmates were all white. Any friendships formed during the school day were put on hold in the afternoon, when the white children and the Indian children went back to their respective homes. There were not any birthday parties or slumber parties or any kinds of parties that were inclusive of both white people and Indian people. In her nineteen years on the reservation, Susan was not invited into a single white person's home. "We never went inside or, you know, socialized with them," she said.

Not all towns on the reservation were like Susan's hometown. "One town was all Native, just next to us, and then we were all white, and then the one up where the BIA offices were, they were mixed," Susan explained. According to Susan, people who were part Indian and part white tended to have government jobs. As a child, Susan learned to snub them. She remembers being envious of the Indians living in all-Indian towns, however. She was particularly jealous of the children. They didn't live near local schools (because schools were located in predominantly white areas), so they were placed in Indian boarding schools. As a child, Susan always wanted to attend a boarding school because, as far as she could tell, that was the only path to playing an instrument in the band.

In her youth, ignorant of abuses children suffered in boarding schools, Susan imagined them to be somewhat glamorous—or, at least much more gratifying than *her* educational experiences, which she begrudgingly shared with snooty white students.

Susan's experiences with discrimination in her predominantly white reservation town were exacerbated by her family's poverty. Susan had three sisters and two brothers, so her mother and father had six mouths to feed in addition to their own. She remembers eating the surplus commodity foods provided by the government. "It's bad when you grow up *really* poor," she said. "In the morning you have oatmeal. And then in the afternoon you have bean soup and fry bread. And in the evening you have leftover bean soup." Dessert was unheard of, and even fresh vegetables were rare, with the exceptions of seasonal corn and squash. Susan cannot recall ever drinking milk. She and her siblings drank Kool-Aid because it was more affordable. "And my dad hated the bread, the white bread," Susan remembered. "He called it cotton bread."

The negative experiences Susan accumulated in her youth continue to shape her general impressions of reservation life. She only occasionally returns to the reservation to visit her sister and, in Susan's words, "give some money to the casino." Susan simply cannot understand why her younger sister continues to live on the reservation when other options exist. "She should retire and move this way, but she wants to live on the reservation," Susan said disapprovingly. "I don't know why." Susan is particularly appalled by the high cost of living on the rez. "I was there and I saw the prices!" she exclaimed. She continued, "Our reservation, I think it only has like two groceries. Well, there's a mini mart now, next to the casino, but in the next town they have a grocery store. It's so expensive there! My sister said, it's just for necessities. And you only buy enough gas to get off the reservation, [then] you go to Bismarck and fill up your gas tank. And go to Walmart." Susan believes that the price markups on the reservation are unnecessary and exploitative. "You would think they would have, you know, cheaper things for the people living there now," Susan said.

Susan compared the tribe's casino to her hometown Indian hospital to further illustrate her point: that urban living is better (in her opinion) than life on the reservation. "It's a *beautiful* casino," Susan said. "It's beautiful," she explained, "because they're catering to tourists." Susan said the casino creates the façade that life on the reservation is good. In reality, the tourists are the only people living in splendor. The locals, in contrast, are struggling to survive. "It looks like Las Vegas, but then when you drive down the road, you'll see where the real people live"— real people like Susan's sister, who worked in housekeeping at the casino for a while. "My sister hated working there," Susan said, "because they took advantage of the labor." Low wages, rigid schedules, harsh rules, and no rewards, said Susan, basically summed up her sister's experiences there.

Susan was particularly appalled by differences in accommodations at the casino, which catered to white tourists, and accommodations at the hospital, which catered to Indians. Susan said everything was "so nice" at the casino, which "had brand new bedding, linens, furniture, towels." In contrast, the hospital was "pathetic." "The sheets?! You could see through them!" Susan said with contempt. Ultimately, Susan sees the reservation as an inaccessible, inconvenient, depressing, and impoverished place. She has kept the promise she made to herself decades ago: to never (again) live in North Dakota. She knows a lot of relocated Indians who feel differently about their reservation homes. According to Susan, many of her friends say they would retire and move back to the rez if they could. "I would *never*," Susan said with conviction.

Among NE Ohio relocators, Susan was unique in her bitter renunciation of reservation life. She was not unique, however, with respect to her decision *not* to return to the reservation. No relocators interviewed for this project, in fact, planned to move back home. Barbara, an enrolled Cherokee, was the only person who expressed genuine interest in returning to her childhood home in Oklahoma Indian territory. Her husband, she said somewhat dejectedly, would never agree to live there, though. Disappointment and resignation cast shadows on her round, copper-toned face. Barbara had high cheekbones and thinning black hair, several strands of which occasionally fell into her line of vision. Once in a while she tugged at the errant hairs and pushed them behind her ears while she talked. Barbara explained that she met her husband when they were both stationed at an Air Force base in Hawaii. After being discharged from the military, the newlywed couple moved to Oklahoma briefly. Family matters, however, called Barbara's husband back to his home state of Ohio, and Barbara has lived there ever since.

"I'd like to go back to Oklahoma someday," she said wistfully. "I like being around Native people, more than the white people, I guess you could say." Her husband, however, never expressed much interest in her Indian identity. "He would never go to powwows with us or any of that stuff. It's just not a part of him," Barbara explained. The corners of her mouth drew downward as she relinquished the thought of returning home. "My grandmother," said Barbara, "she told me, when I was very young, she says, 'When you get married, marry an Indian.' And I wish I would have, you know?"

Despite growing up in poverty, Barbara has fond memories of her childhood in Cherokee country. Her parents divorced when she was just a baby, so Barbara grew up on a farm with her mother and her grandparents. Tilling the soil, planting seeds, growing vegetables, and preparing food for consumption or storage occupy a broad swath of her childhood memories. "We didn't have any money," said Barbara, "so we would can everything for the winter." She continued: "We would can corn, and green beans, and tomatoes, and [we] made sauerkraut, and [my grandparents] had like a corn crib, you know, . . . and the whole thing was filled with potatoes that they had grown all summer, because that was our food for the winter. We had a couple of pigs and they'd butcher those for the winter, and . . . my uncle, he killed deer, so we'd have deer meat or squirrels or rabbits. Um, I guess that was about it," Barbara said, but then her eyes lit up when she remembered one more food from her childhood—a traditional Cherokee dish called "*kanuchi*." "It's like hickory nut," Barbara explained. The nuts are gathered in the fall, dried, shelled, and then pounded until the nut meat can be pressed into little round balls for storage. Before the *kanuchi* is eaten, it is simmered in water and strained. It is "like a soup, but it's not really soup," Barbara said, "and then you add hominy to that and you put sugar in it and it's sweet and—oh my God, it's so delicious!"

Barbara also remembers sleeping outside on hot summer nights. Each evening, before the family slept, her grandfather smudged the whole area (i.e., burned dried herbs to cleanse the space of negative emotions or spirits), said Barbara, to ensure "nothing would harm us." Such traditional Cherokee practices were woven into the family's daily life. Still, the family attended a Christian church every Sunday. Their church was located just down the road from their farmhouse and the sermons were delivered in Cherokee. Barbara's mother spoke Cherokee and English, but her grandparents knew only Cherokee, so that was the language spoken in Barbara's childhood home. When she returned to Oklahoma, after moving to Ohio, she always looked forward to visiting the old Cherokee church and hearing the familiar sounds of a Cherokee sermon. "When I go back now," Barbara said, "they rarely speak any Cherokee because of the children. They didn't maintain the language and stuff, which to me, it's sad." A bit more angrily, Barbara added, "I mean, if I lived there, I would make damn sure my kids knew our language." Barbara does not live there, though, and her children do not know the Cherokee language. In fact, Barbara admits that *she* struggles to interpret her native tongue. "I forgot it," she said, "because I've been gone too long. I always understand a few words, but that's about it."

Barbara enjoys visiting friends and family back in Oklahoma. She also travels to other parts of Indian Country to call on friends and attend powwows. An annual powwow at the Foxwoods Casino in Connecticut is one of her favorites. "It's just a great powwow," Barbara said. "It's your best drums and dancers." But as much as Barbara likes to travel to Indian Country, she appreciates her urban home, too. "I love Cleveland," she said. She did not love it when she first moved to the region, but she has learned to appreciate many things the city has to offer. The only thing missing is Indians. Barbara would like to be surrounded by other Indians; but, she said, "If I want to see my friends, I'll just go visit them at the reservation, you know?"

In contrast to Susan, who vowed *never* to move back to her home reservation, and Barbara, who yearns to return but is resigned to staying in Ohio, Berta and Greg, the Lakota couple introduced in chapter 2, moved back to the rez when they decided to have children. They wanted their children to grow up immersed in Lakota culture. But they also wanted their children to have a "full life," as Berta put it—the kind of life, she and Greg eventually determined, the reservation could not provide. They struggled to get by in the reservation economy for ten years before making the decision to return to Northeast Ohio. It was a difficult decision and one that illustrates the tensions experienced by relocated Indians who see reservations as essential to Indianness yet fear their families will be deprived of basic needs—like health care, education, and work opportunities—if they reside on reservations.

Though Berta and Greg emphasized the bad reservation economy as pivotal to their decision-making process, they also spoke candidly about experiences of discrimination that colored their return-to-rez experience. These experiences may have stood out to Berta and Greg *because* they had been living in Cleveland. "In the city," said Greg, "you don't see so much prejudice against American Indians because they hardly know there's any around!" he exclaimed, before growing serious again. "But when you go around the Dakotas, closer to the reservations, or the city around the reservations," he explained, "the people there are *so* prejudiced. It's bad like it was back in the South when the whites were prejudiced against the blacks, right? And that's just the way it is around the reservations." Berta nodded in affirmation. "Yes, because when you live in a city like this," Berta said, "you don't see the prejudice as bad. You hear prejudice, but you don't see it as targeted on you."

Experiences of discrimination were altogether different in reservation towns and/or towns bordering reservations. Berta described an altercation she had at work after she and Greg moved back to the reservation from Cleveland. Her colleague at a social service agency, a white woman, told Berta about a conversation she had with a different Lakota colleague who purportedly was being insubordinate. Berta's eyes got bigger and bigger as she recounted the story, which ended with a statement that shocked Berta's urban Indian sensibilities. "She made a comment like, 'Hey, I'm a white lady,'" Berta said, seemingly still astonished by the woman's words, "and what I say goes." Berta's jaw dropped. She sat silent for a moment, shaking her head, and then continued: "And I said, 'You know, I would have told you where to go if you said that to me.' And she looked at me like, 'What?!' Like I would dare [speak to her that way]. 'You being white don't mean shit to me!' I told her. 'If someone said that to me, I'd tell them to go to hell. I don't care if you're white or not, you know? . . . I'm not scared of anybody," Berta asserted. "If you're right, you're right. If you're wrong, you're wrong. Just like me!" she said passionately. But Berta knew the woman had grown up on the reservation, and she had been socialized, like many white people living among Indians, to believe that "white equals right." "A lot of people grew up like that," Berta said. She knew white people *and* Indians who actually believed it, people who had internalized this deception. "But I grew up in those times where I spoke up for my rights. I grew up in those militant days," Berta said with pride.

Relocators and Embedded Indianness

Adapting to the urban environment presented some challenges to first-generation relocators, but being Indian did not. For first-generation relocators, being Indian alleviated rather than amplified many ills associated with living in settler society. Having the right to be Indian, in particular, was celebrated by interview respondents old enough to experience racism prior to the civil rights era—relocators relentlessly subjected to the "white equals right" mentality. Such experiences explain why Berta responded to my question regarding "what it means to be Indian." To Berta, being Indian means "the right to be who I am without, you know, without people bothering me about it."

When asked the same question, Gertrude, the Cayuga woman introduced in chapter 2, similarly replied, "Wow, that's powerful, because I just, like I said before, I'm just proud of my heritage and where I come from, and . . . I don't know, just, that really sums it all up, you know?" In the same conversation, however, Gertrude admitted that being Indian had not *always* been easy. When she lived in Ponca City, Oklahoma, with her husband's family, Gertrude said she didn't want to be Indian. "I wanted to be white," she said, "because of being prejudiced against." Gertrude recalled her first encounter with storefront signs indicating "No Indians allowed." "You have to experience that before you know how somebody feels about themselves. When you see all those signs and you're not wanted, it's not a good feeling inside," she said. "A lot of people nowadays—Native people, especially your city people—have not experienced that at all." Because first-generation relocators *have* experienced blatant discrimination on reservations and in border towns, they tend to believe that being Indian in NE Ohio today is *relatively* easy.

Being Indian is not a choice for first-generation relocators. Indian is who and what they are. They grew up on Indian reservations, surrounded by Indian people and Indian cultures, so even in the urban environment, their indigeneity is a taken-for-granted aspect of their identities. They know *of* Indians who, after relocating to the city, willfully shed their identities and discarded their Indianness in efforts to blend into the urban landscape. The relocator participants in this study, however, were not interested in blending in. Even Susan (Dakota), who maintains her identity but not her traditions, is incredulous that Indigenous people abandon their identities. "I know there's a lot of people in Cleveland that are Native and they don't get involved [in the relocator community]. They're just invisible. I don't know how they can live like that!" Susan said with wonder.

First-generation relocators agree that their Indian *perspectives*, their ways of seeing and being in the world, are central to what it means to be Indian. More often than not, they described being Indian as an accumulation of experiences, particularly during early childhood. They disagreed on whether experiencing reservation life played a crucial role, but they shared a common sentiment: that early exposure to Indigenous values and other intangible but distinctly Indigenous ways of thinking and doing is critical to being Indian. "I think what makes it [being Indian] different," Gertrude said, "is a way of life, how you're brought up. Um, you know, you're taught certain things and those things, you might not like them, and you might disagree with your parents at the time, but you know what? Those things are going to come back to you. They're *embedded*, and they're going to come back to you," she said, nodding her head. Since Gertrude's earliest memories are from boarding school, she attributes her embedded Indianness to the lessons she learned as a teenager and young wife living among the Ponca people of Oklahoma. "I was really open minded to everything. I wanted to hear everything that I could," she explained. "I wanted to find out everything, and I did! I learned a lot back then. So that's what I think," Gertrude said confidently. "I really, truly believe that, how you were raised comes into play in a lot of things."

In contrast to Susan, who sees her reservation experience as indispensable to her Indian identity, Gertrude carefully articulated that growing up on an Indian reservation does not make a person Indian. "I don't think that has anything to do with it," Gertrude said. "You could be miles away [from a reservation]." She continued, "If you're not raised Native American, you're not going to be Native American. If you're raised white, or like everybody else, I should say, that's the way you're going to be and you're going to bring your children up that way. But say your parents are raised on the reservation, Native American way, and they moved to the city, both of them. I'll guarantee you they're going to bring some of that tradition with them, down through the ages, through the kids." Gertrude's perspective on Indian identity, which highlights the passage of traditions (and all the stories and memories they sustain) from one generation to the next *across spatial contexts*, aligns with the views of most relocators. Susan, for instance, half-jokingly suggests that her urbanized children "will never know what it's like to be poor and to be a *real* Indian." At the same time, Susan knows that her children are perceived as Indians by every Indigenous member of the Northeast Ohio relocator community. They are Indians because their mother is Indian and they cannot be anything *but* Indians. *Being* Indian, for relocators, is decoupled from *acting* Indian because "Indian" (or "Indigenous") describes populations of people, not repertoires of actions.

Many relocators also believe Indigenous peoples are characterized by persistence. Real Indians are perpetual Indians. Bly, a spunky, fifty-something, Sioux-enrolled and Sioux- and Diné-identified first-generation relocator, voiced this idea—though she struggles with it. Bly has a lusty enthusiasm for life. Her bright, lopsided smile hints at her orneriness, and her mop of black hair bounces and sways when she moves across a room. Despite the great distance between her and her North Dakota reservation home, she remains committed to her teachings, which give her a spiritual purpose and sense of pride in her Indian identity. "I really believe that our people were the very first very spiritual people ever, in this entire world," Bly said, "and I think that's where we gained our strength to endure all the things that happened to us."

> You missed and assimilated and trashed
> and denied your Indian blood.
> —Esther Belin (Diné), "Ruby's Answer"

But not all Indigenous people endured. Some simply called it quits. "There was a lot of American Indians who just totally denied even being American Indian because they were ostracized, they were being killed, there were a lot of things like that," Bly said. She learned this important lesson from her grandmother Little Crow. "That's why [grandma] said it's important for you to never forget who you are." Her grandmother taught her that being Indian is not something you walk away from. Being proud to be Indian means you stick it out, regardless of the consequences. "I'm sure there's a lot of people here in the United States especially," Bly said, "who, a long time ago, they probably might have been American Indian, but because it wasn't cool and it wasn't a good time for them to be American Indian, they said 'No, I'm not,' and they just blended right into the mainstream." Bly continued: "Like I said, my grandma Little Crow, she said that happened a lot. She said she used to see it all the time. They were just like, 'Alright, it's not cool to be American Indian, so I'm gonna take the easy way out.' And she really had a problem with that . . . and I understand what she means because she lived it. She lived it where she was, where people were prejudiced against her [and] gave her a hard time because she was American Indian." Even in the worst of times, Bly's grandmother persevered. She chose to suffer consequences for being Indian rather than relinquish pride in her people or herself. She held weaker Indians, fickle Indians who took the "easy way out," in contempt.

Bly's grandmother's perspective on Indigenous identities (and who is entitled to claim them) is widespread. It is the crux of anthropologist Deborah Davis Jackson's book about urban Anishinaabe Indians. She describes an urban Indian community deeply divided into two factions—one comprised of members with reservation roots, the other comprised of members without. The latter (similar to NE Ohio reclaimers) are reconnecting with Indian identities abandoned by previous generations of family members. Although Jackson powerfully describes the experiences of Indigenous respondents with reservation connections, she dismisses the experiences of people reclaiming Indian identities. The book's title, *Our Elders Lived It*, is not subtle. For Jackson, Indigenous people whose elders "lived it"—who, just like Emma Little Crow, lived on reservations and experienced the hardships of reservation life—are the only Indigenous people whose experiences are worth understanding.

Singer-songwriter Floyd "Red Crow" Westerman even produced a song about unjustified claims to Indianness. Westerman, a legendary figure in Indian Country, was born in 1936 on the Lake Traverse Indian Reservation in South Dakota. Having experienced firsthand reservation hardships and boarding school traumas, Westerman brilliantly articulated these experiences in his music. Several songs on his first album are fashioned from Vine Deloria's "Indian Manifesto."[1] The first track shares the book's title, "Custer Died for Your Sins," and additional tracks, with names like "Missionaries," "Red, White, and Black," and "Here Come the Anthros," are evocative of the book's chapters. In Westerman's homage to Indian "imposters," he sings the following lyrics in his customary straightforward, folksy style: "Where were you when we needed you, our friend? / Where were you when we needed you to bend? / Now you claim to be part Sioux or Cherokee / But where were you when we came close to the end?"

The first time I ever heard this song, Berta sang the lyrics to me. She sighed deeply when she finished. "Everyone wants to be Sioux or Cherokee," she said, "but where were they when we came close to the end, you know? So I really like that song," she said, and then a mischievous grin spread across her face. "I always play that [song] when I go to the pow-wows," she said playfully—*Ohio* powwows, Berta assured me, where too many people inappropriately claim Indianness. "You know," she said, serious again, "it *is* funny that everybody wants to be Indian now, but they weren't here for the hard times, you know, when we had to fight just to be who we are, to have the right to be who we are. Now everybody wants to be Indian. And it makes me sad."

In contrast to Berta, Bly's perspective on unsubstantiated claims to Indianness is more nuanced. She respects her grandmother Little Crow's experiences and opinions, but also knows that some people really struggle to reclaim Indigenous identities. "Because some people, they *know* they have American Indian blood in them," Bly said, "and they really are trying to get involved in the traditional ways." Bly further explained, "They're trying and I feel bad for them because there is no way they can trace their roots, obviously. And they look like, you know, they're basically white American. But I have to give them respect because they're trying to get back to the roots. They're trying to do what's right for them. And I do, I feel for them. . . . You can't help what your ancestors did. And I'm grateful to my family," Bly continued, "that they stuck it out and hung in there and didn't just blend into society, the mainstream." In some respects, Bly sees her indigeneity as a gift from her family, something given to her by loved ones who protected and nurtured Indigenous stories and identities. Bly is immensely grateful to the kinfolk who persevered and preserved her Indigenous teachings. They are the people who made her who she is today: a Sioux- and Diné-identified woman, an uncontested Indian.

Spiritually Minded Peoples

Sustaining Indigenous identities requires the cautious maintenance of Indigenous spiritualities, which are foundational to Indigenous peoples' relationships to the land and to each other. Settler authorities engaged in any means necessary to destroy these relationships, ultimately hoping to transform Indian "heathens" into "civilized" children of (a white, Christian) God. Incensed by Indigenous community members who would not bow to colonial authorities pressuring them to adopt Christianity, Congress outlawed Indigenous spiritualities and all associated activities with passage of the Indian Religious Crimes Code of 1883. The law forbade feasting, dancing, and giveaways and commanded authorities to destroy sacred Indigenous objects and imprison Indigenous spiritual leaders.

In his own sardonic style, Standing Rock Sioux author Vine Deloria[2] provides an abbreviated history of Christian missionaries in Indian Country. In *Custer Died for Your Sins*, he writes, "One of the major problems of the Indian people is the missionary. It has been said of missionaries that when they arrived they had only the Book and we had the land; now we have the Book and they have the land. An old Indian once told me that when the missionaries arrived they fell on their knees and prayed. Then they got up, fell on the Indians, and preyed." Deloria goes on to describe infighting between different Christian denominations intent on saving Indian souls. Their lobbying efforts were rewarded by the federal Office of Indian Affairs in the early 1860s. Catholics, Lutherans, Methodists, and Episcopalians (among others) were awarded exclusive rights to save the souls of people on specific Indian reservations. Once a reservation was assigned to a particular Christian denomination, no other churches were permitted to enter that reservation without permission. "It always bothered me," Deloria writes, "that these churches who would not share pulpits and regarded each other as children of the devil, should have so cold-bloodedly divided up the tribes as if they were choosing sides for touch football."[3] Following this strategic pairing of Indian reservations with Christian denominations, an escalation in the number of Indian congregations led to "a record harvest of red souls"[4] that continued through the early twentieth century. It was a full century later when the American Indian Religious Freedom Act of 1978 finally reinstated US Indigenous peoples' "freedom to believe, express, and exercise" their traditional spiritualities.[5]

Despite insurmountable odds (and prior to the passage of the Religious Freedom Act), Indigenous peoples found ways to maintain their sacred beliefs and practices. They discovered ways to conceal their practices—sometimes in plain sight. For example, late-nineteenth- and early-twentieth-century "powwows," marketed as performances for white audiences, more than likely were cleverly disguised celebrations of Indigenous spiritual practices banned in the United States and Canada.[6] Indian dances were outlawed, but Plains traditions—the styles of drumming, dancing, and dance regalia accompanying Ojibway war dance performances (i.e., the festive precursors to powwows)—were allowable under the guise of white entertainment. Even while Indian cultural genocide was carried out, white people delighted in romantic "reenactments" of Indian celebrations. These customs became the standard image of Indianness on display at Wild West shows and later in Hollywood movies. Thus, this history helps explain both the dominant culture's stereotypic association of Plains Indians' customs with those of all other tribes and the proliferation of Plains songs, dances, and regalia in the contemporary powwow scene.

Syncretic religious practices were crucial to hiding Indigenous spiritualities in plain sight. Religious syncretism refers to blending traditions or borrowing aspects of one religious or spiritual tradition from another. Berta's grandfather, for instance, was both a Lakota medicine man *and* an Episcopalian (Christian) minister. Gertrude's (ex-)father-in-law was a priest in the Native American Church, which in many ways epitomizes religious syncretism with its incorporation of pan-tribal spiritual traditions and Christian beliefs (along with peyote use, as Gertrude discussed). Religious syncretism is a *resourceful* response to settler-colonial attacks on the spiritual core of Indigenous cultures. According to a survey of three thousand tribal citizens located on two of the nation's largest Indian reservations—one in the Southwest and one in the Northern Great Plains—syncretic spiritualities continue to predominate in Indian Country.[7] A whopping 97 percent of survey respondents said it is important to believe in *some* higher power, whether traditional tribal spirituality, Christianity, *or* the Native American Church. Traditional spiritual beliefs were most salient for these tribal citizens, but a majority of respondents who believed in any tradition also said at least one other tradition was "very important."

Relocators across generations similarly noted the importance of spirituality as a commonly embedded but *nonspecific* marker of indigeneity. Spirituality was broadly defined to include tribal traditions, Christian belief systems, or a combination of the two. Some relocators, like Berta, preferred spirituality to religion. "I believe in spiritual ways, but I believe in doing it every day, not just on Sunday," Berta said, explaining what she perceives as a critical distinction between daily Indigenous spiritual practices and the more superficial religious observations of Christians. "That's what I try to teach my boys," she continued. "They grew up with a spiritual calling, but not a religion." Berta said she only recently discovered that her adult sons do not know the Lord's Prayer. "Is that right or is that wrong?!" she said, laughing. "You know, why teach them something that I never believed in but was forced to believe in?" Berta remembers being compelled to recite the Lord's Prayer at the boarding school she attended prior to her family's relocation to Cleveland.

Despite her personal disinterest, Berta does not judge other Indians who elevate Christian belief systems over Indigenous spiritualities. "I think a lot of people live a little differently," Berta said, "and you've got to respect them for that." Occasionally, when visiting her reservation, Berta even attends a Christian church out of respect for her mother and grandfather. She follows the Lakota traditional way, but never pushed it on her boys because she wanted them to "make their own decisions." To Berta, worship cannot be defined by a rigid set of rules, and neither can Indianness—aside from, perhaps, one rule about consistent identification as Indigenous persons *across* generations. For Berta, being Indian and the many things being Indian might entail, such as engagement with traditional Indigenous spiritualities, are not things "white" people have a right to (re)claim.

* * *

Northeast Ohio *reclaimers* also believe that being Indian means having a relationship with the sacred. Like relocators, many reclaimers held syncretic (Christian and Indigenous) beliefs. Dean, Kurt, and Daniel, introduced in chapter 3, talked in depth about the confluence of Christianity and Indian spirituality in their lives. Their syncretic beliefs emerged from the experiences of Dean's father, whose exodus from Oklahoma Indian Territory was abetted by a young Christian couple. The couple, with whom he hitched a ride north and eventually shared living space, taught him about the good works of Jesus. Dean's father adopted the Christian faith and eventually joined the ministry. Dean fondly remembers his father's unusual style of preaching. "People called him the little Indian preacher," Dean said with pride, "and he had a pretty good crowd of people that would come and listen to him." A broad grin spread across Dean's face as he remembered his father on the pulpit. "He'd go on one of those Indian warpaths when he was preaching," Dean said in his gruff voice. "He would holler out, holler out, and give one of them Indian war cries in church!" he said mirthfully, laughing at the memory.

Dean's son Kurt, an ordained minister, also practices syncretic beliefs. His need to justify his blended Christian and Indigenous convictions became apparent when he quickly pivoted from the topic of his personal beliefs to a mini-lecture about the forced assimilation of US Indigenous peoples. "You weren't allowed to speak your language, you weren't allowed to talk about being Native, you was made to shave your hair—all them things," Kurt said angrily. "You became white!" Rationalizing his grandfather's (and subsequently his own) Christianity, Kurt explained, "Grandfather knew of his culture, he practiced his [Indian] traditions, but there was such a mixture of Christianity within it that, you know, when he spoke of the Creator, he also spoke of Jesus and God." Kurt admits that he gets frustrated with reclaimers who talk about the "Indian way" and simultaneously want to "leave Christianity out" of the conversation. This suggestion, Kurt argues, was made impracticable by centuries of forced assimilation and Christianization. "I think you'll find *even in the Native culture*," Kurt explained, "that there's a fine line between Christianity and belief" (emphasis mine). Kurt's language reveals his reluctance to label *his* syncretic reclaimed urban Indigenous beliefs and practices *Native* culture.

Kurt's son, Daniel, agrees that Christianity and Indigenous spirituality are mutually inclusive belief systems. "Dad was a minister, so, I believe in God, Jesus, and the Holy Ghost," Daniel said matter-of-factly. He cannot turn his back on his earliest (Christian) teachings, he explained, despite his interest in Indigenous spiritual traditions. "You can't believe in something with your whole heart and then just one day decide that you don't want to believe that anymore," he said candidly. He explained how he makes sense of his own syncretic beliefs in the context of a conversation he had with a fundamentalist Christian troll online. "I said, look in your Bible. It says your God, the alpha and omega, the beginning and the end, is capable of all things. *All* things," Daniel said with emphasis. "So why is it so hard to believe," Daniel said, his voice cracking, "that your God explained religion to my people [in a way] that *we* would better understand, versus the religion that you were taught, that *you* would understand?" Daniel let out a deep sigh. He continued more calmly. "Like some guy dying on a cross?" he asked, eyebrow raised. "We'd leave it alone," he said, sitting back in his chair, arms folded across his chest. "We don't do death," he said.

Although specific practices vary from tribe to tribe, many Indigenous spiritual traditions do not, as Daniel stated, "do death" the way Christianity does. In a number of traditions, the name of the deceased is no longer said out loud after a period of mourning. In some traditions, the dead are cremated rather than buried and the absence of cemeteries discourages "visits" with people who have passed on. Some Indigenous languages do not have a word for "goodbye" because nothing, not even death, is final from the perspective of Indians, who see time and space as cyclical. Daniel's point: the story of Christ's resurrection would be too unsettling for Indians who conceptualize death and dying very differently than westernized, Christianized peoples.

Some Indians resent Christianity for reasons explained in the works of Deloria and others who document the brutal treatment of Indigenous peoples in the name of a Christian God. Many Indians, however, identify as Christian or at least recognize the significance of Christianity to contemporary Indigenous peoples and communities. Christian, Indigenous, and syncretic belief systems are legitimized within both relocator and reclaimer community contexts. Though members of both groups frequently justified their family members' Christian conversions, reclaimers like Kurt were more defensive than first-generation relocators like Berta, who spoke matter-of-factly about her grandfather's syncretism. This discrepancy in levels of defensiveness results from complex historical and contemporary phenomena leading to first-generation relocators' taken-for-granted identities and reclaimers' more calculated and contested identities.

Reclaimers and Intuitive Indianness

In contrast to first-generation relocators who believe "Indian" is who they *are* rather than what they *do*, reclaimers experience Indianness as a matter of being *and* becoming. Reclaimers do not see themselves as "race shifters." Rather, they believe they were *dis*possessed of the indigeneity they are now (rightfully/righteously) reclaiming. Their Indianness has always existed in their blood and bones. It just needs to be nourished. According to reclaimers, their Indian identities are a combination of divine intervention, biological inheritance, and personal undertaking. The Creator set them on a particular path, and they are responsible for moving forward from there. As one reclaimer said, "I am who I am and who I need to be."

Similar to Cherokee "race shifters" described in Sturm's work, many reclaimers understand being and becoming Indian to be fused by mystical experiences they attribute to their Indigenous bloodlines. Reclaimers, for instance, believe their innate Indianness drew them to learn and practice religio-spiritual philosophies linking the natural and spiritual worlds. Sasha, a short, plump, Lakota-identified reclaimer woman in her thirties, provides a straightforward example of this phenomenon. A self-described introvert who is amiable, engaging, and unflinchingly straightforward, Sasha admits she may sound "hokey" when she confesses that engaging in Indigenous spiritual practices "just felt *right*." Sasha explained, "When I was a teenager . . . I was drawn to more earth-based philosophies and that was, that was really basically it. . . . And then I just started learning a lot and everything felt, uh, it just felt *right*, you know? It felt natural. I mean, learning things was less like learning new things. It was more like remembering stuff I had forgotten—which doesn't make sense, because I'd never learned it in the first place!" Casey, a Cherokee-identified reclaimer in his sixties, described a similar affinity to Indian spiritual practices. After years of experimenting with different religious and spiritual traditions, he finally turned to Indigenous spirituality. "It just clicked," Casey said. "It was how I felt inside and didn't even know it."

Reclaimers also talked about intuitive talents for which they credited their Indian ancestries. Valerie, the Cherokee-identified woman introduced in chapter 3, cannot explain why, but she intuitively knows how to find and use herbs for healing purposes. When friends or family members are sick, she said she can "make up a brew of yellow root and ginseng . . . and then in a couple days they feel better." Valerie spoke proudly about another feat she accomplished inexplicably: tanning an animal hide. According to Valerie, one day she had an uncanny urge to retrieve some road kill she'd spotted. Without thinking, Valerie explained, she stopped the car suddenly, hopped out, and scraped the unfortunate groundhog from the road surface with a shovel. She then proceeded to "take it home, pound a couple nails in it, stretch it out, and smear salt all over it, dip it in ash, soak it in water." The fur fell off, and in a few days, Valerie had a nicely tanned groundhog hide hanging in her garage. Having never tanned a hide before or seen anyone do it, Valerie was perplexed, but also incredibly happy. "I don't know where I got that!" she exclaimed.

Other reclaimers talked about knowledge or talents they acquired with little effort. Casey (Cherokee-identified), for instance, spends his weekends in the summer selling hand-carved Native American–*style* flutes at area powwows. A friendly, attractive man in his early sixties, Casey has a trim, athletic build, cornflower blue eyes, and long, flaxen hair silvering at the temples. He described his affinity for flute making as "kind of weird" because no one in his family, at least not in the generations he remembers, made flutes, and yet he always "kind of knew subconsciously" he would be a flute maker. "When it actually started happening," Casey explained, "it was coming from I don't know where." Some of the requisite knowledge seemed intuitive, and the rest of it, according to Casey, came from "gifting lots of tobacco to elders."

Reclaimers also discussed unexpected feelings of homecoming when they visited Indian reservations. Recall Valerie's experience from chapter 3. According to Valerie (Cherokee-identified), simply visiting the Cherokee nation made her feel "such peace, at home, just as though my inner spirit was where it was supposed to be." Similarly, Sasha, the Lakota-identified woman quoted above, communicated her own experience of homecoming during her first visit to a South Dakotan nation. "You know how when you go to your parents' house, the house you grew up in? You know that feeling you get when you pull in the driveway or walk in the door?" Sasha asked. "It's like, oh! Wow. I'm *home*. I had that feeling the moment we hit there," she explained.

Such feelings of homecoming are common for people reclaiming Indian identities. Even Bly (Sioux), the relocator who expressed empathy for people who are "basically white" but trying to get back to their Indian roots, was familiar with these experiences. "It's funny," Bly said in a conversation about urbanized Indians who are disconnected from other Indians. "A lot of them will say they feel like they're lost, but at the same time, they feel like they're missing something. And once they get back again to the Native community, they're like, 'Oh my goodness! Now this feels right, this feels good. Now I'm okay.'"

Feelings of homecoming are documented in the literature as well. Research conducted by Nancy Lucero (Choctaw), a professor of social work, for instance, reveals that urban Indians returning to their roots experience feelings of affirmation and belonging.[8] Though many urban Indians in Lucero's study talked about "going back" or "returning to the people," this course of action was more symbolic than literal because most study participants (like NE Ohio reclaimers) were disconnected from long-standing Indigenous communities. Some NE Ohio reclaimers with this problem got creative about initiating such "returns." In addition to adopting reservations and being adopted by reservation-based Indians, they also "returned" by remembering wisdom imparted to them by Indian grandparents.

Reclaimers: Remembering Grandparents

Learning to do things the "old way" was important to reclaimers. For reclaimers, the "old ways" referred to activities harkening back to an earlier era—surviving in the wilderness, living off the land, communing with nature. A few reclaimers were fortunate enough to remember Indian grandparents who practiced the "old ways," and they used this expression interchangeably with "Indian ways." Tabatha, an enrolled Cherokee reclaimer in her early fifties, called them "Cherokee ways" and explained that she learned them from her grandparents, who lived in West Virginia. Tabatha grew up in Ohio, but she and her four siblings spent summers in their youth with their Cherokee grandparents.

Tabatha told me about her favorite childhood memories, rooted in West Virginia, on a beautiful October afternoon. Wearing skinny black jeans that accentuated her petite frame and a red Minnie Mouse sweatshirt, Tabatha smiled and waved at me as I pulled my car next to her trailer home. She hugged me tightly before inviting me to sit on the lawn chair beside her. Before I had a chance to speak, she told me she did not believe in "any such thing" as "trailer trash" and she had been living in this trailer park for almost a year now and she really liked it and she liked her neighbors, too. She spoke softly and slowly. Each time a neighbor approached, Tabatha squinted into the bright sunlight, crinkling the honey-colored skin of her face, to determine who it was. She greeted each passerby by name. Tabatha also spoke kindly to several squirrels, a rabbit, and various insects that made appearances during the interview.

Tabatha likened her youthful experiences in West Virginia to those of "the Waltons," characters in a television series about a Depression-era (white) family in the Blue Ridge Mountains. "We had the big old washtub set up in the kitchen," Tabatha recalled, "and the water was boiled on the stove and we went out and got our water for the morning out at the well." "*Everything* was done the old way," she insisted. "Drying meat, preserving it, butchering the hogs and cows in the fall to put up meat for the winter." While her grandfather and brothers hunted deer, rabbits, and squirrels, Tabatha and her grandmother harvested mushrooms, berries, dandelion, and clover. "A lot of our cooking was done with stuff out of the garden," Tabatha explained. "You know, that was also a Cherokee way." Though Barbara (Cherokee), a relocator, described similar childhood experiences, she attributed them to her family's poverty. Tabatha's brother calls them *hillbilly* ways, but his opinion is irrelevant, Tabatha claimed, because he is uninterested in the family's Cherokee past. Only Tabatha and one sister (of five children) cared enough about their Cherokeeness to seek tribal enrollment as adults.

Kurt, the Choctaw-identified director of the reclaimer Indian center, described fond memories of his grandfather as well. Kurt remembers his grandfather sitting in the back yard for hours, perched on an old milk crate, just watching the squirrels and rabbits and birds. When Kurt asked him what he was doing, he simply responded, "Best television there is." During his teens, Kurt regularly sought his grandfather's advice when he was grappling with issues he did not want to share with his parents. Kurt's grandfather taught him to slow down, breathe, and reflect on the things troubling him. If he listened to his inner self, his grandfather told him, Kurt would know what to do. "And I give this advice to people even today," Kurt said. "I say, 'Sssssssh! Listen!' Because you already know what to do. . . . And that, to me, is what being urban Native is about," said Kurt. "Remembering those teachings and slowing yourself down. Enjoying life."

Reclaimers: Seeking Indian Mentors

Many reclaimers did not have Indigenous mentors (or Indigenous identities) in their youth. Rather, they sought mentorship as adults, after deciding to nurture previously dormant Indigenous identities. Sasha (Lakota-identified), for instance, always knew she was Native. Her Indigenous heritage—the only thing passed to her from an estranged Native Hawaiian father—was what set her apart from the rest of her family. Sasha had dark, sepia-toned skin, mahogany eyes, and black-brown hair, but her family was white. "My mother, my half-sister, and my step-father all have light brown hair, they sunburn really easily, and they have blue eyes," Sasha explained. "From the time that I can remember," Sasha said, "when I'm with my family, people assume I'm a family friend. When I was growing up, because there's an eight- or nine-year gap between me and my sister, people would assume I was the babysitter. I've always had that feeling of separateness, of not belonging," Sasha said, reflecting on her experience. "It's pretty much the way it's always been."

Sasha's "separateness" impacts her Indigenous identity, too. Her grandmother, adopted as a child, discovered her Blackfoot heritage as an adult, but Sasha did not grow up with Blackfoot traditions. She never knew her Native Hawaiian father, so she "didn't really identify with that so much, either. I identify mostly with the Lakota because they were my teachers," Sasha said. "I generally say I'm Blackfoot Lakota," she clarified, "because I think that's kind of a nod to both my biological heritage and what I think is really more important, which is the traditions and teachings and wisdom that have been, you know, passed on to me."

When Sasha decided to learn more about her Native roots, she was intent on finding "real Indian" mentors. "I think it's important that you learn from someone who knows what they're doing," Sasha said, "who actually knows the traditions, who has some sort of history there." She continued: "I was taught my traditions by real Indians, you know, quote/unquote real Indians. I mean straight off the rez, born and raised and practicing their traditions their entire lives. Um, I think it's important that your traditions are real and not made up. I don't think your blood quotient matters. I don't think the color of your skin should matter. The only thing that I get upset and irritated about is when I see people just making stuff up [chuckles], you know? Or bastardizing traditions." Sasha used the example of burning sage to explain what she meant by "making stuff up." "I see people burning sage *all the time*," she said, rolling her eyes. She was taught that sage is sacred and should be used discriminately. "It's like a spring clean, almost," she explained. "It's for when you get down, and for whatever reason, *really* feel that you need to cleanse." So when Sasha sees people burning sage, she asks them why. "And they don't know the answers!" she said with exasperation. "They're doing things because it seems cool, or they're changing traditions . . . without actually understanding why the tradition works a certain way." Such behavior is unacceptable to Sasha.

Sasha's commitments to understanding *why* traditions and practices exist and *how* to engage them led her to establish relationships with reservation-based Indians. These adoptive kin provided her with mentorship and cultural experiences unavailable in Ohio. According to anthropologist Susan Applegate Krouse (Cherokee), this strategy of establishing kinship ties through adoption is fairly common among urban Indians seeking cultural competency and authentication of their indigeneity.[9] It was not a particularly common strategy among NE Ohio reclaimers. Only a few reclaimers, including Sasha and her (ex-)husband, Kenai, put forth such effort.

Sasha's story of reclamation is entangled with Kenai's. Prior to hooking up, they both identified as part-Indian, but they did not engage in Indigenous practices. "At that point in my life, I was kind of aimless," Sasha admitted. "I was twenty-one and my biggest concern was, you know, how many beers can I get out of the bartender tonight?" Sasha laughed. She certainly was not looking for a steady boyfriend. When Kenai entered her life, however, things just felt right. "[He] helped lead me to that path," she said. "It sounds so hokey, *again*," she said, giggling, "but I think it was one of the reasons we were brought together." "After Kenai and I were married, we went out to Sun Dance and that was where we met the [adoptive Indian] family," Sasha explained. "It was from them that I learned most everything."

Though the couple divorced, Sasha's and Kenai's lives remain deeply entwined. They coparent their son, Max, and remain committed to their Lakota identities. Kenai also credits Sasha for leading him down the right path, away from youthful recklessness and toward the Indigenous identity his mother always tried, albeit stealthily, to instill in him. Kenai said he was always drawn to the Indian heritage his mother secretively relayed. "She said her job was to plant the seed," Kenai explained, "so I would go find it without her." Ultimately it was Sasha (and his uncles, discussed below) who helped him find it.

In contrast to Sasha, Kenai's mousy brown hair and walnut-colored skin give him a vaguely nonwhite appearance. Most people, according to Kenai, assume he is white. Unlike other relocators, who bemoan their whitened complexions, Kenai admits that passing as white is convenient. "A lot of days it's not good to be Indian, you know? It's easier just to slip in under the wire. I can walk in anywhere," Kenai said, "and people don't know anything." After his mother died, however, Kenai made "slipping under the wire" more difficult for himself. In honor of her memory, he legally replaced his (somewhat estranged) father's Arabic surname with his mother's maiden name, which sounded Indian even to people wholly ignorant of all things Indigenous.

During a four-hour interview, Kenai described his mixed heritage in frenetic, fidgety detail, whispering feverishly (we were at a library) while bouncing, wriggling, and incessantly apologizing for his attention-deficit/hyperactivity (ADHD) disorder. Kenai said he identified solely as Arabic in his early life. His proud, patriarchal Arabic father was quite insistent on this point because he disapproved of Kenai's mother's Indian background. He forbade his wife from sharing what he referred to as her "primitive" culture with *his* boys. Kenai's mother mostly obeyed her husband's authority. Occasionally, however, she committed small acts of resistance, sharing bits and pieces of her family's traditions with Kenai and his brother. Kenai patiently gathered the precious pieces and, in time, they grew into an identity he felt compelled to inhabit.

According to Lakota tradition, no one *decides* to participate in Sun Dance, but rather, people receive dreams or visions calling them to become Sun Dancers. Kenai had had Sun Dance dreams since he was a small child, but he did not *know* they were Sun Dance dreams until he was older. Not long after he and Sasha married, Kenai went to his uncles, his mother's brothers, for guidance, and they helped him see that he was being called to Sun Dance. So he and Sasha traveled to South Dakota.

In South Dakota, Kenai learned to be Indian from men unrelated (biologically) to his mother, but whom he learned to call uncle, or "Ate" [a: teI]. Acquiring traditional knowledge from them, Kenai conceded, entailed "a lot of suffering." In hindsight, he understands and respects the process because he knows *why* his uncles put him to work: Indigenous learning traditions are active. Indigenous *learning* necessitates *doing*. "I was the one cutting the wood, and I was the one doing anything and everything that needed done," Kenai said. "See, my uncles would do these things to me, and then teach me why they did it." In addition to completing these manual chores, Kenai entered the world of Sun Dance, an annual Lakota ceremony that takes place over nine days. The dancers, or "pledgers," offer flesh sacrifices for the renewal and restoration of the Lakota people. The complex ceremony culminates in "tree day," during which each pledger's chest is pierced with a piece of bone attached to a rawhide strap. The strap tethers the pledgers to a central pole, and throughout the day, the pledgers dance and pull backwards until the bone pieces rip free from their bodies. "It's like a whole new world," Kenai said hoarsely. "It proves itself to you."

Kenai was not the only reclaimer man who received mentorship from adoptive uncles. Other NE Ohio reclaimers described the serendipitous ways they became acquainted with "uncles" who became mentors, and the significant impacts of their uncles' mentorship on their lives. Casey, the Cherokee-identified maker of Native American–style flutes, had numerous mentors over the course of his lifetime. "I'm still meeting people that I consider teachers and elders," said Casey, "and they don't necessarily have to be older than me." They are not all Cherokee, either. When Casey was younger, he was intensely interested in the sacred. He vociferously read about world religions and different spiritualities. What is the most important lesson he learned? "If you need a teacher," Casey responded, "a teacher will show up. And it's true, and they have over the years. I'm still meeting people that I consider teachers and elders.

. . . When you find people that still walk the old paths," Casey explained, "they can tell where your heart is. And if your heart's in the right place, then they'll open up."

Casey is especially grateful to his adoptive uncle, Elmer, whom he describes as a full-blood Indian enrolled in the Eastern Band of Cherokee Indians. "You know, if he accepts me as one of his nephews," Casey said defensively, "then I'm fine with that." Historically, Casey said, "the Cherokee were really big on adopting. . . . That's just the way the Chero- kee were," Casey explained, "and my uncle tells stories, Uncle Elmer, he tells stories of how they would bring people in. They even raised white babies and they *became* Cherokee, you know?" Folks like his uncle, who practice the "old ways," said Casey, do not measure Indianness by blood quantum or lineage. "The man is just a walking book of knowledge for Cherokee everything," Casey said admiringly.

Floyd is a forty-something reclaimer easily mistaken for a Harley enthusiast. He is a big guy, broad shouldered and ample bellied, with fair skin, a long, silver-streaked goatee, and silvering hair he wears in a single, skinny braid that stops around the midpoint of his back. Floyd is a consummate prankster and, despite his tough appearance, a tender, sentimental man. Floyd's father, who identifies as one-quarter Blackfoot, was not around for Floyd's early years. According to Floyd, when his fa- ther left his mother, he basically divorced the whole family. Despite his absence, Floyd's (non-Indian) mother decided that her children should learn about their Indian roots. The "American Indian Movement was going pretty good," Floyd explained, and likely inspired his mother's ac- tions. She sent her children to the local Indian Center with a family of mixed-blood Indians in the neighborhood. "They made it okay to feel proud about being Indian," Floyd said. "And then, you knew there was other kids like you, that were mixed blood, and they were okay with it."

Although Floyd celebrated his Indian heritage as a child, he "drifted away" from this part of his identity during adolescence. "I just kept get- ting further and further away from the path," Floyd said. He dropped out of high school and admits he "got into using drugs really hard." In his midtwenties, he was arrested on drug charges. "I was looking at fifteen years," Floyd said, shaking his head in disbelief, "but the judge, out of the kindness of his heart, just put me on probation. And I had to promise to put myself in a program . . . and life just started getting better." One good thing led to another. Floyd and his father started hanging out. "And my dad, just out of the blue one day, said, 'Let's go to a powwow.' And I'm like, 'Yeah, right on. Let's go to a powwow!' I ain't been to one since I was a kid, you know? And it just sounded like the right thing to do. And then when we got there," Floyd continued, "it just *felt* like the right thing." At the powwow, Floyd reconnected with childhood friends who greeted him with smiles and hugs. "Then I sat down at the drum and was singing with them—and then, it was like a couple powwows later, here comes Oscar and he grabbed me by my ear, you know, like 'Here!' He was mad at me."

Floyd was young when he met Oscar, whom he describes as "a full-blooded, carded Canadian Indian." "He's watched me grow up," said Floyd. "And I don't know, maybe he thought he saw something good in me at one time, you know?" From Floyd's perspective, he was just a poor, mixed-up, mixed-blood youth in his twenties (at the time) who had been in and out of the powwow circle *and* the county jail. Yet, Oscar took him under his wing. From that point forward, Oscar annually took Floyd "home" with him to his reservation to participate in ceremonies, for which Floyd remains deeply grateful. "I call him Uncle," Floyd said. "He's my adopted uncle—or, father really. He's treated me like his son." Floyd's eyes filled with tears. "I could go on for days about that one," Floyd said. "I won't, because it will make me cry."

Indian mentors did not always materialize when needed. Sadie and Neville, a young, Indian-identified couple in their early thirties, struggled to find "real Indian" mentors. They did not struggle to find one another, however. In fact, they met online long before online dating was common or trendy. Neville thought Sadie's identification as a "tree hugging dirt worshipper" was hilarious, and Sadie was drawn to the Indian imagery on Neville's profile. After they lived together for several years, the couple's tiny, cluttered abode divulged the same Indigenous subtext that led to their mutual attraction. A deluge of Indian miscellanea engaged my senses upon entering—a medicine wheel poster hanging on the front door, regalia pieces suspended from the walls, the smells of sage and cooking oil and burnt coffee, a big, round drum taking up space in the corner. Even the computer screen displayed the shadow of a buffalo in the sunset.

The droll couple became quite animated when describing their encounter with "phony" Indians. "We learned *lots* of good things," Sadie said, forcing her rosy-pale, youthful, round face into a smile. She paused for effect, then added, "how *not* to be." Sadie and Neville said it all began when they accepted an invitation from an unknown Indian organization to participate in a meeting and dance exhibition. "We had a lot of basic 'Indian 101' craft and spiritual knowledge," Sadie said, "and we made them look good with that knowledge." The couple, for instance, already knew how to powwow dance. They knew how to make traditional Eastern Woodlands regalia. They even knew how to construct a porcupine roach (a male headdress worn for powwow dancing), though it was an arduous and time-consuming task. Between the cost of materials and the intensive labor, porcupine roaches are worth anywhere from three hundred to twelve hundred dollars. Much to their dismay, Sadie and Neville suggest they were conned into making one for free. They expected payment, but when they finished the roach, the organization's director, the woman who commissioned them, refused to remunerate them. "We kind of got used," Neville said, raising his thick, tawny brows, which extended across the great expanse of his forehead. It was not the couple's first insight into the unscrupulous character of the group, but it was the last. They got out. "It was one of these, 'You too can be Indian for three easy payments of $19.95' type of groups," Sadie said sardonically. "But we didn't know about it until after the fact," Neville added, regretfully shaking his head.

This disheartening incident did not stop Sadie and Neville from trying to find Indian mentors. They agreed, however, that finding mentors who practiced the Indian traditions they claimed, which, combined, included Lenape, Blackfoot, Nanticoke, Cherokee, and Lakota, was implausible. Eventually the couple connected with a Canadian Anishinaabe elder, thanks to the recommendation of a friend, from whom they received guidance. Sadie and Neville met the elder at a buffalo dinner in southern Ohio, and not long afterward, decided to have their young twins "named"—meaning, given Indian names during a special naming ceremony over which the elder presided. "And then we went to the first powwow," Neville said, "and we started learning some of their ways." About a year later, Sadie and Neville participated in naming ceremonies where they each received *their* Indian names. Sadie felt ambivalent about learning Anishinaabe traditions (rather than Lenape or Blackfoot, the ancestries she claims), but Neville was enthusiastic. "The stuff he teaches is a good way," Neville said. "It's a *great* way, but it's hard," he said, amending his previous statement. Perhaps most importantly for Sadie and Neville, this "great way" is available to anyone. "According to the paperwork we got when we asked for names," Sadie said, "it doesn't matter if you're pink, purple, blue, green, brown, red, white, [or] yellow." She continued: "It doesn't matter if you're male, female, gay, straight, whatever. If you want to follow these traditions, then follow the traditions and walk that pathway and go do what everybody else had to do to walk this way. That's what the paper says. It doesn't matter what you are. If this is what you're dreaming and this is what you feel called to do, then do it." Though Sadie and Neville felt called to do it, they admitted that it was not easy. As Sadie pointed out, traveling internationally for ceremonies and visits with the elder added a layer of complexity: "It's like six hundred bucks to and from, like the whole round trip in gas, and then it takes twenty-four hours if you drive nonstop, and you have to have a passport or equivalent now. . . . And you have to have somewhere to stay. And you've got to be careful what you take, because if you don't have papers for your [eagle] feathers, you run into that whole thing." Traveling to Canada post-9/11 was a logistical nightmare, Sadie said, so she resigned herself to receiving her mentor's guidance mostly by phone. She did not like it, but it reduced her chances of being fined up to twenty-five thousand dollars for carrying unauthorized eagle feathers across an international border. She did not have "papers" for her feathers because her Indian identity was not documented. To Sadie, participating in ceremony without her hard-earned feathers, however, was unthinkable.

Despite the travails associated with being Indian in urban NE Ohio, relocators and reclaimers embrace their Indian identities. For relocators, stories of struggle embed indigeneity in themselves and their children. Relocators are confident that their stories, passed on by ancestors and alive within themselves, will lead their children to brighter futures. For reclaimers, stories of (somewhat mystical) identification correspond with experiences of gratification as they work to reclaim Indian identities and practices in the present. Some reclaimers reminisce about the "old ways" of Indian grandparents, while others toil to learn and experience the "old ways" for themselves. Reclaimers, for the most part, fail to consider whether "old ways" are simply dated practices engaged by any number of people (across racial and ethnic identities) alive in previous eras. Their understandings of Indianness are shaped by societal images that locate Indians in the long-ago past rather than the here-and-now present. Moreover, as Sadie and Neville attest, reclamation attempts do not always proceed smoothly. Reclaimers, however, remain committed to reclaiming and embracing Indian identities.

5

Doing and Discovering Indigeneity

Due to their unique relationships to Indigenous peoples and the past, relocators and reclaimers embrace Indian identities differently. In turn, they evince different styles of communicating Indigenous ideas, identities, and teachings to their children and grandchildren. Reclaimer adults focus intensively on learning and engaging Indian practices, or what many reclaimers call "the old ways." They aspire to learn tribally specific customs, but most reclaimers lack access to knowledgeable tribal members or mentors. As a result, many NE Ohio reclaimers learn and practice pan-Indian customs. In meticulous detail, they pass what they learn to their children. Contrary to reclaimers, relocators' commitments to Indian identities are somewhat decoupled from precise and measured actions. Because relocator adults primarily perceive their indigeneity as something they *are* rather than something they *do*, they tend to concentrate socialization efforts on engendering Indigenous perspectives and values in relocator youth, rather than teaching them how to *act* Indian. This more holistic yet less specific socialization strategy creates identity confusion for some urban Indian youth, who struggle to understand who they are amid controlling images and political definitions of Indianness in US society.

Reclaimers' Commitments to Practicing and Passing on Indian Traditions

Bein' Indian's a state of mind. It's how you hold yourself and
present yourself and live your life day to day.
—Floyd (Blackfoot- and Ojibwa-identified)

For many NE Ohio reclaimers, being and becoming Indian are full-time and primary commitments. Indians "didn't just go pray and do spiritual things one day a week or three days a week," Sasha (Lakota-identified) said fervently. "Everything is so intertwined," she continued, "that it's hard to separate the religion and the culture." Kenai, Sasha's ex-husband, expressed a similar sentiment, admitting that he did not initially want to be a Sun Dancer, despite his Sun Dance dreams, because of the life-encompassing nature of Indigenous spirituality. "I didn't want to do that," Kenai said. "I like being Catholic. You get to do whatever you want all week, go to church on Sunday, and it's all better." Now Kenai is a Sun Dancer, and he accepts his spiritual commitments. "That's why I sing [Indian songs] at my desk at work," Kenai explained, "'cause if I don't, I'm gonna be just like every other brain-dead white dude out there." What *really* matters, said Floyd, the sentimental German-, Blackfoot-, and Ojibwe-identified reclaimer, is putting forth the effort. "How can I live in a good way?" he asked. "How can I *walk* in a good way?" In response to his own questions, Floyd stated, "remembering my teachings, using my tobacco, and trying to pass on [traditions] to my children."

Many reclaimers expressed these beliefs, but experienced tensions between the Indigenous cultures they *wanted* to participate in and the dominant white culture they felt compelled to participate in. In contrast to NE Ohio relocators who grew up on Indian reservations and moved to the urban environment, reclaimers did not experience urbanity and indigeneity as two sides of the same coin. They preferred indigeneity, but their daily subsistence depended on necessary interactions with dominant social institutions. The newness of their Indian ethnic cultures made it difficult for reclaimers to shift back and forth seamlessly between their previous identities and their Indian identities. Neville, the multitribally identified reclaimer introduced in chapter 4, compared himself to a circus entertainer spinning plates precariously situated atop long, skinny poles. "It's a balancing act," Neville said. "You've got to balance a plate, run over here, balance this plate. It gets really hard!" Yet, as difficult as it is to keep all the plates spinning, it is worse if they fall and break into pieces.

Reclaimers opt to toil over the bits and pieces of broken Indianness their Indian ancestors left for them. It is laborious, but (committed) reclaimers consciously choose daily sacrifices of time and resources over sacrificing their Indian identities and Indian futures. They are committed to learning and practicing Indian traditions and passing them to their children. After all, they nearly lost their Indian identities due to preceding generations' *lack* of commitment. Now they need to make up for lost time, and despite the strain being Indian adds to their lives, they believe their hard work improves their lives and the lives of their children, grandchildren, great-grandchildren, and so forth.

Reclaimers' Tobacco Offerings

Combining prayer with "gifting" or "laying" tobacco is a ritual practiced by many reclaimers. Tribes vary in their specific relationships with tobacco, but in many North and South American Indigenous cultures, tobacco is a sacred, ceremonial item that enables communication with the spirits. It is scattered on the ground as an offering to the Creator and used for prayers and ceremonies. According to Tabatha (Cherokee), this practice is central to living in "a Native way." "Of course you start your mornings with morning prayers to the four directions and to the Creator," Tabatha said. "It helps ground you, I think. It just starts your day off good. No matter what goes on the rest of the day," she continued, "you're prepared for it." Floyd agreed that praying with tobacco every day is important, but admitted that he sometimes forgets. "And [I] just can't figure out why [I'm] having a bad day," he said, "and then it just dawns on [me]." Some days Floyd needs someone else to remind him. Now, when his wife notices that he is exceptionally cranky, she tells him to "throw some tobacco down and shut up!" Even Floyd's granddaughter occasionally reminds him to pray. "That just hits you in the heart," Floyd said, beaming with pride. "She understands my teachings."

Some reclaimers keep a pouch of dried, loose-leaf tobacco handy at all times because, as Sadie (Lenape- and Blackfoot-identified) indicated, it is "like money of the spirits." Sadie talked about her recent transaction with two cross orb weaver spiders residing in the exterior windows of her home. "Because I dreamt [about] spiders and that's obviously the animal I'm working with or learning from," Sadie explained, "I took a little shell and I put some tobacco in the shell outside in the window." The tobacco was Sadie's expression of gratitude. In return, the spiders permitted her to observe and learn from their actions. Floyd said, "You never know when you'll see an eagle, or a hawk, or something hits you. . . . So, yeah, you keep tobacco with you all the time." Tabatha also carries a tobacco pouch because she loves collecting rocks. "Everywhere I go, I've got to have rocks," said Tabatha. "When I find interesting rocks, I give back. You know, you don't take without giving."

Reclaimers say it is particularly important to offer tobacco to people from whom you seek guidance. It is a way to show your respect. "The minute someone pulls out tobacco, things get serious." This inside joke is frequently invoked by reclaimers in a lighthearted manner, but the subject matter is serious. Tobacco means business. Kenai, for instance, talked about the first time his young son, Max, approached him with tobacco. Max wanted to "put a bustle on" and powwow dance with the *men* (not the boys), but he needed his father's blessing. Max's grown-up offering to his father—the man whose guidance he sought—deeply moved Kenai. At that precise moment in Kenai's life, he was contemplating whether to focus on his Indigenous or Arabic traditions. When Max approached him with tobacco, "right there was my answer," Kenai said. Max understanding the importance of tobacco meant that his socialization into Indian ways was, so far, a success.

Several reclaimers taught *me* the art of tobacco offering. Matu, a heavy-set multitribally identified man in his twenties, broke it down for me during an interview. "Say I have a major question to ask you," Matu said matter-of-factly. "Instead of just walking up to you and asking you, I'd have to buy Tops [loose-leaf tobacco widely available at gas stations and convenience stores]." Matu acted out the scene for my benefit. "You go up to them," Matu said, stepping toward me and extending his hand, "and you have it in your hand and you shake their hand and say 'I have a question for you.'" Matu smiled cunningly, and then, with dramatic flair, he executed a stealth handshake-transfer of the tobacco into my hand. The maneuver approximated the smooth exchange of drugs and money in a Hollywood blockbuster film. He turned to me, winked and nodded confidently, and then sat back down. "Use tobacco," Matu reiterated. "You don't have to be Native to ask," he assured me. "Just ask. But make sure you do it the right way, the way *they* were taught."

Floyd also taught me a lesson about tobacco currency. At a reclaimer community gathering, Kenai and I teased Floyd about canceling his interview with me earlier in the week. Floyd shrugged to indicate his disinterest. Kenai seemed momentarily at a loss, but then almost gleefully shouted, "Give him some tobacco! Then he'll have to do it." I actually had a pouch of loose-leaf tobacco in my purse—not for spiritual "use" but for "abuse," as the anti-smoking PSAs on Indian Center walls make clear. Certainly, I thought, gifting it to Floyd *now* would seem insincere. I decided to wait. Then, for some reason I cannot explain, I jokingly mentioned the canceled interview to Floyd again as we were cleaning tables and rearranging chairs at the end of the night. He stopped what he was doing and looked me in the eye. "Give me some tobacco," he said, exasperation in his voice. "Stay right where you are!" I shouted over my shoulder as I dashed toward my purse on the other side of the room. I rummaged around, found the tobacco, scuttled back to where Floyd was waiting, and laid the pouch in his hands. I took a step back and held my breath. "So, when do you want to meet?" Floyd asked.

I never again showed up for an interview with a reclaimer community member empty-handed, and my tobacco offerings were always appreciated. I gave Kurt, the Choctaw-identified reclaimer Indian Center director, a tobacco-filled sandwich bag at the beginning of our interview, and while talking about the importance of listening, *really* listening, and learning from the people around you, he picked it up. "It's simple things like this," Kurt said. "You've been taught, so maybe this is expected of you now, since you know, see?" With slow and deliberate speech, he continued: "It's good. And it surprises us who use our traditions and do this because it makes me respect you more. Because you're asking of my knowledge and you're asking me to give, and uh, this makes it better because this will go in my prayers not only for myself, but for you, to guide you and help you through your journey." Despite my initial discomfort, most reclaimers, like Kurt, so graciously received the gift that I learned to enjoy the ritual. Engaging in this practice with relocators, however, was unthinkable to me. A few relocators might have appreciated a tobacco offering, but I feared such an act (of earnest gratitude) would shift some relocators' perceptions of me from friend to pretendian.

Reclaimers' Other Spiritual Practices

Reclaimers engage in other practices that encourage mindfulness and reflection in the midst of day-to-day life. For instance, many reclaimers regularly make "spirit plates"—platefuls of food set aside for the spirits at mealtime. Different components of the meal are piled onto a plate and left outside as an offering. Making spirit plates, reclaimers say, is a tribute to the ancestors and an expression of gratitude for the many gifts bestowed by the Creator. When the spirit plate is made to nourish a particular spirit—like a family member who recently "walked on" into the spirit world—its contents reflect the food preferences of the person being remembered. If Aunt Eunice had a serious sweet tooth, for instance, the plate might be filled with candy, doughnuts, and Little Debbie snack cakes (with a small side of something more nutritious). Ideally, according to reclaimers, spirit plates are a daily practice, but they conceded that the hustle and bustle of everyday life sometimes thwart their efforts. "Like me," Kenai admitted. "I'll just run in the kitchen and grab something [to eat] when I'm hungry." Because Kenai tries be a good role model for his son, he is more vigilant about the practice when Max is around.

Smudging, or burning dried herbs such as sage or cedar for cleansing purposes, is another common reclaimer practice. Reclaimers told me about smudging their bodies before praying and their clothes before participating in ceremony. They smudge their houses at different times throughout the year. One reclaimer even smudged his house before I arrived for our scheduled interview. "Just because that's something you do," he said. "You want your house to be clean and so I smudged the house." Smudging is a time-honored ritual at powwows, too. The powwow circle—initially a sectioned-off area of grass in the middle of a park, recreational area, or gymnasium—*becomes* "a holy spot," according to Floyd, after a respected Indian elder "smudges the circle and lays tobacco down in the four directions. . . . And when you go in [the powwow circle], while you're dancing and having a good time—which you're supposed to—you should also be praying, you know? And remembering who you're dancing for, you know? You're dancing for your children and your elders and your ancestors, and for your future generations to come." Similar to the laying of tobacco, the practice of smudging signals a transformation from the mundane to the sacred.

Sasha talked about the challenge of teaching practices like smudging to children. "I have to put more thought into it than I thought I would have to," she said. Because smudging, for Sasha, is somewhat habitual, she assumed her son Max would learn by observing her. As Max got older, however, Sasha realized he was not picking up important details. "A lot of things come up, just little tiny things," Sasha said, "that I realize I never explained to him or told him that he needed to do." Now she thinks she has the hang of it. She explained, "I try to make it part of everyday life. Well, it *is* part of everyday life, but having a child, I try to talk about it more. Like, this is how you smudge a house and this is why we're doing it. And, we start at the west because we're a Sun Dance family and we want to honor the west first, but most people start in the east because the east is where everything begins." Sasha's efforts to socialize Max require her to demonstrate, describe, interpret, and justify nearly every action she takes. It can get a little intense, she admits, to sustain this seemingly endless chatter. The important thing, however, is Max's exposure to all the "little tiny things" that make a big difference in his understanding of Indian ways.

Sasha also showed me how she smudges before making prayer ties, which, to the lay observer, are little satchels of tobacco made with scrap material and twine. It is the *process* of making prayer ties that matters, Sasha assured me. "You just have tobacco and you just kind of put a prayer, you know, think a prayer," she explained. "You put it [the prayer and the tobacco] into the material and you wrap it up and tie it. That's pretty much it." After I asked Sasha numerous questions about the process, she said, "You know what? Let me just go get some scissors and I'll show you." Sasha proceeded to gather the necessary materials—tobacco, pieces of scrap material, imitation sinew thread, scissors, sage, a lighter. She lit the small bundle of sage. "This is one of the times that I do use sage to smudge," she said, "because it's a prayer and I think it should be really cleansing for you." Sasha took a deep breath and began making prayer ties, slowly and methodically. She pinched tobacco between her fingers and held it close to her heart for a moment while sitting silently with her eyes closed. She then placed the tobacco in the center of the material and pinched the edges of the material together before she tied the little bundle off with the sinew and retrieved more tobacco from the pouch. She explained every step of the process her first time through, then silently continued until she had four little tobacco bundles next to her. "I find it very relaxing to make prayer ties, and sometimes," said Sasha, "I'll do it like a meditation exercise. If you want to try it," she offered, "I have tons of scrap material. I don't throw any material away." She pointed to the other side of the living room, bringing my attention to several storage bins and bags overflowing with colorful pieces of fabric and leather.

Sasha's stockpile of scrap materials was emblematic of other reclaimer practices, like being thrifty and making things "the old way," meaning at home and by hand, rather than purchasing them from the store. Reclaimers tout "do-it-yourself" philosophies, which they link to their reclaimed Indianness. Sadie (Lenape- and Blackfoot-identified), for instance, told me about her recent trip to the food bank. When prompted to choose items from "the special shelf," she helped herself to cornmeal, buckwheat flour, and flax seed instead of the more popular "cookies and chips and crap like that." Sadie's choices surprised the food bank volunteers. "I make from scratch," Sadie said matter-of-factly. "I can make five loaves of bread with this."

Reclaimers and Crafting

Reclaimers also associate crafting with their Indianness. Crafting knowledge, skills, and preferences vary significantly among reclaimers, but all craft making is celebrated. Valerie (Cherokee-identified), for instance, likes to tan leather for drum covers. She looks forward to learning how to make moccasins. Tabatha (Cherokee) enjoys making dream catchers because she "likes the idea of it" even though they are not a Cherokee tradition. Sasha (Lakota-identified) also makes dream catchers *because* they are a Lakota tradition. Recently, Sasha explained, she has been teaching her son, Max, to make dream catchers, which requires a *lot* of explanation. For Max to really understand this practice, Sasha emphasized, he needs to know *why* he is doing it in addition to *how*. "You start talking about spider medicine and how that works," Sasha said, "and how you would use it and how spiders use it and . . . how you use that information, those lessons the spider taught us."

Sadie (Lenape- and Blackfoot-identified) also discussed crafting as an important aspect of her and her children's socialization into Indian ways. "Growing up," she said, "we'd all make crafts." "We" included Sadie's mother and grandmother, who both died when Sadie was young. Sadie fondly remembers their weekly crafting sessions, hosted by a family friend on Thursday nights. Sadie described the scene: "They'd put on coffee, and everyone brought a dish or some sort of food, and you sat around and drank coffee and did crafts and worked on whatever you needed to work on. And the kids played, and you came and went when you needed to, and that was it. It just was. So to me, that's normal," Sadie said. "There *should* be the getting together and doing of the crafts." The importance of crafting is reinforced by Sadie's Canadian mentors. "Up north, when the crafts come out," Sadie said, "they say that's when the spirits will come. And when people are crafting and talking, that's when you learn the most."

Reclaimers also express pride in crafting their own powwow regalia. Sasha (Lakota-identified), for instance, showed me her handmade jingle dress, covered with the tell-tale tinkling "bells" of conically rolled aluminum lids from chewing tobacco canisters. Metal cones are available for purchase, but Sasha collected Copenhagen lids until she had enough for her dress. "I think it's important to make your own regalia," she explained. Ever in instructional mode, Sasha then warned, "When you're working on sacred things or on your regalia or anything like that, you don't want to do it with a bad heart because you don't want to have those feelings, that negativity, going into your stuff." This "rule" makes crafting spiritual and creative. To Sasha, it perfectly aligns with Indianness.

Reclaimers' Nature-Based Practices

Deep appreciation for the natural world, said many reclaimers, is central to Indianness. Numerous reclaimers said natural, outdoor settings made them feel more in tune with their Indian identities. Observing nature, reclaimers suggested, enabled them, as Indians, to understand the earth's rhythms and use the earth's resources in appropriate and sustainable ways. To illustrate this point, Sadie (Lenape- and Blackfoot-identified) talked about the fall holiday she calls "feasting," *not* "Thanksgiving." If people paid attention to nature, Sadie maintained, they would feast earlier in the year when produce is still plentiful. In turn, they would conserve their food in November, when their (NE Ohio) gardens are bare. Sadie said her Canadian mentors, for example, feast in September because winter arrives earlier in the north. Sadie, on the other hand, tends to feast in October—but not on the same date each year. "We feast," she said, "when our leaves around the house are almost down."

According to Sadie's traditions, falling leaves also mean it is time to feed the spirits and put them to sleep for winter. When the leaves begin to bud again in the springtime, it is time to wake the spirits up again and feed them. Sadie wants her children to understand these teachings, too, so she does not let them play on their tree swing until the tree has leaves. The tree should be "awake" first. It is more difficult, Sadie admitted, to enforce these rules as the children get older. They "had a rough time" with it last year, Sadie said, and she fears it will only become more complicated as they advance in age. How will she explain why their school friends follow very different rules?

Whereas some reclaimers learn the value of nature's lessons from their mentors, others, like Valerie (Cherokee-identified), believe their affinity for the natural world is inherent. According to Valerie, being Indian "explains kind of why I feel much more comfortable outdoors in nature than I do being enclosed." She talked about visiting Oconaluftee Indian Village in Cherokee, North Carolina, where "you can actually see how they used to live back in the old, old days. . . . I would just as soon go back to that age," Valerie said. "Give me the woods, a knife." Some reclaimers, like Valerie, associate respect for nature with living in a more "natural" state they believe existed (only) in the (imagined) past. According to Kurt (Choctaw-identified), it was not uncommon for reclaimers to express a desire to return to the "old, old days." Kurt said he frequently warns people against this romanticized vision of old-timey Indianness. Kurt replayed a typical conversation:

RECLAIMER: God, I'd love to go back to those days.
KURT: What days?
RECLAIMER: You know, when Natives were Natives.
KURT: Oh, so you'd like to get up in the morning and go hunt for your food? The women worked from the time they got up until the time they went to bed. Children worked. They were children, but they were still instructed on what to do and still had certain duties to do.

Kurt shook his head and exclaimed, "Our young people today couldn't survive! And that really discourages me, too." He continued: "If something would happen tomorrow, I still have some of those Native instincts in me that were taught to me from my grandfather and my father. And my oldest son [Daniel], he has them. But my youngest ones? They scare me because they represent our next generation, who, if something would happen tomorrow, the electric could go out, if something major happened, they wouldn't know how to survive. They could not survive." Kurt described an apocalyptic scenario in which department stores and grocery stores disappeared and food and clean water were scarce. Referring to his youngest children or perhaps members of the millennial generation more generally, Kurt asked, "Would they know how to boil water? Would they know how to hunt without a gun? Would they know how to clothe themselves?" He sighed.

Kenai (Lakota-identified), Sasha's ex-husband and Max's father, took this idea one step further, stating that wilderness skills are obligatory because they *comprise* Indian culture. "You need to know how to live," Kenai stated. "My son has to know how to make a bow. He has to know how to skin [an animal]. He *has* to," Kenai said, "or he's not traditional." Kenai did not explain *why* activities like building bows and skinning animals are compulsory for contemporary Indigenous people living in urban environments. He simply stated, "It's our Sun Dance religion. That's the way we live."

Tabatha (Cherokee), who spent summers with her grandparents in West Virginia, talked about her love of the outdoors and her concern for the environment. "Going on vacation is not living in a hotel room," Tabatha said. "To me, it's being out in the woods with my tent . . . getting up in the morning and getting that campfire going and cooking right over an open fire and just communing, you know, getting back to nature." Tabatha takes her grandson camping because, as she put it, "every child should know how to live off the land. I mean, who knows what's going to happen?" she asked. Like Kurt, Tabatha expressed concern about an apocalyptic event—one that ends with the earth rejecting its abusive human inhabitants: "It is going to throw us off, you know, just like a bucking horse."[1] Tabatha was silent for a moment, then asked, "Do you remember seeing the old commercials, where the Indian's standing in front of that big pile of trash and he's got that one single tear going down his face?" She paused. "That's the way it feels with me," she said.

Tabatha's reference to this decades-old commercial indicates its impact on her. She relates to the "crying Indian" (1971) public service announcement (PSA) because she *feels* his sorrow. Unfortunately, the commercial's "many duplicities," according to historian Finis Dunaway, are unknown to many Americans.[2] According to Dunaway, author of *Seeing Green: The Use and Abuse of American Environmental Images*, the "crying Indian" PSA became "the quintessential symbol of environmental idealism" despite being paid for by *corporate* polluters intent on framing pollution as an individual-level phenomenon. In a piece written for the *Chicago Tribune*, Dunaway brilliantly captures the mood of the PSA:

> It's probably the most famous tear in American history: Iron Eyes Cody, an actor in Native American garb, paddles a birch bark canoe on water that seems, at first, tranquil and pristine, but becomes increasingly polluted along his journey. He pulls his boat ashore and walks toward a bustling freeway. As the lone Indian ponders the polluted landscape, a passenger hurls a paper bag out a car window. The bag bursts on the ground, scattering fast-food wrappers all over the Indian's beaded moccasins. In a stern voice, the narrator comments: "Some people have a deep, abiding respect for the natural beauty that was once this country. And some people don't." The camera zooms in on Iron Eyes Cody's face to reveal a single tear falling, ever so slowly, down his cheek.

"At the moment the tear appears," Dunaway writes, "the narrator, in a baritone voice, intones: 'People start pollution. People can stop it.'"

Dunaway notes that deflecting blame for environmental pollution away from industry is the *second* duplicity of this advertisement commissioned by the "Make America Beautiful" campaign. The first duplicity involves the fraudulent Indian identity of Iron Eyes Cody, who claimed Cherokee-Cree descent but was Italian American. The actor, whose given name was Espera de Corti, "played Indian" in commercials, movies, and life. Yet, the crying Indian's *authenticity*, Dunaway aptly notes, is necessary for viewers to embrace "authentic" Indigenous culture "*that was once this country*" over "commercial" contemporary culture (emphasis added). The central idea and third duplicity driving home the PSA's propagandized point is Indianness as anachronism, as though the crying Indian emerged from a pristine past to grieve the polluted present.

The "crying Indian" PSA is a compelling example of how ruling elites homogenize memories[3] of Indianness in the United States. "Make America Beautiful" and innumerable other political and corporate campaigns manipulate people's memories by repeatedly portraying authentic Indianness as something existing only in the pristine, natural world of the "old, old days." In the PSA, people cruising down the highway littering fast-food waste is juxtaposed with a lone Indian traveling by birch bark canoe. The Indian's antiquity is further indicated by his long braids, bone choker, and fringed leather clothing.[4] The commercial—as well as innumerable images used to sell corporate products (e.g., Argo cornstarch, Calumet baking powder, Jeep Cherokee vehicles, Money House Blessing air fresheners)[5]—teaches audience members to dissociate Indigenous peoples from contemporary (industrialized, urban, built) environments. This dissociation normalizes and justifies the "disappearance" of Indigenous peoples in modern times. Moreover, the scene falsely dichotomizes "nature" and "technology," disguising the complexities of Indigenous knowledges existing in the past, present, and future. Ultimately, the subtle messages relayed by the "crying Indian" signify *colonial unknowing*. Colonialism, racism, and capitalism are deemed irrelevant. The takeaway, instead, is that Indians cannot exist here and, importantly, *would not even want to* exist here. Their so-called natural demise was inevitable. White people remain *innocent* of everything, except (perhaps) littering.

Indigenous and Indigenous-identified residents of Northeast Ohio are exposed to the same idealized memories of Indianness. As the above section and remainder of this chapter reveal, *reclaimers* are more likely to internalize them. Without positive Indigenous role models in their day-to-day lives, reclaimers' understandings of indigeneity overlap and become entangled with settler-imposed images of Indianness. While engaged in processes of identity making and Indian becoming, some reclaimers unwittingly enact stereotypes that reproduce notions of homogenized and antiquated Indianness. In this way, reclaimers perpetuate colonial unknowing. Relocators, in contrast, neither imagined a singular past for all Indigenous peoples nor romanticized the pasts of any Indigenous peoples. They did not vocalize desires to return to some vague conceptualization of the "old, old days." Not a single relocator discussed the necessity of knowing wilderness survival skills. Additionally, relocators rarely commented on the specifics of Indigenous peoples' practices. At community engagements, relocators ceremoniously used tobacco and composed spirit plates, but few relocators highlighted these practices as intrinsic to being or behaving like an Indian. Relocators suggested, instead, that the pan-Indian community's ethnic diversity, coupled with the great distances between their urban and reservation homes, made practicing their unique traditions quite difficult.

> We made powwows because we needed a place to be together. Something intertribal, something old, something to make us money, something we could work toward, for our jewelry, our songs, our dances, our drum.
> —Tommy Orange (Cheyenne and Arapaho), *There, There*

Doing and Discovering Indianness in the Pan-Indian Powwow Circuit

Due to a general lack of Indigenous gatherings, both relocators and reclaimers participated in Ohio's pan-Indian powwow scene. Across both communities, members generally agree that Ohio's powwows are important because they affirm ties to an Indian community, cultivate pride in Indian identities, and provide instruction in pan-Indian ways.[6] Powwows, a relatively modern cultural phenomenon, developed from "war dances" of the Omaha and Pawnee nations, spread to other Plains tribes, and then moved eastward to the Ojibwa.[7] Eventually adopted by many Indian nations and off-reservation Indian communities, powwows are now a common feature of contemporary pan-Indian culture. The *lack* of federally recognized tribes in Ohio likely contributes to the abundance and popularity of powwows in the region. During Ohio's powwow season from May to September, "powwow hopping" or "being on the circuit"—i.e., moving from one powwow to the next—is a popular activity among reclaimers, relocators, and more than a few self-identified white people who "caught the powwow bug."

Relocators and reclaimers introduce their children to powwows early in life. "My children," said Gertrude (Cayuga), "went into the circle at a very young age. When they learned to walk, they were in there." Berta's granddaughter, Farah, was "brought up in the powwows," according to Farah's mother, Melissa (Native Hawaiian–identified). "That's what Berta's family did," Melissa said. "Soon as they could walk, you make them a little outfit and you send them out there." Melissa said her daughter Farah "was probably home from the hospital a couple of days" when she attended her first powwow.

Reclaimers, like Kurt's son Daniel (Choctaw-identified), also emphasized the importance of powwows in their lives. Daniel said most of his good friends are "powwow people," and he even met his wife, Tyra (Cherokee-identified), on the powwow circuit. Daniel and Tyra, in turn, introduced their first-born son to the powwow circle when he was only months old. I witnessed this happy occasion. After the powwow emcee cleared the circle, announced the ceremony, and recited a prayer, the young couple, surrounded by siblings, parents, and grandparents, carried their tiny son in his tiny regalia around the powwow circle. When the small familial troupe, walking in step with the beat of the drum, completed a full revolution around the circle, the powwow dancers joyously entered. Together with the family, dancers and spectators welcomed the baby boy into the local pan-Indian powwow scene.

Relocators and reclaimers also similarly talked about urban Indian youths' *mostly* enthusiastic participation in powwows. Parents and grandparents try to strike a balance between encouraging children's participation and preventing powwow fatigue. Berta, a Lakota relocator, for instance, said that her oldest granddaughter is always excited for powwow season to begin, but eventually experiences some burnout: "[She] calls me every week—'Grandma, when's the next powwow? When's the next powwow?' [But] once she starts going to powwows, she's like, 'Every weekend I've got to powwow. I just want to go to a movie with my friends!' So I say, 'Okay, next week you don't go with us. You go to the movies,' but she ends up going with us anyway, you know, [because] she can't live without the powwows, either." Berta smiled at the thought. Sasha, a Lakota-identified reclaimer, also talked about her son's enthusiasm for powwowing—especially now that he and his father had completed his men's traditional outfit. "He's so proud of it," Sasha said, beaming. "It's so cute." Though Max loves to powwow, Sasha admits that some days are "a struggle." "I don't want to push him and force him," she said, "because I know that will send him running the other direction." As a result, Sasha tries not to impose powwows or other celebrations of Indianness on Max. "I think a lot of it is just making sure that it stays fun for him," Sasha explained. "That it is a joy for him, like it's a joy for me or for Kenai."

Despite general agreement about powwows as meaningful sites for social interaction and children's socialization, NE Ohio Indians' opinions about the primary functions of powwows vary. Relocators generally emphasize the social aspects of powwows, whereas reclaimers tend to emphasize the spiritual elements of powwows. These sentiments, however, do not divide evenly across the two pathways to urban Indian identity. Samantha, a second-generation Cherokee relocator, for instance, said she attends powwows for social reasons now, but misses the spiritual element of dancing "jingle," a medicine dance. "Most people who dance say you should only think good thoughts when you're dancing, especially with jingle dress," Samantha explained. "They say, you know, you shouldn't swear, you should be respectful. So I guess it is different, going [to a powwow] as a spectator in your street clothes. There's just something missing." At the same time, Samantha expressed no misgivings about purchasing her jingle dress and other regalia—"I don't sew," she said unself-consciously—whereas Sasha, the Lakota-identified reclaimer who also dances jingle, emphasized the importance of making her own.

Samantha also talked about dancing jingle competitively. "I definitely like to compete," Samantha said. "I notice when I compete, I don't see anything around me. . . . I'm just in the zone, they call it. And I like that feeling." When Samantha danced, she participated in dozens of jingle dance competitions. Now, when Samantha cannot attend powwows, even as a spectator, she gets her "fix" watching competitive powwow dancing on YouTube. Samantha's perspective distinctly contrasts those of Sadie and Neville (multitribally identified reclaimers). They believe that competitive dancing cheapens the entire powwow experience. "That, to me, is like putting a price on how well you are able to dance," Neville said. "The spirits don't care how you dance!" he exclaimed. To further illustrate his point, Neville directed me to search for "team jingle dress" on the powwows.com website. "Team jingle dress dancing!" Sadie excitedly chimed in. "That's when there's like five or six women dancing together at the same time, getting their cones going the same way. I mean, I'm sure it's hard and it takes lots of practice," Sadie continued, "but it's one of those, um, okay, where have we lost the tradition in that one?" Sadie and Neville are particularly offended by jingle dance competitions because the jingle dance—the dance category in which Samantha competed—should, in their opinion, only be used medicinally.

Not all reclaimers thought of regional powwows as spiritual events. In fact, Kenai (Lakota-identified) was somewhat dismissive of NE Ohio

Indians who emphasized the spiritual aspects of powwows. "It's a freaking powwow," Kenai said somewhat irritably, "and they try to turn it into this ceremony and all this other bullshit. It's a powwow, you know what I mean? It's like a really pimped ass family picnic," Kenai continued. "*That's* what it is. You're supposed to go and have a blast. It ain't all like wOOOoooOOOooo [spooky ghost noise], you know?" Yet, Kenai said he understands why some reclaimers attach mystical significance to Ohio powwows. "That's all some people have," he said. "That's all they know." Kenai sighed. "They don't know what a *yuwipi* [Lakota healing ceremony] is, they don't know what a sweat lodge is," he said, shaking his head. He recognizes that he is fortunate to have Indian mentors and a reservation home to which he travels for ceremonies. Many reclaimers, according to Kenai, rely exclusively on powwows and other urban, pan-Indian events to *experience* their Indian identities.

In contrast to reclaimers, relocators spoke rather casually about powwows as money-making opportunities. For Monica and Sam, an elder relocator couple who are Diné- and Mexican-identified, powwows are a primary source of income. According to their adult granddaughter, Sandra, who spent summer weekends in her youth with her grandparents on the powwow circuit, money making is the *primary* reason for powwows. "It's a business," she said matter-of-factly. Her grandparents "obviously care" about the local Native community, she explained, but powwow vending takes a lot of preparation and business savvy. Sandra rattled off a list of tasks her grandparents complete to make their living: "They have to travel [to the Southwest] and get their jewelry, kachina dolls, pottery, pay that person, and then hope to sell them, pay for tents, you know, whatever set up they're going to have. . . . It's for a good cause," Sandra said, "but it's a business."

Socializing Later-Generation Relocators

Pan-Indian powwows, though appreciated by most relocator families, are considered only secondary sites of socialization by relocators. Though Berta (Lakota) attends NE Ohio powwows to socialize now, she used to treat them primarily as money-making ventures. She used the money to travel home to her reservation. Selling her hand-crafted jewelry, dream catchers, and moccasins, Berta sometimes made up to a thousand dollars in one weekend. "Every time I did a cultural event, I would make extra money," Berta said, "and I would pack my kids up and go home to the reservation!" Berta laughed at the memory. Now she requires dialysis, so the long trip is implausible. She explained, "Now, you know, it's real hard for me to get around, but every holiday I would go home, take my kids home, to every cultural event on the reservation—for every name giving, *every* event that happened, I would go home to the reservation. As soon as Easter vacation hit, we would head back to the reservation, . . . as soon as Thanksgiving hit, we would go back to the reservation." These trips home were everything to Berta. They helped her stay connected to her family and community *and* introduced her urban Indian children to reservation life—a necessity, as far as Berta was concerned.

Barbara (Cherokee) and her daughter, Samantha (Cherokee), agree that reservation visits are essential experiences for Native children growing up in urban environments. Samantha, of course, danced jingle at competitive powwows, but she said powwows did not help her "identify with [her] Cherokee side." When Samantha was younger, Barbara regularly took her to Oklahoma. "In Oklahoma," Samantha said, "[mom] tried to immerse me more in the Cherokee aspects [of Indianness]— like taking me to our stomp dances. And she used to take me into the Cherokee Baptist Church." Samantha is grateful her mother exposed her to more than "just powwows."

Sandra, in contrast, is thankful her grandparents Monica and Sam nurtured her Native identity through their involvement in regional powwows, but wishes she knew more about her Indigenous heritage. Now in her twenties, Sandra is self-conscious about her limited knowledge of the family's Indian roots. Her mother is Italian but, Sandra said, "I don't identify with that because I lived with my dad and my dad was so strong in my life and my grandparents were so strong in my life, that's who I identify with." Like her grandparents and father, Sandra identifies as Native and Mexican. "It's complicated!" Sandra said, stating that Native and Mexican are arbitrary distinctions that resulted from a haphazardly drawn international border. She continued: "Just where the border was drawn, people got crossed over. Our families must have been right there at the time. So they were Native living there, but yet considered Mexicans. So it's kind of a weird line there, all depending on where that border was drawn and what sides the family picked. They almost had to pick, you know, were you Native or were you Mexican? Or were you Native-Mexican?" Sandra thinks her great-grandparents were Spanish speaking, but she doesn't know for sure. She has asked her grandparents, Monica and Sam, "several times" for clarification, but said, "I think *they* don't really know where, exactly, they came from."

Sandra expressed sorrow for her little sisters, who also will grow up unacquainted with their racial and ethnic heritages. "They know about *powwows*," Sandra said. "They know as much as I do. But there's nothing for them to see outside of that. I mean, outside of 'powwow world,' you know, this little mini-construction of a world." Sandra sighed. "There's nothing outside of that for them to know about Native life or Native people." Still, Sandra insisted, "powwows are so important" for Native children living in NE Ohio. "It's the only thing still here that we can do," she said glumly.

Many (but not all) first-generation relocators believed it was important for their children and grandchildren to learn their specific cultural traditions. Although pan-Indian powwows served an important purpose— bringing urban Indigenous people together and providing space to talk about their contemporary experiences—some relocators argued that they were not effective "substitutes" for tribally specific customs. They pointed out that some tribes do not even recognize powwows as traditional gatherings. To better represent the community and to avoid homogenization, a few relocators suggested that multiple gathering formats be adopted. Giveaways and potluck-style dinner events, they argued, would provide needed diversity. Adding variety to relocator community events would not teach youth specific tribal customs, however.

First-generation relocators simultaneously acknowledged that the urban environment was not particularly conducive to socializing youth in holistic ways. The reservation environment, with dense networks of family, friends, teachers, healers, and other spiritual leaders, could not be recreated in NE Ohio. Tribal ceremonies could not be recreated in NE Ohio. NE Ohio lands did not have the same histories as sacred homelands. They could not tell the same stories. Ultimately, NE Ohio could not provide the same sustenance first-generation relocators received in Indiancentric spaces, immersed in tribal cultures, speaking Indigenous languages.

How could relocator elders, then, possibly communicate all the knowledge they received from so many sources to relocator youth? Their relocation bus tickets did not come with manuals for maintaining cultural traditions. Additionally, to survive in the city, relocators needed to work. They worked menial jobs, multiple jobs, second and third shifts to make ends meet. For many relocators, exhaustion prevented them from teaching their children what seemed unteachable—the wealth of cultural knowledge available (though not always received by young people) at home in Indian nations. Finally, relocator elders asked, To what use could their children and grandchildren put this knowledge if there were some way to teach it? The Indians with whom relocators communed in the urban environment were from distinctive tribes with unique customs. First-generation relocators enjoyed learning about different customs from each other, but collectively engaging such customs was neither feasible nor desirable.

The taken-for-granted ways in which first-generation relocators experienced their own identities complicated things further. Their identities resulted from enculturation in particular Indigenous societies and belonging in particular Indigenous communities. They knew they were Indians and nothing could change that fact. What they did or how they did it was irrelevant. Further, relationships with other relocators, Indians with different perspectives and different customs, more firmly established what first-generation relocators already knew: there existed no recipe for being Indian, no instructions for achieving Indianness.

For all these reasons and more, first-generation relocators did not concentrate their energies on the hows and whys of tribe-specific practices. Rather, they tried to provide their children and grandchildren with more general understandings of what being Indian means. They created opportunities for urban Indian youth to socialize with other Indians in the local community and, when possible, at home on Indian reservations. Trips home to tribal homelands, however, were fleeting. They were costly in terms of time and travel expenses and never lasted long enough for urban Indian children to absorb the cultural customs of their parents or grandparents.

Many first-generation relocators focused their socialization efforts on instilling in children the Indigenous *values* they believed Indians held in common, rather than pan-Indian and/or tribally variable practices.

Berta (Lakota), for example, was adamant that *everyone* needed to understand that indigeneity is inconsistent across individuals and tribal nations. As a reservation resident, as a boarding school student, and even today, in the urban environment, Berta said people expect her to fit *their* expectations of Indians. She, however, *knows* what she is "supposed to be" (as she indicated in the quotation at the beginning of the book). To Berta, indigeneity is constituted by deep-rooted *knowing* that contradicts dominant ways of knowing. Berta steadfastly embodies and enacts this understanding of indigeneity and encourages her children to do the same. She and her husband, Greg, consciously impressed upon their children Indigenous ways of *knowing* rather than Indigenous ways of acting.

For Berta and Greg, Indigenous ways of knowing are predicated on profound *respect*. They concentrated their socialization efforts on imparting this value to their children. To illustrate, Berta explained the difficulties of moving her boys from their reservation home, the only home they knew in their first ten years of existence, to the urban environment. "It was really hard for them at first," Berta said. She recalled their confusion about other children's behaviors at school: "They would come home and say, 'Mom, the kid at school yelled at the teacher!' I mean, that was unheard of because our number one thing we teach our children is respect. . . . And it was really hard for them to come to this culture where people didn't learn respect. It was really difficult for them, but like I said, my husband and I both talked with them so they would realize that there are different ways to approach life, not just overpowering people." If the boys talked disparagingly about another child or a family acquaintance, Berta said she gently chided them, saying, "That's his right, you know. He has the right to be who he wants to be. If he wants to believe that, then that's his right. You don't have to believe what he believes." More than anything else, Berta said she and Greg wanted their boys to be respectful and fair-minded. "We more or less bombarded them with that," she said.

When asked *how* she and Greg bombarded the boys with Lakota culture, Berta talked about watching Hollywood movies together as a family and then engaging the boys in a dialogue about them. "So we always made discussions of every movie we saw," Berta said. One movie they discussed, Berta recalled, was *War of the Roses* (1989). This black comedy was about a wealthy husband and wife who, in the midst of a tumultuous divorce, went to great lengths to oust the other spouse from the house they both wanted to keep. After the film, Berta said her sons disagreed about which character deserved the house. "My one son said, 'She picked it,' and then my other son said, 'But it was his money!' . . . We would have discussions like that, you know? I think," said Berta, "that kept them pretty much fair-minded." For Berta and Greg, socializing their Lakotan boys in the *urban environment* meant nurturing *who they are* as Indigenous people. It meant teaching them how to embody Indigenous values like respect and fair-mindedness—values that maintain Indigenous ways of being in the world. Though Berta did not mention it, the couple's strategic utilization of movies and movie-based discussions to socialize their children aligns with Indigenous storytelling traditions used to teach young people for centuries.

Second-Generation Relocators and Early Identity Confusion

The Indigenous identities of children socialized in urban environments are not quite as rooted or unshakeable as the identities of relocator elders. Second- and later-generation relocators said they always knew they were "Indians," but as children, they struggled to understand what that meant. Many young relocators recalled early childhood confusion about their racial and ethnic heritages. As a small child, Samantha (Cherokee), for instance, recognized that her mother was different from her friends' (white) mothers. "[M]y mom was darker," Samantha noted, and she also said some things, like "come here," in Cherokee. "So I think," said Samantha, "I kind of knew I was different from other people who just had white parents." Samantha noticed the differences, in other words, but did not know how to label them.

Moreover, urban Indian children's immersion in the dominant culture—replete with settler-constructed images of primitive, violent, drunken, caricatured, and romanticized Indianness—skewed their perceptions of who or what Indigenous peoples were. Because representations of Indianness so uniformly contradicted their experiences as Indians, they did not understand how their Indian identities were linked or connected to "Indians" as portrayed in popular culture. Second- and later-generation relocators provided examples of mistakes they made during childhood as they tried to figure things out. Some young

people, for instance, mimicked "Indians" they saw on television, scream-
ing "Woowoowoowoowoowoo!" while dancing around in circles. One
young relocator specifically remembered being reprimanded for this
behavior, despite having no understanding of what it meant or why it
was "bad." This information is something she learned in time. Another
young relocator recalled harboring prejudicial feelings toward "Indians"
on television because they appeared to be "crazy" and did not seem re-
motely related to the "Indians" in his own life.

Some young relocators were confused by other Indian *people* in their
midst. Sandra (Native- and Mexican-identified), for instance, said she
grappled with her relationship to other members of the pan-Indian relocator community. As a child, she remembers thinking that community
gatherings were "weird," and she never knew "what to think about the
people there." "I just knew they were different from what I considered
normal," Sandra reflected, "but different in [the same] ways I was different, but *more* different than I thought I was." That is to say, as a child
Sandra perceived herself as *unlike* many of the white people around her,
but *more* like the white people than the Indians she knew (who, in her
estimation, were even *less* like the white people than herself). Across
scenarios, Sandra considered the white people to be normal or typical
and the nonwhite people like herself to be nonnormative or atypical.
"Yeah," Sandra said, "there was a lot of questions as a kid because it is so
different from what you see on TV."

Second- and later-generation relocators also struggled with ideas regarding fractionated or segmented Indianness. They were too young and
naïve to understand how Indian bodies and bloodlines were divvied up,
quantified, and legitimated (or not). Many young Natives were still fig-
uring out what it meant to be "Indian" when they were confronted by
gradations of Indianness, too. One second-generation relocator, for instance, said she would never forget an interaction she had with a teacher
after revealing she was Indian. The teacher asked, "Well, how much are
you?" and she proudly replied, "I'm a quarter!" She'd heard her mother
say so. In her mind, however, her "quarter" Indianness had something
to do with a twenty-five-cent piece because that was the only "quarter"
with which she was familiar.

Even full-blood Indians are divided into different tribal pieces and
parts. With more than 570 federally recognized Indian nations in the

United States, the possibilities are practically endless. Many tribes do not recognize the Indian blood of another tribe's enrolled members, so even full-blood Indians are sometimes denied full-blood status when their (full-blood) parents are enrolled in different tribes. For example, Berta and Greg are both enrolled as full-blood Lakota, but in *different* Lakota nations. Because the different nations use different blood quantum guidelines, their children do not automatically qualify for full-blood status. Berta explained: "We're allowed to sign our children up under *either* his [name] or my name. But his reservation, they only count his blood, so the kids would be considered half-blood. That's it. Period. But my reservation, they count all Sioux blood, so that means his half and my half. The kids are considered full-blood [by my tribe], which they are. So, of course we enrolled them in my tribe."

In Indian Country and beyond, full-blood Indians occupy a higher status than mixed-blood Indians.[8] This phenomenon results from historical constructions and enduring memories of Indianness as something wholly unique, and therefore utterly unlike whiteness and/or Europeanness. Full-blood Indians, whose bloodlines are perceived as "undiluted" by European or other blood, are consequently perceived as more authentic. Berta and Greg know their children are full-blood Lakota Indians irrespective of their tribal enrollment, but they also know that tribal documentation matters. As Berta indicates, "of course" she and Greg strategically enrolled their children in *her* Lakota nation because this decision resulted in documentation of their children's full-blood status. Importantly, the children's recognition as full-blood Indians protects the family's Lakota citizenship status for future generations. If the children were enrolled as half-bloods instead, non-Indian child-bearing partnerships (or even half- or quarter-Indian partnerships) would rapidly diminish their bloodlines, resulting in blood quanta deemed too trivial for enrollment purposes in fewer generations. That the actual composition of their children's blood remains the same is inconsequential.

Berta's and Greg's enrollment considerations illustrate how some families strategically negotiate blood quantum politics. Though Indigenous studies scholars openly discuss the *dangers* of strategic essentialism, i.e., the calculated utilization of blood-based metrics to establish Indian citizenship and legal rights, such sweeping considerations are less likely to inform familial enrollment decisions. For many families, the best path forward is the one most protective of family members' tribal citizenship status. Even scholars committed to decolonization, who recognize the settler state's role in quantifying Indigenous bloodlines in the first place, recognize that maintaining Native distinctiveness is a primary, though "semimournful," means of protecting Indigenous sovereignty in the current sociopolitical climate.[9] (See chapter 1 for a more thorough discussion of scholarly debates about the benefits and drawbacks of using blood quantum metrics.)

Issues of blood quantum and tribal enrollment are incredibly complex, so it is not surprising that urban Indian children—who often embody complicated combinations of Indian and non-Indian blood—are confused by language dissecting their bodies and quantifying their belongingness in one group or another. Berta and Greg relayed a story about their young grandson, who was understandably befuddled by issues of blood and belonging. Berta explained that her grandson "knows there is a difference" between tribes because both of his parents, her Lakota son and her Diné (Navajo) daughter-in-law, are proud of their heritages. When the grandson overheard Berta and Greg refer to him as "Navajo-Sioux," however, the child insisted *he* was Sioux and his sister was Navajo. "He pushed it off on his sister," Berta said. "He didn't want to be *that*, you know?" Laughing and shaking her head, Berta exclaimed, "It's just crazy that he would say something like that!" Berta made light of her grandson's youthful naivety, but she understood why the child was unable to comprehend his combined heritage. "Even though they're all Indian, full-blooded Indian, society deems you to be half of this or half of that," Berta said disapprovingly, herself seemingly bewildered by such nonsensical quantifications.

Non-Indian children in part-Indian families also experience identity confusion in the urban environment. With some amusement, Berta and Greg talked about two little girls, named Maddie and Piper, who are not blood relations, but whom they call their granddaughters. They are the white daughters of their white ex-daughter-in-law, Sarah, who is now married to the young girls' father, also a white man. Sarah's oldest daughter, Mallory, however, is Berta's and Greg's biological granddaughter. As such, Mallory is half-blood Lakota (i.e., the child of a full-blood Lakota man and a white woman).

Berta and Greg maintain a very close relationship with their (biological) granddaughter, Mallory, and as a result, they have a close relationship with Sarah's "new" family, i.e., her husband and their two girls. Thus, when Berta and Greg visit Mallory, they also visit Maddie and Piper, and when Mallory visits Berta and Greg, her half-sisters frequently accompany her. Maddie and Piper are too young to recognize that Berta and Greg are not *their* biological grandparents, but they are old enough to know that their sister and (adoptive) grandparents are "Indians." Understandably, the young (white) girls think they are Indian, too, and they asked their parents if they could dance at powwows like their big sister Mallory. "At first their parents didn't want to let them," Berta said, but "I told them, 'If they want to dance, let them dance.'"

Sarah and her husband eventually relented, and now Maddie and Piper regularly dance at powwows. Their powwow participation, said Berta, seems to exacerbate the girls' confusion about their racial-ethnic identities. Additionally, Berta admitted, she is responsible for muddying matters further: "When they say, 'We're Indian, right grandma?' I say, 'Yeah.'" Berta said she just does not have the heart to tell them otherwise. "They're so cute!" Berta exclaimed. "And everyone says, 'But they're not Indian!' And I say, 'No, they're not, but that's okay, you know? They can play Indian with us. I don't think it's going to hurt them.'" Greg wholeheartedly agreed with Berta (as he was prone to do). "They'll learn the culture," Greg said. "I mean, that's more education for them." "When they get older," Berta said confidently, "they'll understand the differences—you know, that I'm not their real grandma."

Indian Identity Salience and Later-Generation Relocators

Eventually, second- and later-generation relocators grow out of their childhood confusion. Just as Maddie and Piper will understand that they are *not* Indians when they get older, urban Indian children understand that they *are* Indians—even if their lives do not resemble depictions of Indianness in the dominant settler-colonial culture. At some point, many young relocators experience distress about their inability to *look* like pop-cultural portrayals of Indians. For instance, Sandra (Native- and Mexican-identified), a third-generation relocator, expressed disappointment in her "light skin." She confessed that she "was always kind of envious" of "girls who looked more Native" than she. Her sisters are among those she envies. "They are like four shades darker than me!"

Sandra lamented. Samantha (Cherokee) also expressed annoyance about her light complexion, which diminished others' abilities to identify her as Indian. Her mother, who (according to Samantha) is "dark-skinned and looks more Native," was always careful to introduce Samantha to relocator community outsiders *as her daughter* to underscore Samantha's Native bloodline and identity. Barbara (Samantha's mother) took particular care to use this strategy at out-of-state powwows. "I always just found that annoying," Samantha sighed, "like I have to prove I'm Native to them by my mom." Though both young women asserted that their "darker" and/or "dark-skinned" relatives appeared more Native than they, neither Sandra nor Samantha recognized their (relatively minor) roles in reifying stereotypes about "dark-skinned" Indianness.

Relatedly, Berta talked about her young (mixed-blood) granddaughter's discontentment with her physical appearance, which did not resemble her grandmother's. "She used to want her hair [to be] black so bad when she was little," Berta said. Berta explained, "I used to comb my hair, and then I would brush her hair and I would say, 'Okay, now take all of the hair out [of the brush] and put it in the trash.' And then when she was taking the hair out of the brush, she would see my black hair and she would say, 'Ha! My hair is turning black!' She was so happy that her hair was turning black. She was just little, but she was just so proud!" Berta said, laughing. When Berta's granddaughter turned eighteen, she dyed her hair black. "It didn't look good to me," Berta chuckled, "but she really liked that dark hair."

The blonde-haired, blue-eyed child's desire to look more Indian undoubtedly resulted from the barrage of messages she received about how "real" Indians look—including unintentional messages from her grandmother. Berta said that she constantly reminds people that Indians "come in every shade." "I tell people we come in all colors, just like everybody else," she said. Berta also confessed, however, that she once said her granddaughter (the one who dyed her hair black) looked "*wasichu*" (like a white person). She had taken her granddaughter with her to visit family back home on the reservation: "All the uncles and aunts . . . would say, 'Eh, she really looks *wasichu*,' which means she looks white, you know. And so I said, 'Yeah, she does kind of look *wasichu*.' And then I looked at the door and she walked in. She understood that word, '*wasichu*,' and she says, 'Grandma! You said I was Indian!' And I said, 'Oh, babe, you are Indian.' I said, 'Sometimes you look *wasichu*.' I didn't know how to explain myself!" Berta laughed as she relayed the story, but it was likely jarring for her impressionable granddaughter to hear her Native grandmother say she sometimes looks *wasichu*.

For some second- and later-generation relocators, recognizing their nonlikeness with stereotypical portrayals of Indians coincided with broader awareness of oppressions experienced by Indigenous peoples.[10] Their commitments to Indigenous identities and Indigenous peoples grew stronger as they grew older and more informed. Samantha (Cherokee), a lifelong NE Ohio resident, for instance, said that the salience of her Indigenous identity increased during high school and further intensified during college, culminating in her decision to enroll in a master's degree program. At the time of our interview, Samantha was soon departing for graduate school to work with an Indigenous professor of clinical psychology on research based in an Indigenous community. Samantha was excited to embark on this new adventure and felt confident in her decision to pursue a career of service to Indigenous peoples.

Samantha also understood, however, that her experiences as an urban Indigenous woman were different from the experiences of Indigenous individuals who (in Samantha's words) "grew up where they do their ceremonials" and "speak their language." Though Samantha is an enrolled Cherokee who occasionally visits reservation-based family with her mother, during our interview she said she identified as "more of a pan-Indian" because, she explained, "I have a universal sense of connection [with Indigenous people], than specifically with my tribe." Samantha said she discovered just how different her perspective was when she participated in an internship program with other young Native women in Oklahoma the previous summer. They "thought it was weird" that she embraced a pan-Indian identity. "Some of the people from Oklahoma, those Indians, they're very rooted in their specific tribe, and to me that's just, I don't know, it's kind of different for me." Samantha thought perhaps her pan-Indian identity resulted from "going to [out-of-state] powwows and being friends with so many different tribes."

College was a turning point discussed by several relocators in their twenties. At this juncture of their lives, they became more fully committed to the advancement of Indigenous peoples generally, as opposed to personal advancements and/or achievements.[11] As a whole, however, young adult relocators had different levels of commitment to Indigenous identities and communities. Susan (Dakota), for instance, said only one of her five children seemed interested in their Native heritage. "Now that they're older," Susan said, her children *identify* as Native and Puerto Rican (on their father's side), but their Native identities, for the most part, do not impact their day-to-day lives. Growing up, their primary experiences with Indigenous peoples and cultures were powwows. "Yeah, they had that kind of exposure. But like I said, my older daughter is the only one who loves that kind of culture, the Native languages and stuff." In contrast, Susan said her other daughter, who lives in the Southwest and is married to a Mexican American man, "is more into her husband's culture."

Sandra, a third-generation relocator, said she, too, was becoming more invested in her Mexican (rather than Native) heritage. Throughout her interview, Sandra identified as "Mexican and Native," "Italian and Mexican and Native," and "Italian and Mexican" (dropping "Native" altogether). Sandra said her Mexican identity is what led to her romantic involvement (and recent engagement) to a Mexican and African American man. She appreciates their "diversity" and looks forward to a "life of mixture," but thinks she and her fiancé's shared Mexican heritage "probably" will be more dominant in her future family because she does not know if people like her grandparents, who are "getting old," will "be able to keep [the relocator community] alive forever."

Though most second- and later-generation relocators minimally *identify* as Indians, Barbara (Cherokee) said her adult son (Cherokee, second-generation) wholly denies his Indian heritage. "He hates Indians," she said, then continued, "I think he's embarrassed to be Native. It makes me mad. . . . I think maybe he got teased in high school or something, because you can obviously know that I'm different. I'm not white. So you know, I don't know. I don't know. He thinks Indians, we all drink or we're drunks or bad people or something, I don't know. So we don't talk about it. . . . He doesn't even acknowledge that he's Native," Barbara said despondently. "Even at his wedding, which really offended me!" she exclaimed. The best man at the wedding noted the bride's "Irish and Italian" heritage, Barbara said, but he "never said [her son] was Native American, which really pissed me off. Yeah, I thought—what am I, *white*?!" As she relayed the story, Barbara's hurt and anger were palpable. Barbara admitted she was so upset on her son's wedding night that she cornered him: "I said, 'I'm *not white*,' like that, really mean to him, and he just looked at me, you know. I think I said, 'I'm not a damn white person,' or something to that effect. So, who knows?"

Barbara's son, who did not acknowledge his Cherokee roots, was anomalous among young adult (second- and later-generation) relocators. These relocators differently *prioritized* their Indigenous identities, but generally *recognized* their Indigenous heritages. Several second- and later-generation relocators, upon reaching young adulthood, developed strong and relatively broad commitments to Indigenous identities, peoples, and communities. Like Samantha (Cherokee), who discussed her "pan-Indian" orientation, these young adult relocators were socialized in urban, pan-Indian environments in which they learned to recognize *all* Indigenous peoples as their relations. A majority of young adult relocators with whom I was associated felt deep pride in their Indigenous heritages, and although they did not organize their lives around the advancement of Indigenous causes, they stayed connected and involved with the urban pan-Indian relocator community. Inevitably, some second- and later-generation relocators, like Susan's children, were rather nonchalant about their Indigenous heritages. Because they rarely participated in relocator community events, I was not well acquainted with them, and therefore remain uninformed about their perspectives.

Across these outcomes, relocator parents did their best to nurture the Indigenous identities of children raised in NE Ohio. Some parents' general focus on Indigenous *perspectives* rather than practices limited youths' knowledge of tribally specific cultures. This approach to socializing youth was strategic nonetheless. For many Indigenous peoples, articulating a worldview is prioritized over thinking about "things" (like tobacco offerings) that reduce Indigenous perspectives to practices.[12] Many first-generation relocators focused on embedding Indigenous identities grounded in Indigenous value systems in their children and grandchildren. Relocator elders, that is, understood Indigenous values and meaning systems as *most* crucial to sustaining Indigenous ways of thinking about and engaging with the world. Due to their socialization and the logistics of everyday life, only a few young adult relocators in

NE Ohio remained connected to and concerned with the affairs of their tribal nations. Home reservations were located some distance from NE Ohio, making visits difficult, costly, and time-consuming. Young adult relocators attended ceremonies and other significant reservation-based gatherings when they could, but, like their parents, they were often compelled to prioritize more immediate issues affecting their lives. Family, work, and urban pan-Indian community affairs directly impacted their day-to-day existences, and therefore required sustained (daily) attentions.

Reclaimers' emphasis on learning and engaging in singular, somewhat disjointed practices like laying tobacco, smudging, and crafting, in contrast, was constraining. Reclaimers' affinities for these kinds of practices likely grew from desires to engage their Indigenous identities in tangible and transferable ways. Like memories and stories about reclaimers' Indigenous pasts, such practices could be passed from one person to the next with relative ease. They were, in a sense, (constructed) collective memories in material form.[13] Like material memories commemorated in a museum, they were largely removed from the Indigenous contexts, stories, and perspectives that gave them power. Only a small minority of reclaimers, like Sasha (Lakota-identified), remained steadfast (to the degree possible) about understanding and engaging Indigenous worldviews.

The diligence with which such reclaimers repeated and rehearsed practice-able (and therefore practical) memories, however, could not resolve tensions and/or obstructions resulting from their distance and disconnectedness from long-standing Indigenous communities. Collectively, reclaimers tended to reproduce reductive ideas about Indigenous peoples and cultures. They learned and internalized stereotypes about Indigenous peoples due to their own socialization in US settler society. Many reclaimers, for instance, imagined Indianness as something that existed more authentically in the past. Such reclaimers found it difficult to envision authentic Indianness in a metropolis, and accordingly, they consistently reified false understandings of Indians as people who belong elsewhere—whether in the past or in (settler-constructed) Indian territories of the present (i.e., tribal nations and reservation lands). Reclaimers' frequent and romanticized references to the "old ways" of noble warriors and nature-loving Indians are illustrative.

6

Urban Indian Troubles

A primary trouble with being Indian in the NE Ohio environment is negotiating authentic identities amid false memories of Indianness propagated in US settler society. This theme emerged in chapter 5 and is further elucidated here. Relocators' troubles revolve around glamorized images of Indians that inspire Northeast Ohioans to sentimentalize and possess Indianness. For relocators, the Cleveland MLB franchise and its fans consistently have been the worst perpetrators of this possessiveness. This chapter reveals how Cleveland's MLB team has, through its promotion of regional stories of romanticized Indianness, amplified processes of colonial unknowing and reproduced *white settler space* in NE Ohio.[1] "White settler space" is defined as environments that normalize and secure white settler interests through subordination and cooptation of the Indigenous *other*.[2] Another (related) trouble elucidated by relocators is regional residents who are not really Indians *but pretend to be*. Their possession of fake Indian identities, relocators maintain, distorts perceptions of Indigenous peoples. Many relocators accuse reclaimers of "wannabe" Indianness. Reclaimers agree that Indian stereotypes are harmful because they decrease people's abilities to recognize Indians in urban spaces. More troublesome to reclaimers, however, are "political Indians" who dismiss the efforts and identities of people (like themselves) working to reclaim and revive Indigenous heritages. Reclaimers specifically accuse relocators of engaging in counterproductive "Indian politics."

Relocators and the Trouble with Romantic Notions of Indianness

First-generation relocators, who recall the severity of their early lives on reservations, generally agree that being Indian in NE Ohio is easier than being Indian on or near Indian reservations. In NE Ohio they have better access to critical resources (like jobs and health care) and fewer run-ins with people who don't like Indians simply because they are Indians. First-generation relocators also agree that they experience racial *misclassification* more often than racial *discrimination* in this urban environment. (Importantly, many relocators revoke this claim when the topic of Cleveland's MLB team arises.) "Around here," Barbara (Cherokee) said, "people just kind of look at you. Because you're different. Because you're not white." NE Ohioans are not skilled at locating Indigenous people within US racial-ethnic schemas, and Barbara does not appreciate the quizzical stares resulting from their mystification.

Relocators said they are frequently mistaken for Latinx or Asian-identified persons—the brown populations with which NE Ohioans seem most familiar. Racialized stereotypes are likely the cause of people's misclassifications, many relocators agreed, but they also believed most people made this mistake due to ignorance rather than prejudice. Some relocators turned experiences of racial misidentification into a game. Berta (Lakota), for instance, said she enjoys making people guess when they ask "what" she is. "They'll name every nationality in the book, and I tell them, no, no, no, no!" she said, chuckling. Bly (Sioux) is so accustomed to being racially misclassified that she lights up when reminiscing about *one* experience of identity validation at a grocery store. Bly said when a white man at the grocery store asked if she was American Indian, she replied, "'Yes, I am!' I said—'I am so amazed! You are the first person who actually got it right the very first time!' [Laughs.] And he just looked at me and he smiled and he said, 'I just knew it.' . . . And I said—'That is so nice. Thank you! You made my day.' I think I told him that, too, and he started laughing. Yeah, it was cool." Bly said she could not resist asking the man if he had spent some time out West, and he nodded an affirmation. As Bly speculated, he only knew she was Indian because he was familiar with Indigenous peoples *outside* NE Ohio.

Relocators also conceded, however, that NE Ohioans' romantic fascination with Indianness is exasperating. Regional residents' understanding of indigeneity as a contemporary *identity* is overwritten by stereotypical images of Indians that abound in US society. Ohioans, according to relocators, seem particularly enamored with settler-constructed versions of Indianness that sentimentalize noble Indian warriors of America's wild western frontier. As sociologist Laurel Davis-Delano[3] indicates, this version of Indianness was aggrandized in settlers' stories of conquest and incorporated into settlers' identities. It is somewhat predictable, then, that many NE Ohioans exoticize Indianness. They do not *see* Indigenous people in Ohio (even when they interact with Indigenous people in Ohio) and consequently assume Indians do not live in this space. Further, they are oblivious to Ohio's Indigenous history and abide (unknowingly) by settler logics that take white possession of Indigenous lands and peoples for granted. Relocators, as a result, often find themselves fielding exhausting questions, like, "Are you a *real* Indian?" "Do you live in a teepee?" "Where are your feathers?" "Can I touch your hair [or regalia, or drum, or feathers]?"

Sasha (Lakota-identified) is a reclaimer rather than a relocator, but her discussion of how people treat her—a dark-skinned, black-haired, Indian-identified woman—at NE Ohio powwows powerfully illustrates the exoticization of Indianness in the NE Ohio context. Sasha described a specific but not anomalous encounter with a white powwow attendee who introduced herself and then asked Sasha for her name: "And I said, 'My name is Sasha.' And she said, 'No, what's your *Indian* name?' And I said, 'My name is Sasha.' And she said, 'No, no, honey, what's your *Indian* name?'" At this point, Sasha said she was dumbfounded. "Why would I tell a perfect stranger something [personal] like that?" Sasha asked. "So," Sasha said, grinning, "I told her my name was Sunkmánitu Thánka Ob Wačí, which is 'Dances with Wolves.'"

Sasha laughed heartily at her own joke, but then grew serious again, noting, "I think sometimes it's almost like too much familiarity." For instance, Sasha said, people often want to touch her. "They want to touch parts of my outfit," Sasha said. "They touch my hair," she continued. "And I'm just like—who does that?!" she squealed. "Who goes around touching people?" Sasha shook her head incredulously, adding, "It's like being pregnant all over again, [when] complete strangers would come up and touch my stomach." Sasha paused, reflecting on these experiences. "Maybe it's just something different, people get some sense of intimacy there," she said slowly, formulating the thoughts as she spoke them. "Yeah, like if it's exotic to them," she said more confidently, "they think they have a right to put their hands on it, you know?" Clearly, white people in Ohio are fascinated by Indigenous people, whom they perceive as foreign (ironically) and exotic. Their over-familiarity and assumed "right" to touch Indigenous people, however, falls in line with Aileen Moreton-Robinson's ideas regarding the "white possessive."[4] If white ownership of Indigenous lands and even Indigenous bodies is perceived as common sense, then denials of Indigenous sovereignty over Indigenous lands *and* bodies inevitably results.

These examples illustrate how fascination and over-familiarity with Indianness (as represented in US settler society) inspire presumably "well-meaning" but devastatingly ignorant white people to speak to Indigenous people in offensive ways. Inaccurate assumptions, earnest questions, and unenlightened jokes reveal the limits of people's knowledge about Indigenous peoples. Routinely experiencing such unabashed ignorance frustrates, saddens, and angers relocators, who cannot seem to escape unwanted attention from white people captivated by them. Consider this example. About a dozen relocators attended a small-town street fair called "Heritage Days." The women sold fry bread, Indian tacos, and *wojape* (berry pudding) from a small vending stand. The community's young people participated in live powwow dancing exhibitions at the top of every hour. The first part of the day was sunny, but the afternoon was mired with cloudy grey skies and rain, rain, rain. Each time it seemed the rain might let up, it rained more. John (Diné, aka Navajo), a second-generation relocator, returned to the vending stand after performing dances for a dwindling crowd. He was dressed in full regalia, which attracted the attention of a white, middle-aged man at a nearby vending stand. The man shouted, "Hey! Did you do a rain dance or something?!" The white man looked at John expectantly, a huge grin spreading across his face. John looked at him, surprised, then awkwardly half-smiled. John's first reaction was to avoid being rude. At the same time, he did not wish to condone the white man's comment. As Monica (Diné- and Mexican-identified), a first-generation relocator, overheard the comment, an irrepressible frown creased her face. She emitted a soft "hmmph!" and cast her eyes downward. John's mother, Janice (Diné, first generation), a habitual joker, pointed with her lips toward John and said, "You should have told him you did a rain dance right around his tent!" The women snickered in appreciation of Janice, who skillfully deflected their feelings of irritation and hurt with a humorous quip.

Relocators do not appreciate this kind of attention. They prefer to be left alone. As Berta noted, "People always think that we're different, special. They put us on a pedestal, you know, like we're the chosen people, etcetera, etcetera, and they look at us like that." She provided an example: "We went to this powwow and they [white people] were all looking at us, you know. We're all sitting and talking and everything amongst ourselves. And then somebody said something and I said, '*Bullshit!*' I said it real loud, you know? And then they [the white people] all looked at me, like—'What did she say?!' Like they couldn't believe I was cussing and stuff."

According to Berta, the white onlookers were aghast at her behavior—as though "Indian people don't say those words or something," she said. "But," Berta continued, "I tell people, we're just like you. We get mad, we get bad feelings, we get hurt feelings, you know. We'll say bad words. We're nothing special." Berta, in other words, frequently must tell NE Ohioans that Indigenous people are *people* because settler-constructed images of Indianness so deftly and comprehensively erase and replace Indigenous people's *humanity*.

Another Trouble: Cleveland's Other "Indians"

As racially misclassified *brown* people, relocators say they sometimes experience discrimination, but relocators generally agree that NE Ohioans seldom act with intentional hostility toward them because they are *Indians*. That is, relocators are not the target of NE Ohioans' hostilities as long as their behaviors align with NE Ohioans' romantic notions of Indianness. When relocators insist on being treated with *dignity* and *respect*, however—for instance, when they called on Cleveland's MLB team to dispense with its fraudulent "Indians" identity—NE Ohioans revealed the possessiveness and aggressiveness lurking just beneath the surface of their Indian idolatry. For many relocators, dealing with random people's romantic fantasies about Indianness was an annoyance that paled in comparison to the incessant abuses they endured as a result of the Cleveland baseball team's fraudulent "Indians" identity.

Indigenous people's perspectives on Native-themed mascots are diverse,[5] but resistance to Cleveland's "Indians" imagery was a central project of the relocator community for over half a century. Many relocators experienced the team's name and mascot as environmental assaults on their Indian identities. Prior to moving their families "off the reservation" and into Cleveland's "Indians" territory, they were oblivious to the prevalence and popularity of Native-themed sports mascots. When they arrived in Cleveland, the Wahoo image triggered feelings of embarrassment, loathing, and unease. Berta's mother, in partnership with Russell Means, was one of the first people to draw attention to Cleveland's mascot problem. She was concerned that her children and other urban Indian children might *internalize* the Wahoo image—a maniacally grinning, feather-wearing, red-faced "Indian" mascot—and consequently reject their indigeneity. Coming to Cleveland on relocation was risky; she refused to stand by idly while her family's Indigenous roots dug into Cleveland's colonized, Wahoo-laced soil.

In the 1970s, Berta's mother knew what scholarship on Native-themed mascots now reveals—the saturation of any environment with appropriated Indianness is noxious for *all* people living in that space. Research conducted in the last three decades across the social science disciplines documents the negative impacts of Native-themed mascots on both Native and non-Native people.[6] Experimental research confirms Berta's mother's primary concerns—that Native-themed mascotry has deleterious impacts on Native children's self-esteem and overall psychological well-being.[7] Even when Native children have positive associations with Native-themed mascots, the mascots lead to decreased self-esteem. They are "inordinately powerful communicators" of what Indianness is and who Indians are, and consequently, "remind American Indians of the limited ways in which others see them."[8] Other experimental work indicates that *non-Natives'* exposure to Native-themed mascots increases their negative stereotyping and prejudicial attitudes *toward* Native peoples.[9] One study even shows that exposure to the Chief Wahoo image specifically activates *only* negative stereotypes.[10] These findings are bolstered by survey research indicating that supporters of Indian mascots are more likely to exhibit prejudicial attitudes toward Indigenous peoples[11] and are more likely to minimize the impacts of racial discrimination on members of all racialized groups.[12]

Scholars and activists working to eradicate Native-themed mascots tend to frame the issue in terms of racial discrimination, inclusion, and equal rights. Kevin Bruyneels, political science professor and author of *The Third Space of Sovereignty: The Postcolonial Politics of US-Indigenous Relations*, however, convincingly argues that such analyses are incomplete. The problem, states Bruyneels, is "not the charge of racism itself, but that it has become hegemonic in the debate." He maintains that the appropriation of Indianness in any form is a "mnemonic device" that denies settler violence against Indigenous peoples and settler usurpation of Indigenous lands. Native-themed mascotry, in other words, derives from constructed stories settlers tell to manipulate settler memories—specifically, remembrances of Indians as historical rather than contemporary beings.[13] Indians from *history* are easily parlayed into settler-colonial traditions that "supplant and replace" the stories, memories, histories, and realities of US Indigenous peoples. To support this point, Bruyneels discusses the historical period—the late-nineteenth and early-twentieth centuries—when sports teams (and other corporate entities) were most likely to adopt Native-themed mascots and/or logos. It is not a coincidence, Bruyneels asserts, that this rise in "symbolic indigeneity" occurred when settler policies of displacement and assimilation, like the General Allotment Act, thoroughly and effectively diminished and marginalized Indigenous populations.

The Cleveland MLB franchise adopted its name during this period, and for more than a century, the "Indians" baseball team was the region's favored "tribe." Cleveland baseball fans knew little about the histories or realities of Northeast Ohio's Indigenous peoples, but they embraced the memories, traditions, and identities sustained by the franchise's simulated Indianness. *These* memories, which compelled regional residents to support and identify with Cleveland's "home team," were told and retold across generations of family members living in Northeast Ohio. Accordingly, understanding experiences of Indigenous identity in Northeast Ohio necessitates some engagement with this very different "Indians" identity, which has thrived in the NE Ohio context since 1915, the year baseball writers selected "Indians" as a replacement for the team's former name, the Naps.[14] This history of the team's naming, as noted in the introduction, was overwritten by the fabricated memory that Louis Sockalexis, the team's and league's first American Indian ball player, inspired the name.[15] That the name was intended to honor Louis Sockalexis, a citizen of the Penobscot Nation, is contradicted by the degrading stereotypical imagery that has always accompanied the "Indians" name. To announce the new name, in fact, the Cleveland *Plain Dealer* "published a large cartoon featuring figures in stereotypical Indian attire and headdresses along with the caption 'Ki Yi Wangh Woop! Their Indians!'" [sic].[16] The cartoon Indian mascot, created by seventeen-year-old logo draftsman Walter Goldbach, first appeared on team uniforms in 1948. In 1951, the mascot's image was revised to have a smaller nose and red (instead of yellow) skin, and in 1952, the mascot became known as "Chief Wahoo."[17]

Following the MLB commissioner's 2018 determination that "Chief Wahoo" was "no longer appropriate for on-field use,"[18] Wahoo finally was removed from team uniforms and stadium signage. The mascot, however, did not and will not completely disappear. In a *Belt Magazine* article about the "secret history" of Wahoo, author Brad Ricca recognizes this bleak reality: "Let's be honest: Could there ever be a Cleveland without Chief Wahoo? And I don't mean in terms of any eventual change in name or logo, but in the sheer amount of *stuff* that the Chief is already stitched in, ironed on, applied to, and inked in. . . . Wahoo in Cleveland is like infrastructure: it is way down in the bowels of things." Wahoo, of course, is deeper in the "bowels of things" than Ricca recognizes. The icon not only continues to exist on all the *stuff* but also maintains a stronghold in NE Ohioans' memories, histories, and identities. Scholar and author Thomas King (Greek and Cherokee descent) would say that Wahoo is "loose in the world," and therefore "cannot be called back."[19]

"People, Not Mascots!"

Since the 1970s, relocators and allies resisted the Cleveland team's "Indians" identity. In 1972, under the directorship of Russell Means (Oglala Lakota), the Cleveland Indian Center became the primary complainant in a $9 million lawsuit against the Cleveland MLB team.[20] The Indian Center accused the team of promoting imagery that was "racist, degrading, and demeaning" to Indigenous peoples.[21] The case, based on group libel, was settled privately in 1983, but the community's resistance to the team's defamatory imagery never waned.[22] In 1992, the relocator community created a nonprofit organization devoted to eradicating the Cleveland team's Native-themed mascot. In addition to educational campaigns and discussions with local political leaders, the organization hosted half a dozen protests annually outside Cleveland stadium. Each year, members of the Indigenous-led, multiracial group kicked off the baseball season with a conference and protest. Local academics, national

American Indian Movement (AIM) leaders, and activists from across the Midwest convened to discuss harms caused by and strategies for eliminating Native-themed mascots.

The "opening day" protest, the biggest of the year, was attended by local members of the nonprofit protest organization, out-of-state allies, and approximately one to two dozen local residents. This event always received some (albeit not enough) local media attention. It was one of few occasions each year (e.g., Thanksgiving) when NE Ohioans recognized the *continuing existence* of Indigenous peoples. The kind of recognition Indigenous protestors received on opening day, however, was anything but informed or respectful. Occasionally game-goers gave protestors a "thumbs up" or other supportive gesture, but a majority of Cleveland baseball fans interacting with protestors were venomous. They were protective of *their* "Indians" and quickly asserted *their* ownership of the team's name, mascot, and stories. Fans' behaviors outside Cleveland baseball stadium, in fact, elucidated fans' perceptions of entitlement and possession of Indianness in Cleveland. Fan behaviors also revealed their collective hostilities toward Indigenous people asking to be treated with dignity.

> How can you figure this honors us when we're
> telling you it is dishonorable?! What is it that
> you don't understand about that?!
> —Bly (Sioux)

Relocators and their allies agree that fans' treatment of protestors outside Cleveland stadium exposes an important truth: Native-themed mascots are not about honor but rather *ownership*. Fans' angry invectives, such as "Get a job!," "Go back where you came from!," and "We won, so get lost!" expose fans' unsettling animus toward Indigenous people demanding justice. Susan (Dakota), a protest participant for over a decade, described protests as "emotionally draining" experiences of "mass abuse." "It's like you're attacking them [fans] personally," Susan explained. Attending a protest, relocators attested, was an eye-opening experience. Berta (Lakota), for instance, invited an acquaintance, a white woman who previously did not "see anything wrong" with the ball team's mascot, to a protest, hoping to challenge her perspective. It did. After witnessing fans' abusive behaviors, Berta said the woman resolved never to purchase or wear Wahoo paraphernalia again.

Consider this scene, repeated annually for decades: as hordes of celebratory, enthusiastic baseball fans make their way to the stadium entrance gates, a multiracial group of protestors peacefully stands in the tree lawn with paperboard signs conveying a variety of messages, like "People, not mascots," "Play baseball, not Indian," "Sacred symbols are not toys," and "Racism hurts everybody." For the protest's duration, approximately two (pregame) hours, baseball fans collectively and hatefully haze protestors, subjecting them to an endless stream of taunts, obscene gestures, and other cruelties—i.e., the "mass abuse" to which Susan referred. Disgruntled fans guffaw in disgust, exaggeratedly shaking their heads from side to side. Many fans flip protestors the bird. Some fans yell "Go Tribe!" or "Go Indians!" or "I love Chief Wahoo!" while others perform the "tomahawk chop" or some variation of a "war whoop," clapping their outstretched hands to their lips and screeching "*aye yi yi yi yi yi yi yi yi!*" or "*woo woo woo woo woo woo woo!*" Fans shout everything from "You're fucking stupid!" to "Go fuck yourself!" to "Get a job, you fucking loser!" They chide protestors for being "overly politically correct," yelling, "It's just a game!" "It's only a mascot!" "It doesn't mean anything!" and "It's harmless!" Fans (usually men) lift their shirts and lower their socks to reveal bright red Wahoo tattoos on bellies, backs, shoulders, and calves. On occasion, a particularly angry (often inebriated) red-faced fan singles out a protestor and screams into their face, "*It's a tradition!*" On more than one occasion, an outraged fan *spit* on an Indigenous protestor.

Fans' feelings of anger and disgust are fomented by the MLB team's clever manipulation of fans' memories, including the fabricated "Sockalexis story." On one occasion, for instance, a twenty-something white man insisted that each protestor take one of his flyers—two pages copied directly from the "Indians history" section of the baseball franchise's Media Guide. The section, highlighted in yellow and purportedly drawn from a 1915 Cleveland *Plain Dealer* news article, read, "Many years ago there was an Indian named Sockalexis who was the star of the Cleveland baseball club. As batter, fielder and baserunner he was a marvel. Sockalexis . . . naturally came to be regarded as the whole team. The 'fans' throughout the country began to call the Clevelanders the 'Indians.' It was an honorable name. . . . It has now been decided to revive this name . . . [which] will recall fine traditions." This fictional tale resonates with fans because it is a familiar cultural narrative. Fans, in turn, reiterate the "Sockalexis story" to justify their possessive investment in the team's "Indians" identity.

Many "Indians" fans asserted that they were *celebrating* rather than *appropriating* Indianness. Numerous fans viciously admonished Indigenous protestors for refusing to accept the "honor" bestowed on them. At one protest, a beet-faced, fifty-something white man marched back and forth along the protest line and, between gulps of air, repeatedly screeched, "You took this, what was meant to be an *honor*, and ruined it with your lies!" Another angry fan, a forty-something white woman, approached a Diné protestor and, pointing to the Wahoo on her shirt, screamed, *"You should be proud! You should be proud!"* To avoid the saliva spurting from her angry mouth, the protestor took a step backward. Calmly he asked the woman, "Do you really think I look like that?" Her eyes darted frantically from the protestor's face to the Wahoo face and back. Finally she walked away, muttering, "No, but who cares?" to which the protestor whispered a response: "Me."

Fans also claimed ownership over Indianness by "playing Indian" in various ways. Some fans claimed Indigenous ancestry and concluded that if *they*, as Indian persons, were not offended, nobody should be offended.[23] Other fans played Indian in more theatrical ways, with costumes, makeup, and other props. They wore fake headdresses, carried foam hatchets, donned "war paint," and even dressed in *red face*, literally transforming themselves into anthropomorphized Chief Wahoo heads situated atop human bodies. Such impersonations of Indianness, protestors maintained, dehumanized Indigenous peoples, dismissed Indigenous histories, and mocked Indigenous cultures. Fans, in response, derisively shook their heads, flipped the bird, or callously laughed at the people asking for some semblance of respect.

Rather than examine their position when Natives and allies vocalized concerns about the team's name and mascot, fans defended it, grasping onto any "evidence" or arguments to support their claims. Fans, for instance, frequently told Indigenous protestors that Indigenous people *support* rather than oppose Indian mascots. They cited problematic opinion polls—like an Annenberg poll from 2004 and a *Washington Post*

poll from 2016—purportedly suggesting that Indigenous people find Indian mascots to be unproblematic, while remaining indifferent to the
resounding denunciation of Native-themed mascots by virtually every
major Indigenous organization in the United States, including many
tribal nations and confederations.[24] Fans also suggested that the absence
of *Indigenous* protestors at the stadium proved that Indigenous people
were not offended by Native-themed mascots. Indigenous protestors
were at the stadium, but fans' utter ignorance of Indigenous realities and
over-exposure to settler-constructed images of Indianness prevented
them from recognizing the indigeneity of people standing in front of
them. The actions of a thirty-something white man are illustrative: the
fan pointed at each protestor and shouted their perceived "race": "white,
white, white, black, white, hmm [pause], maybe Chinese?" Three of
these protestors, two labeled "white" and the man guessed to be "Chinese," were Indigenous people.

When confronted by Indigenous protestors, Cleveland baseball fans
could not deny Indigenous peoples' existence. They continued to deny
Indigenous people's truths, however, and fans' emotional reactions to
Indigenous protestors provide critical insight into the co-constitutive,
interlocking relationship between settler colonialism and white supremacy. Illustrating deeply rooted beliefs in racialized white-settler
superiority, baseball fans disguised their disgust for Indigenous peoples
through performances conveying (empty) sentiments of concern. In
racialized-emotions scholarship, *disguised* racialized disgust legitimizes
whites' hostile feelings by transforming them into socially acceptable
but ultimately empty sentiments of caring.[25] These sentiments, void of
genuine empathy, are never backed by action. In NE Ohio, fans (angrily) feigned concern for Indigenous peoples by accusing protestors of
prioritizing the *wrong* Indigenous issues. Alcoholism and asthma, fans
patronizingly asserted, were among the problems Native people *should*
be addressing—*not* a "harmless mascot."

An illuminating example of this phenomenon involves a white man
fan, approximately thirty years old, who drew attention to himself at
home opening protests in back-to-back years. The first year, he stood
across the sidewalk from protestors, clutching a neon orange poster
board sign with "forget real people, protest mascots!" scrawled on it.
For the duration of his counterprotest, he crossly yelled at protestors,

indicating that he once lived (however temporarily) on the Pine Ridge reservation and saw firsthand "the devastation of Native America" and the "real issues" facing Native peoples—*real* issues, he maintained, that had *nothing* to do with Indian mascots.

The second year, this same fan, covered head to toe in Wahoo paraphernalia, initiated a heated conversation with an Indigenous protestor holding a sign that read, "I'm in a tribe already, *thanks*, and I don't feel 'honored' to be in yours!" For approximately ten minutes, he fulminated about the *real* issues wreaking havoc in Indigenous communities. He told the protestor she was wasting her time worrying about a "silly mascot" that represented *baseball*, not Indians. The protestor patiently listened, then explained her perspective. People often tell her she should not be offended by Wahoo because Wahoo doesn't make them "think of real Indians." "Then when *do* you think of Indians?" she asked, before articulating her views on Native-themed mascots. When the protestor finished, the Wahoo-wearing Cleveland fan thanked her for her time and shook her hand. "We'll just have to agree to disagree," he said as he walked away. Despite his professed concern for "real [Indigenous] people" suffering, the counterprotestor was apathetic to the concerns of the Indigenous woman protestor. He flatly refused to acknowledge that his cherished "Indians" mascot inhibits empathetic understanding of Indigenous peoples and perspectives.

Cleveland baseball fans' callous indifference toward Indigenous people's requests for dignity and respect is not a regional quirk. NE Ohioans are not unique in their wanton and collective disregard for Indigenous peoples and their stories, histories, spiritualities, traditions, and identities. This gross lack of empathy for Indigenous peoples occurs locally, nationally, and globally due to the inundation of settler societies with dehumanizing images that reduce Indigenous people to caricature and historical relic. Cornel Pewewardy, a Comanchee-Kiowa professor of education, refers to this phenomenon as "dysconscious racism"[26]—a "habit of mind" that uncritically accepts white dominance and leads to distortions of thought and action regarding racialized social inequities. Pewewardy suggests that Native-themed mascots are "a symptom of 'dysconscious racism' and form of cultural violence that operates at a psychological level."[27] Muscogee sociologist Dwanna McKay (formerly Robertson) refers to this phenomenon as "legitimized racism"[28]—racial discrimination that is institutionally sanctioned and normalized to the extent that it seems "right or reasonable"[29] even to individuals who believe they are unprejudiced and nondiscriminatory. Ultimately, legitimized racism, according to McKay, is "multilayered, intersectional, and dynamic racism" that "becomes *simultaneously overt and invisible* within social norms and social institutions."[30] Both Pewewardy and McKay articulate the critical relationship between *repeated* exposure to symbolic violence against Indigenous peoples and the desensitization of entire populations to the *realities* of Indigenous peoples.

While I agree with their analyses, I (additionally) wish to expose the settler-colonial roots of the racialized stories and collective memories that socialize US residents to lack empathy for Indigenous peoples. The Cleveland MLB franchise is merely one entity contributing to "epistemologies of ignorance" regarding still-existing US settler colonialism, but in the NE Ohio context, it has been a powerful institution responsible for shaping regional ignorance of and apathy toward Indigenous peoples' realities. Prominent, well-known stories circulating *where people live* shape regional culture, and thereby contribute to fluidity in how people think about things. I suggest the Cleveland MLB team's stories about "Indians" have intensified and legitimized white/settler meaning making that normalizes white possession of *NE Ohio* territory and "*Indians*" identity. Fans' reactions to protestors expose not only how the MLB team's "Indians" mascotry invisibilizes the local Indigenous population but also how Native-themed mascots ameliorate authentic concern for Indigenous struggles and replace it with paternalistic and/or hostile attitudes toward Indigenous peoples. Fans' responses to protestors reveal an epistemological orientation that refuses to recognize the perspectives of Indigenous peoples—perhaps *most* especially when they are engaged in resistance to colonial definition and domination. Rather, fans assert their ignorance (of ongoing settler-colonial realities) *as* knowledge that deflects white/settler responsibility for racialized injustice in their community. In sum, Cleveland's MLB team unequivocally reproduces white settler space that justifies white settler domination, Indian identity cooptation, and Indigenous peoples' vilification.

An Inescapable "Enduring Smear"

Indigenous protestors outside Cleveland baseball stadium understood they were entering a hostile environment, but all Indigenous residents of NE Ohio, whether or not they participated in protests, were continuously confronted with the team's images, stories, and memories of Indianness.[31] The team's name and logos were displayed on everything from storefronts and billboards to bumper stickers, baby clothes, and beer bottles, serving as a constant reminder to *all* Ohio residents, Indigenous or not, that "Indians" are not *really* people—not modern people who live, learn, love, work, and play in the greater Cleveland metropolitan area. The inability to escape the baseball team's fraudulent "Indians" identity, which erased relocators' contemporary existence, their very *humanity*, was a constant source of stress in many relocators' daily lives. They described countless disturbing encounters with "Indians" imagery and coworkers, teachers, and family members desensitized to it.

Like sports fans across the country, Northeast Ohioans enjoyed celebrating their favorite "home team" in workspaces. The legitimation of racism against Indigenous peoples disconnected the dots linking the MLB team's "Indians" identity to other acts of discrimination against historically marginalized groups in the United States. As a result, Indigenous people living and working in regions with prominent Native-themed mascots, such as NE Ohio, are not protected from defamatory, dehumanizing imagery depicting members of their racialized group in their workspaces. Bly (Sioux), for instance, talked about work colleagues who rebuked her for coordinating a "diversity day" event focused on the Indian mascot issue. Once Bly's coworkers realized *both* guest speakers *opposed* Cleveland's "Indians" identity, they became irritated. Bly's coworkers believed it was only fair to explore both sides of the mascot debate. "We had people actually get up and walk out [of the event] because they did not like it," Bly said. "I wasn't too popular for a while."

The MLB team's Indianness also infiltrated educational settings, which were already hostile environments for many Indigenous children. US educational systems historically stripped Indigenous children of their languages, cultures, homelands, and identities, and this assimilative process continues today in less explicit but entirely normative ways. US public K–12 schools, for instance, continue to imprint *all* young people, Indigenous or not, with settler understandings of US history that exclude the stories of US Indigenous peoples. More often than not, Native children and their classmates are exposed to *dis*information about US Indigenous peoples, which perpetuates controlling images of indigeneity and creates dissonance and psychological distress for Native children.[32] Consider the "traditional" Thanksgiving play enacted by young people year after year in classrooms across the United States. In addition to learning objectively false information about Indigenous peoples and US history, children, dressed in construction paper "headdresses" and "pilgrim hats," also learn that "playing Indian" is acceptable.[33]

When Samantha (Cherokee) recalls "lessons" she received about Indians in her NE Ohio elementary school, she gets upset. "We had to make these necklaces out of macaroni beads," Samantha recalled, "and we made a hat with fake feathers and our 'Indian name.'" She remembers feeling uneasy about participating in make-believe Indianness even as a child. As a college-educated, proud Cherokee adult, she is horrified.

These curricular problems were exacerbated by Cleveland's other "Indians," according to relocator parents. In NE Ohio, school "team spirit days" encouraged students and teachers to wear "Indians" gear. Some NE Ohio schools even hosted annual field trips to Cleveland's MLB stadium. Melissa (Native Hawaiian–identified) said she experienced anxiety each year she had to decide whether her daughter should attend the game or stay home on the day of the field trip. Either option potentially resulted in experiences of exclusion for her daughter, a third-generation relocator. "When she goes," Melissa sighed, "I tell her to love the game and not the name. And that's where I leave it." Susan's (Dakota) granddaughter, also a third-generation relocator, was only six years old, but Susan knew she was not safe from so-called spirit days. "I'm so afraid they're going to have a spirit day at her school," Susan said, explaining that she intended to "have the talk" with her granddaughter about the team's imagery, but hoped to wait until her granddaughter was old enough to understand. Ultimately, Susan did not get to dictate the terms or times of her granddaughter's lesson. "I'm thinking this year," Susan said, "I'll probably tell her more about it, explain more to her."

Berta (Lakota) remembered baseball season was a rough time for her (now adult) children when they were in school. They were teased year-round for being Indian, but the teasing intensified "during the season of the Wahoo," as Berta called it. She explained: "It makes them ashamed of who they are, you know, because people make fun, 'woowoowoo!' and stuff like that. That's how people identify them, you know? In fact," Berta said, "one of the teachers called one of my boys a Wahoo at school!" She shook her head in dismay. "I think it really works on our children's self-esteem," Berta explained, "and I think our children's self-esteem is one of the biggest things we have, you know?" "I want my children to be proud of who they are," Berta said passionately, "not ashamed of their people, their culture."

Even at home, relocators could not escape Cleveland's mocking "Indians" visage. Samantha (Cherokee), for instance, recalled the night her boyfriend picked her up for a date wearing a Chief Wahoo t-shirt. "And I was like, that's so racist. Why would you wear that?" Though Samantha meant what she said, she admitted she said it as though she was joking to save him from feeling embarrassed or ashamed. Susan (Dakota) talked about an awkward situation she had with someone on her husband's side of the family—a proud grandmother who sent Susan a picture of her new grandson "with Wahoo everywhere!" Susan said the baby was wearing a Wahoo hat and Wahoo t-shirt and was positioned next to a Wahoo baseball and Wahoo bat. Susan's eyes widened as she remembered her first glimpse of the photo. "I thought, 'Oh, I'm not going to hang this up! I'm not going to frame this picture!'" But she didn't know what to do because she didn't want to offend the woman who sent the picture. Susan also said she continuously worried that her Indigenous grandchildren's *other* grandparents, who took them to baseball games, would eventually buy them Wahoo t-shirts and other "Indians" paraphernalia.

Despite their frustrations, relocators did not blame *individuals* for the stressors and hostilities they experienced as Indigenous people in "Indians" country. They did not fault the team's *fans* but rather criticized the team's owners and local political leaders and structural racism. Relocators compassionately insisted that most people—neighbors, coworkers, friends, and even some of their own family members—simply did not know what they were doing. They were not *intentionally* participating in discrimination against Indigenous folks because they did not even know (any) Indigenous folks. The troubles were not caused and would not be resolved by individuals. Rather, they were deeply embedded in the local environment. The "troubles" relocators experienced resulted from the fact that settlers attempted to displace, erase, and, finally, replace Indigenous peoples with ugly, inanimate, ahistorical icons that extended white settler space far beyond the Cleveland MLB stadium.

Yet Another (Relocator) Trouble: Wannabe Indians

According to many relocators, NE Ohioans' romantic fascination with Indianness creates another problem: Indian *wannabes*. Wannabes, from relocators' perspectives, are non-Indians so entranced with Indianness that they adopt Indian identities and *play Indian* in earnest. When relocators discussed this phenomenon, they consistently used the "wannabe" label, but a number of other referents—like "fake Indians," "Johnny-come-lately Indians," "census Indians," and "pretendians"—are used by Indigenous people. Other terms, like "race shifters,"[34] "false faces,"[35] and "ethnic frauds,"[36] are used in scholarship about this phenomenon, which documents decades of exponential growth in the US Indigenous population for which *identity change* (or race shifting) remains the primary explanation.[37] The unyielding nature of this phenomenon increases the urgency with which it must be addressed. Recently, in the midst of the COVID-19 pandemic, Native studies scholar Kim Tallbear (Sisseton Wahpeton) suggested we are (also) in the midst of a "Pretendian Pandemic." Using Philip J. Deloria's *Playing Indian* as a jumping-off point, Tallbear elucidates centuries-long trends in faking Indianness that seem too formidable (at this point) to "push back" against. Tallbear's new sense of hopelessness about the issue is due to her belief that too many Indigenous people "with less lived experience in Indigenous community" are finding "common cause" with pretendians.[38]

In chapter 1 I provide a fuller discussion of how constructions of "false face" Indianness in US sociocultural spheres lead people (Native and non-Native) to conflate settler-constructed fraudulent Indianness with more authentic Indigenous identities (i.e., *relational* indigeneity recognized in long-standing Indigenous communities). These muddled understandings, embedded in centuries of settler-colonial logics and legal policies, threaten Indigenous sovereignty, Indigenous resources, and, consequently, Indigenous persistence. Joanne Barker (Lenape) succinctly captures these ideas in the introduction to *Critically Sovereign: Indigenous Gender, Sexuality, and Feminist Studies*: "Because international and state recognition of Indigenous rights is predicated on the cultural authenticity of a certain kind of Indigeneity, the costumed affiliations undermine the legitimacy of Indigenous claims to sovereignty and self-determination by rendering Indigenous culture and identity obsolete but for the costume."[39] I remind readers now of this earlier discussion because it is crucial to comprehend the significant impacts "race shifting" (for lack of a better term)[40] has on Indigenous peoples' *material* and social-psychological well-being.

The scholarly literature on this topic offers various, nuanced explanations for race shifting, but these explanations roughly fit into two prominent themes: one that elucidates settlers' possessive investment in whiteness—i.e., white settlers' assumed right to possess Indigenous identities, appropriate Indigenous cultures, and consume Indigenous resources—and one that elucidates settler-colonial policies that extinguished (or at least attempted to extinguish) the Indigenous stories, histories, and identities of formerly Indigenous people with renewed interest in Indigenous identities. These explanations overlap and interconnect in complex ways. As Circe Sturm, author of *Becoming Indian: The Struggle over Cherokee Identity in the Twentieth Century*, suggests, the "messiness" of "contingent, variable, contradictory, and incomplete" processes of race shifting "is what leads to different interpretations."[41]

Much academic literature and other media discussing race shifters focus on dangers "wannabes" pose to the sovereignty of recognized Indian nations. Circe Sturm, who is primarily concerned with self-identified Cherokee *groups* seeking state and/or federal recognition, suggests that state recognition is problematic because it "creates public and legal confusion, undermines perceptions of Cherokee historical and cultural authenticity, and defies the principle that sovereignty is fundamentally based on nation-to-nation relationships."[42] Queer Cherokee activist and author Rebecca Nagle, in contrast, deems all varieties of race shifting problematic. Nagle suggests that "pretendians" undermine tribal sovereignty by "perpetuat[ing] the myth that Native identity is determined by the individual, not the tribe or community."[43]

Although a majority of relocators agreed that problematic "wannabe" Indianness results from *white possessiveness* rather than Indigenous *dis*possession, relocators' concerns with "wannabes" did not center on sovereignty. I suggest that relocators' distance from tribal nations, coupled with their long-term participation in urban, pan-Indian community affairs, affected their perspectives on this issue. In NE Ohio, Indian wannabes (perhaps) seemed too far removed from Indigenous nations to influence or negatively impact them. Relocators, after all, *felt* this distance in their own lives. They understood how difficult it was to participate culturally or politically in their respective nations. They also understood how impracticable it was to access tribal resources to which they were entitled as enrolled tribal members. Relocators, consequently, were less likely to imagine a scenario by which (white) Ohioans claiming Indian identities could wreak havoc on their home communities in distant Indian nations.

Relocators, however, shared other concerns about pretendians in NE Ohio. Some relocators, like Bly (Sioux, first generation), perceived wannabes as competitors for the scant resources available to Indigenous peoples in Ohio. Bly suggested that greed was the motivation of many white people who mysteriously *become* Indians. "It has nothing to do with being brought up or proud to be American Indian," Bly said. "They see an advantage and that's what they want."

Samantha (Cherokee), a second-generation relocator, relayed the befuddlement she experiences when confronted with pretend Indianness. She said she cannot understand why people think they can claim Indian identities simply "because they admire our culture so much." "I think it's fine if you like Native art, and you're a non-Native and you buy art pieces and stuff," she continued, "but I think it's different when you buy things at a powwow and think you can wear them and then suddenly become a Native." Even worse, said Samantha, is when "they think they can do ceremonial or spiritual type things that don't belong to them. . . . That just makes me think of that guy who did the sweat lodge and killed all those people," Samantha said, referring to self-help author and new age "guru" James Arthur Ray, who was convicted of manslaughter for causing the death of three people in his Arizona sweat lodge. "And the first thing I said was, leave that to Native Americans. That's *our* thing. Obviously, you don't know what you're doing."

Samantha's comments resonated with other relocators who believed that the problem with pretendians was twofold: when white people assume ownership and control over Indigenous definitions and representations, they reify settler-constructed memories that distort people's perceptions of indigeneity; relatedly, they bastardize Indigenous traditions. Wannabes, relocators insisted, promote a "whitened" version of Indianness that celebrates white complexions and white assumptions about Indigenous beliefs and behaviors. According to Melissa (Native Hawaiian–identified), "people who claim to be Native, [but] can't prove it" are "always seen" and "always heard." "And they don't *look* Indian!" she huffed. "They don't even have any of the characteristics of being Native," Melissa said disgustedly. "I can see where non-Natives would assume that all the real Indians are gone."

Berta also talked about how physical differences between pretend Indians and Native people inevitably reify the false notion that Indigenous peoples exist only as a tragic sidebar in US history. With agitation creeping into her voice, Berta stated, "People think that that's what we all look like, you know what I'm saying? There is real Indians [*sic*]. We are real Indians out there. We're not make-believing or playing Indian for that day. It's a way of life with us. And yet people will play Indian on weekends just to get money, just to get attention, and stuff like that." According to relocators, wannabes don't *act* like Indigenous people, either. Their perceptions of Indianness are skewed, so they enact skewed versions of Indianness. Berta said their outlandish performances make it easy for "real" Indians to identify them. "You can always tell when the Indian is not an Indian in this area," said Berta, "because they have names like Searching Bear, Walking Moccasins—crazy names like that! . . . So you can always tell because they overkill." They overkill because the only stories they know about Indians are romantic fantasies created by and perpetuated in US settler society. Pretend Indians, many relocators agreed, learn, enact, and retell these fantastical stories to their children, loved ones, friends, acquaintances, and strangers, who repeat the stories over and over again.

Berta, Greg, and other relocators suggested that pretend Indians do not *intentionally* talk about and enact fraudulent Indianness. Rather, they say and do offensive things because they lack exposure to more authentic Indigenous customs. "They're giving wrong information to people," Berta explained, "saying, 'Oh, this is what we used to do a long time ago.'" "*No!*" Berta said forcefully. "We never did that. We *never* did that," she said, shaking her head. "They just make up stuff. And I think in the long run," Berta sighed, "it's more harmful to us because people expect us to act like that and we tell them 'no, that's not the way it is,' you know?" Berta continued: "And they sing songs that are inappropriate. You sing certain songs during the day, certain songs at powwows, and some people will sing a song they heard and they're just copying the song and it's inappropriate because it's not even their song. It is a family song that you've got to get permission to sing. You know what I'm saying? In Indian culture, that's what you do." Berta further explained that due to her status as a respected elder in the Ohio powwow circuit, powwow people rely on her to help curb such disruptive and disrespectful behaviors. "If you see something that's wrong," Berta said, "you have to bring it up [to the arena director] and then they'll correct it." Sometimes the offender is asked to leave the powwow circle. Removal from the circle, in fact, is precisely what happened when Berta reported a woman powwow dancer dressed in what Greg described as "a little skimpy mini-skirt jingle dress . . . open, so you could see her skin all the way down."[44]

Across generations, many relocator community members deeply respect Berta as a community elder whose knowledge, experiences, and understandings matter. Many relocators, therefore, are influenced by Berta's unnuanced perspective on pretend Indianness. "All those are wannabes," Berta said of reclaimer community members. "They're trying," she said, perhaps recognizing reclaimers' efforts to lighten her otherwise outright repudiation of reclaimers' Indian identities. In reference to the reclaimer community's annual powwow, Berta said, "We go, you know, because they think it's honoring us, but they do a lot of inappropriate things." Berta frowned. "And, eh, it's kind of sickening to go to that, you know, to see it."

I spent time with numerous members of the relocator community at reclaimer community powwows. Notably, relocators did not participate in this powwow the same way they participated in other powwows. For instance, relocator children who almost always danced did not dance at this powwow. Instead, they ran around with other relocator children or assisted parents and grandparents at vending booths, selling wares like fry bread and Indian tacos, silver jewelry, beaded moccasins, and how-to books for conducting genealogical research. Berta admitted she likes to play the music of Lakota activist and folk singer Floyd Westerman at this kind of powwow. When she steps away from her vending table to rest, she presses "play" on her portable stereo and the singer's stark voice wafts through the air: "Where were you when we needed you, our friend? / Where were you when we needed you to bend? / And now you claim to be part Sioux or Cherokee / But where were you when we came close to the end?"

Berta pauses the song so she can hear the powwow emcee announce the next event: a special guest, an out-of-state flutist and winner of numerous Native American Music Awards, or NAMIs, will treat the crowd to several hit songs. The emcee introduces the flutist by name, nation, and reservation and asks the crowd to give him a big round of applause. As powwow attendees stand, clap, whistle, and shout, the young flutist, an obese, twenty-something, round-faced man with sweaty, shimmering, cocoa-colored skin and a single braid cascading down his back, slowly walks to the middle of the powwow circle. Timidly he thanks the crowd. His next words are so quiet that they are inaudible. He raises his flute to his lips and begins to play.

Casey, the (regrettably, in his opinion) blonde-haired, blue-eyed, Cherokee-identified reclaimer, watched the flutist from the front of his vending pavilion. Only moments earlier, Casey grinned broadly while reporting the recent sale of a rather expensive Native American–style woodland flute, a flute pricey enough to recoup his powwow expenses. Upon hearing the emcee announce the award-winning flutist, Casey's grin fizzled and a scowl took its place. "I just don't know how anyone who calls himself a Native American flute player could play a flute that someone else made," he muttered. "That just doesn't make sense to me! I could *never* play someone else's flute," he grumbled. "Making the flute is part of the whole identity of being a flute player!" Casey exclaimed.

Casey's pride in his own craftsmanship heightened his aggravation. He crafts his flutes from start to finish. He finds fallen tree limbs, hollows them out with a hot iron rod, fashions them into flutes, and, finally, decorates them with hand carvings and inlaid stones. Sometimes Casey's flutes sell for fifteen hundred and even two thousand dollars, but they are not *genuine* Native American flutes because Casey is not a *genuine* Indian according to the US government. It vexes Casey that the federal Indian Arts and Crafts Act (1990) dictates the terms of his flute sales, limits his artisan income, and invalidates his Indigenous identity. Casey's palpable bitterness comes from a lifetime of rejection. He sees himself as a Native person who "walks the walk" and does things "the right way," yet other people constantly question and invalidate his Indian identity.

Reclaimers and the Trouble with Being an Indian-Identified Person in NE Ohio

Casey (Cherokee-identified) and other reclaimers discussed two troubles that complicate being Indian in NE Ohio. The first trouble—finding the time, people, and space necessary to learn about and practice the Indigenous cultures they are reclaiming—is discussed throughout the book. The second trouble, discussed here, is experiencing seemingly relentless invalidations of their Indian identities. Many reclaimers agreed that false images of Indianness are at least partially to blame, but *all* reclaimers talked about another burdensome source of their identity-related distress: "Indian politics." In conversations among reclaimers, the use of this well-worn expression was accompanied by an exchange of knowing nods. Indian politics, as reclaimers understood the term, referred to disparaging and sometimes malicious activities of full-blood or tribally enrolled Indians who denied the identities of other (mixed-blood or nonenrolled) Indians. Such politics utterly complicated being Indian in NE Ohio, said reclaimers, because they infected nearly every space occupied by Indians of different enrollment statuses. According to reclaimers, relocators and other "political" Indians used a variety of tactics to publicly discredit reclaimers' identities.

Further, reclaimers accused members of the NE Ohio relocator community of being the worst offenders. Sasha (Lakota-identified), for instance, described relocators as "very exclusionary." "I don't know why," she mused, because where they live is "not the big hot spot for Indians, either! There's no big rez there or anything." Relocators do not need a rez, reclaimers agreed, to make other urban Indians feel like "outsiders." They have a cliquish, insular community that, according to reclaimers, epitomizes Indian politics. "*They* have a lot of political issues," Oda (Delaware- and Blackfoot-identified) said in reference to relocators. "I just do not understand the people that are so caught up in that [Indian politics], that they only run with other 'bloods,'" she concluded with a sigh.

Powwows are particularly important cultural events for reclaimers, so experiencing invalidation of their identities in this space is acutely disheartening. "At powwows," Floyd (Blackfoot- and Ojibwa-identified) said, "you get looks and you hear people whispering." According to Floyd, some "full-bloods" put people down at powwows simply because they "don't look like the Hollywood Indian." "I've been called a 'wannabe' myself . . . because my skin is white, you know?" Defensively, Floyd added, "I'm mixed blood. I'm not full-blood Indian. I never claimed to be." Calling people "wannabes" is not the meanest thing full-bloods do, either, Floyd warned. "I've been to powwows," he said, "and this never happened to me, but I've seen it happen—where full-bloods . . . cut the string on a guy's bustle because his bustle looked better than theirs, you know? Just dumb stuff." Such antics (and/or rumors of such antics) create powwow environments reclaimers perceive as hostile.

Kenai (Lakota-identified) also expressed frustration with the "political" nature of Ohio powwows: "There's just so much BS that goes along with being Indian in Ohio. . . . You have the full-bloods who don't want, like, the nonenrolled members and then the nonenrolled members are irritated because the 'skins[45] treat 'em bad. It's too political! . . . That's why I hide my face when I dance. I cover my stuff up 'cause you know, I'm just there to dance." Kenai's strategy for avoiding the unwelcome, invalidating stares of "full-blood" Indians is to dance in an elaborate feather roach (a headdress worn by men) that covers three-quarters of his face. His indigeneity cannot be denied if no one knows who he is or what he looks like. Other reclaimers talked about how powwow "politics" inform their decisions regarding which or whether to attend area powwows. Danna (Odawa) said she avoided powwows for years because of "the politics." "A lot of elders think there's like a kind of a cookie-cutter Indian," Danna explained. "Like, if you do something wrong, then, oh! You're *so* disrespectful!"

Reclaimers collectively expressed annoyance with "powwow police," people who, according to Floyd (Blackfoot- and Ojibwa-identified), scoff at dancers for doing things "wrong," simply "because you're not doing *their* traditions." "You have to go with what your teachings are," Floyd said. Reclaimers admit they occasionally make mistakes—many of them are new to Indian culture, after all—but they think the bigger issue is that relocators and other full-bloods intentionally humiliate reclaimers whether or not they are doing things "wrong." Rather than celebrate the state's intertribal diversity, reclaimers believe that relocators and other full-bloods try to stomp it out by insinuating that there is a *right* way for everyone to dance and dress and sing. "You have people who are from one tradition and then people from another tradition," Sadie (Lenape- and Blackfoot-identified) explained. "See, some people dance backwards without shoes on. They do. I've seen it. And some people don't. Well, the people who don't get up in the people who do's crap, saying they're doing their religion, culture, whatever, wrong. . . . That's the kind of 'politics' stuff," Sadie said incredulously. "Oh, you hold your pipe this way, or you give your tobacco that way."

Reclaimers talked openly about their experiences of identity inval- idation. They are fully aware that some Indians believe they are fake Indians. They admitted that such identity rebukes are annoying, both- ersome, and/or burdensome, but never said they were hurtful (despite evidence that they are). Rather than reflecting on their experiences and trying to understand the perspectives of tribally enrolled Indigenous people, many reclaimers deflected feelings of hurt, doubt, sadness, guilt, and envy by reducing all the debates, concerns, and conundrums about Indigenous identity to a single word: "politics." Moreover, reclaimers thoroughly individualized the issue of Indigenous identity by suggesting that "political" Indians, rather than federal or tribal governments, were responsible for their experiences of invalidation. "I think that some peo- ple get this feeling of superiority," said Sasha (Lakota-identified). "They have a way of making outsiders feel like outsiders." Floyd (Blackfoot- and Ojibwa-identified) echoed this sentiment. "That all goes with that prejudice thing," he said. Making no effort to hide his contempt, Floyd continued, "That's people thinking they're better than other people be- cause they carry a card, you know? They got a piece of plastic that says 'I'm Indian,' and you don't." Reclaimers turned this idea into a running joke. Mimicking so-called political Indians and "powwow police," they gleefully yelled, "That's not how *my* people do it!" as though chastising one another for doing Indianness wrong.

Nonenrolled reclaimers consistently said things that illustrated their lack of engagement with issues of Indigenous nationhood, citizenship, or sovereignty. They maintained, for instance, that they *knew* they were Indian and did not need a "piece of paper" or "plastic" (Certificate of Degree of Indian Blood, tribal identification card) or "number" (tribal identification number) to prove it. They dismissed so-called political Indians as people who took pride in being certified as Indian by the US government, but rarely mentioned Indian *nations'* roles in determining tribal citizenship. They said things like "being Indian is a state of mind"; "it's not the blood that counts, it's the heart"; and, what really matters is "walking the red road" or "walking the walk." Reclaimers used this latter phrase to distinguish themselves from enrolled Natives who, in their opinions, too frequently "talked the talk." In this way, many reclaimers defended their Indian identities while invalidating the identities of "political" Indians, whom they accused of acting like settlers. Politics, reclaimers suggested, was the federal government's tactic to destroy Indigenous peoples, communities, and cultures. It was not, reclaimers argued, a traditional or acceptable Indigenous strategy. Historically, Indians did not quantify Indigenous blood or break it down into discrete, measurable units. An Indian was either accepted as a member of the community or not. (That this idea is foundational to the identity beliefs of members of long-standing Indigenous communities was lost on a majority of reclaimers, who relied on their acceptance in the urban, pan-Indian reclaimer community, established in 2001, as "proof" of their community membership.)

In contrast to "political" relocators, reclaimers saw themselves (and their Indian identity claims) as apolitical and unbiased. As Spokane scholar-poet Gloria Bird once said, however, "Being Indian in the United States is inherently political." Reclaimers cannot avoid Indian politics simply by declaring nonparticipation. Indian nations are *polities*, so Indian identities cannot be depoliticized. Depoliticizing Indian identities, in fact, *decontextualizes* indigeneity and endorses stories and memories that deem forgettable and irrelevant so much of Indigenous peoples' histories. Reclaimers' declarations of apolitical Indianness construct new rules of remembrance that dismiss Indigenous peoples' histories of resistance to settler-colonial erasure, as well as their ongoing struggles for sovereignty and self-definition—including the right to define who belongs to/within their tribal communities.

Despite reclaimers' desires to be "apolitical," the political realities of Indigenous identity cannot be dismissed because centuries of policies politicizing Indianness cannot be erased or reversed. It is not possible for Indigenous people to return to (imagined) pre-settler-colonial Indigenous identities. In fact, in their attempts to do so, reclaimers inadvertently bolster settler-imposed memories of an ahistorical indigeneity that exists in a mythological "pure-past" untouched and uncontaminated by settler colonialism. Yet, in telling and retelling and collectively embracing stories about apolitical indigeneity, reclaimers alleviated some of the uneasiness they experienced as individuals with disputed Indian identities.

Reclaimers often unwittingly contradicted their spoken nonchalance about other Native people's dismissals of their identities. When they discussed the issue, the edge in their voices, their defensive retorts, and their sad, defeated tones all suggested that their bravado was a defense tactic. The following story about Casey (Cherokee-identified) illustrates this point. The invited guest of a local parks association, Casey spent the evening telling Native stories and playing several of his handcrafted flutes to approximately sixty park enthusiasts. During his performance he saw what he described as a "hardcore" "Native guy" who made him "a little bit" nervous. Casey said the man was making "all kinds of facial expressions" that led Casey to believe he did not approve of his flute playing. Casey discussed these observations the following morning while tending to his vending pavilion at the reclaimer community powwow. Minutes later, the man Casey saw the previous evening popped his head into Casey's pavilion, held his hand out to Casey, and gruffly said, "Hey! You did a nice job last night." Casey politely thanked him. As soon as the man walked away, Casey exclaimed, "That just made my day!" Grinning from ear to ear, Casey practically shouted, "I feel great!" and then he repeated, "That just made my day." Like many reclaimers, Casey insists that "the rolls and blood quantum and all of that" do not "really matter." With respect to other Native people suggesting that he is merely a pretend Indian, Casey states, "It's like they're slandering your ancestors, who are their ancestors, so it really makes little sense to me." And because he can "walk [his] talk," Casey maintains, skeptical Native people usually eventually come around to accepting him as their Native kin. Yet, Casey's euphoria after a brief but affirming exchange between himself and a person he deemed incontrovertibly Indian reveals his vulnerability.

Reclaimers also revealed vulnerabilities in conversations about family members dismissing their Indian identities. Valerie (Cherokee-identified) said she abhors that her ex-husband constantly refers to her as Mexican in front of their daughters. She explained, "I get really angry at that because I am Native American. There's no doubt in my mind. I mean, I may not have that little card that says I'm Native American, but I *know* that I am. And yet, for him to still tell them. . . . You know, your mom is Mexican. And [my daughter] jokingly, now she says, it's just a joke to say, 'Well, mom, when the Census comes out, I'm marking Mexican.'"

Valerie knows her daughter's banter is good-natured, but it still hurts—especially since Valerie failed in her efforts to acquire her "Indian card." Similarly, Casey spoke exasperatedly about his ex-wife, who mocked his assertions of Indian identity. "She would tell me, 'You're not Indian. Quit it! Quit trying to act like an Indian!'" Casey said, "And it would just irritate me to no end because I never tried to force my beliefs on her." Other reclaimers complained about siblings who were uninterested, dismissive, or even disdainful about the family's Indigenous heritage. Tabatha (Cherokee), for instance, said she gets into heated debates with her brother, who insists that the family's ethnicity is "hillbilly."

Reclaimers' identities are also invalidated in public spaces. Because they tire of being mistaken for white or (occasionally) Hispanic people, some reclaimers make efforts to signal their Indianness to people they encounter in their day-to-day lives. They adorn themselves, their cars, or their living or work spaces with accoutrements that will be read as "Indian" by the people around them. Some reclaimers have experienced demoralizing identity invalidation their entire lives. Kurt's son, Daniel (Choctaw-identified), for example, remembers being teased by *kindergarten* classmates who refused to acknowledge his Native identity. Only after his grandfather, Dean, visited Daniel's class dressed in full regalia were his classmates willing to concede that he was Native. Sadie (Lenape- and Blackfoot-identified) experienced similar difficulties during childhood, the most heartrending of which occurred soon after her mother's death. Within days of Sadie's return to (high) school after a brief bereavement leave, school authorities held a random locker search for drugs and other contraband. When they found Sadie's prayer ties—tiny tobacco bundles from her mother's funeral—they accused her of smoking the tobacco and threatened to expel her from school. School personnel were skeptical of Sadie's explanation *and* her Indianness. She was only absolved of the "deviant" act after members of Sadie's family and the local Native community convinced school authorities that Sadie did, in fact, identify as a Native person and the tobacco bundles were for spiritual use.

As an adult, Sadie tries to prevent awkward interactions and unintentional denials of her identity by using clothing and jewelry to signal her Indian identity to others. This strategy does not always work, though, as was the case during Sadie's last visit to the food bank. The food bank volunteer checked the box for "white" on Sadie's intake form, "even though," Sadie said, "I had my big fat NATIVE sweatshirt on and my bone turtle and my bone earrings and my beadwork!" Sadie corrected the woman's mistake, explaining that she was Native. The volunteer responded with a puzzled expression, so Sadie reiterated, a bit more firmly, "I'm *Native American*." After Sadie stated her identity two more times, the food bank volunteer finally changed Sadie's race on the intake form. Sadie also gets annoyed when people mistake her boy child for a girl child. (Sadie has one of each.) She said she constantly must explain that her family is Native and her son has "long hair just like his daddy. And then," Sadie said, completely exasperated, "if I *still* get the stupid dumb dog look, I say, [loudly] '*We're Indians!*'" Tabatha (Cherokee) talked about similar efforts to avoid seemingly endless questions about her Native identity. She described the frustration she always experiences job hunting: "Every job interview that I've ever gone to, when I put down that I'm Native American—'Well, you don't look Native American.' So I'll just wear my Indian jacket and my Indian jewelry and my moccasins to my interviews and that way it just eliminates that part of the interview, you know? It eliminates the part that makes me angry." Reclaimers' identity signaling does not work every time, but it works often enough. Even occasionally avoiding a "stupid dumb dog look" is better than explaining their identities to every single person they meet. That said, they do not seem to realize that their attempts to signal their Indian identities with clothing, jewelry, bumper stickers, etc., can backfire, too, such as when relocators like Berta (Lakota) consider the actions they take to be "overkill."

Not all reclaimers accentuate their Indian identities with exterior décor. Kurt (Choctaw-identified), for instance, explained how his perspective on this strategy shifted over time. When he was younger, he wore his hair long. "Because it was a way of [gaining] acceptance," Kurt explained. And it seemed to work. Several years ago, however, Kurt decided to resist "playing into the stereotype." "Not all Natives wore long hair!" he said animatedly. "You know, that's another [stereotype] because Cherokee shaved the front part of their head and had hair in the back. Your Pawnee either would have a mohawk or a shaved head like myself. . . . I got to a point," Kurt explained, "where the Creator told me, 'You know what, Kurt? You need to portray the urban American Indian and that urban American Indian no longer looks like this.' And I didn't want to play into the stereotype no more. So," Kurt said a bit triumphantly, "I shaved the head."

With a hint of sarcasm, Kurt declared himself "the urban American Indian poster boy." He continued, "Really, what we're portraying here is—I'm Indian. Hear me roar! Accept me for who I am and not as what you see or portray as Native American. Because I get so upset with individuals who point fingers. And honestly, I know some full bloods who can't tell you nothing about their culture. And they're *full* blood, you know?!" Kurt's frustration developed over many years. For as long as he can remember, both Native and non-Native people have denied his Native identity. Yet, Kurt has always identified as Native. He even committed his life to serving Native people. To the best of his ability, he lives according to Native values and belief systems. According to Kurt, he is exasperated because his actions seldom receive the same scrutiny as his appearance.

The troubles with being Indian in Northeast Ohio tend to emanate from settler-constructed stories, images, and ideas about Indianness. Relocators, more than anything, want people to stop fixating on and attempting to possess Indianness. They resist Indian mascotry and wannabe Indianness—the phenomena they deem most central to their oppression as urban Indians in Northeast Ohio—by publicly asserting their rights to define Indigenous identities for themselves and others. Denying reclaimers' Indian identities is only one facet of a broader resistance strategy. Reclaimers, on the other hand, want people around them, including relocators, to recognize them as Indians. They resist invalidation of their identities by impugning Indian "politics," feigning indifference to others' denials of their identities, decontextualizing Indianness, and accentuating their Indian identities by wearing Indiancentric attire, hairstyles, and/or accessories. The next chapter explores how reclaimers and relocators negotiate these troubles within their respective communities.

7

Urban Indian Communities

Boundaries and Tensions

The troubles reclaimers and relocators experience as Indian and Indian-identified people living in Northeast Ohio contributed to their unique urban pan-Indian community formations. Both reclaimers and relocators needed spaces of belonging. Reclaimers needed a welcoming community where they experienced feelings of acceptance as (predominantly) tribally nonenrolled, Indian-identified people interested in reclaiming Indigenous identities and traditions. Relocators, in contrast, needed an insulated community where they could engage with other Indigenous people who understood them, and at the same time, avoid ignorant people with stereotypical understandings of Indianness. Within their respective communities, reclaimers and relocators simultaneously engaged in "memory work" and "identity work" that affirmed their (respective) definitions of their collective situations as either relocated Indians or Indian-identified people reclaiming indigeneity. Their community work coalesced in boundary-making strategies that created tensions *within* community groups and exacerbated tensions *between* them.

Reclaimers: "Bringing the People Together"

Kurt's father, Dean (Choctaw-identified), founded the nonprofit reclaimer community organization in 2001 after serving on the board of a different urban Indian Center. Dean was dissatisfied with the way they did things. "They went more or less the white man way, more than the Indian way," Dean said. "I like to keep the culture going on, you know, moving on," Dean explained. "Not put it back where it was before." Dean recalled a time when Indian culture was nearly dormant. "It was going downhill there one time, and it started back when the doors come open for it," Dean said. "So we better get in and show people the American Indians are still around here. A lot of people . . . think that we already vanished and gone." "I got this Indian Center interested in parades and stuff like that," Dean said, "and we let people know the American Indians are still alive." Importantly, Dean ensured that his Indian Center was "inclusive to everybody" because, according to Dean, that is the "Indian way." "It's bringing the people together and showing the Indians can work with the whites and the whites can work with the Indians. . . . I learn your way and you learn my way," Dean said, "and this way here we can get things done."

Seven years after Dean founded the reclaimer community organization, his son Kurt took over its directorship. Dean delighted in passing leadership responsibilities to his son. "That feels real good," Dean said, "to have somebody take your place. It's good to sit back . . . and watch the young generation take over." Kurt, said Dean, will take the organization "farther and farther and farther" because he has skills— "with computers and stuff like that"—required of twenty-first-century leaders. Under Kurt's leadership, however, one thing remains the same: all are welcome. Making membership available to people of all races and ethnicities enables Kurt to carry on Dean's work and simplifies the community's commitments to NE Ohio Natives. Documentation is not a membership requirement, whether or not individuals claim Native identities. If a person identifies as Native, participates in reclaimer community activities, and, in Kurt's words, tries "to practice their culture in a good way," reclaimers generally recognize them as Native.

"Policing" Indianness at the community center would cut the heart out of the organization's mission—which, for Kurt, is personal and professional. Kurt's Indigenous ancestry is undocumented, so he understands reclaimers' struggles for recognition in a society that rejects their Indian identities. "A lot of folks," Kurt explained, "get this mysterious vision or fantasy of what a Native is—the long black hair flowing in the wind, the feathers waving to you in the air, dark skinned." "What people don't realize," he said, "is that a lot of Natives born today, they're not full-bloods. They're not even half-bloods. They may be quarter or thirty-second bloods. Does that make them any less Native or any less Indian?" Kurt asked. "So it's eye-opening information that is sort of my job to take out there and teach agencies and governments in this state to be aware and understand. Most of your Natives are not born on a reservation today," Kurt concluded, "but that doesn't make them any less Native."

Kurt works to promote "cultural awareness" that can improve the circumstances of urban Indians' lives. He is disappointed that terms like "wannabe" continue to plague people genuinely interested in *reclaiming* Indian identities. Kurt supports DNA testing and wishes it was considered sufficient evidence of Indigenous ancestry because obtaining tribal enrollment is beyond the reach of so many individuals. He does not understand why people "have to prove they are part of a tribe somewhere" to receive compensation for the oppression experienced by generations of their family members. Kurt, for instance, cannot prove *he* is part of a tribe, but he knows he is Choctaw. He knows his grandfather was born in Oklahoma Indian Territory and migrated north as a teenager. Kurt knows his grandfather was a coal miner in Kentucky, and then in West Virginia. Kurt also knows *his* father, Dean, was born in West Virginia and migrated to Northeast Ohio after serving in the Marines. Kurt knows these aspects of his family history because his family members passed their stories down through the generations. They never denied their Indian identities or even tried to hide them. Rather, the family's separation from their Indigenous community of origin resulted from one young person's desire to ease his mother's burden and begin life anew in a place promising some semblance of the "American Dream." This person was Kurt's grandfather, and though his Indianness slowed *his* progress toward the dream, his grandson and great-grandson—Kurt and Daniel—live in a time and place where it can be realized.

Reclaimers' Stories and Recollections

Kurt and Dean both shared their family's story during interviews, but interestingly, Kurt shared another story, too. It is not *his* family's story, but he heard it (and likely repeated it) countless times. It is a collectively "remembered" memory of many North Americans reclaiming Indigenous identities—one that assures people of their Indigenous ancestry despite their disconnectedness from contemporary Indigenous communities.[1] Every scholar interested in Indigenous identity is aware of it and many scholars make light of it. It surfaces with such regularity, in fact, that it has transmuted into a joke among many Indigenous people and their allies. It is the story of a family in hiding.

In defense of reclaimers who cannot prove they are "part of a tribe," Kurt told his version of the story. "Now, let's go back in history," Kurt began, "and let's think about this for a minute." Kurt continued:

> So, we're living in our little community, and in the middle of the night our door gets kicked in. Soldiers come in and look at us and say, "You've got five minutes. We're moving you out of here." We're questioning, "Why? Where?" Some of us get shot, some of us are beaten, some of our women are raped, some of our children are killed. Fear is immediately sent into us. So what's our scenario? Well, we grab our family and we do what we're told. Other individuals, warriors, for instance—those who are the watchful eyes—sometimes looked out and saw what was going on, grabbed their families. If I see my neighbors and I see something happening down my street, well . . . I'm taking my family. I'm hitting out the back door. And that's what some of them did. Some went to Canada, hid out. Some went into the mountains where they couldn't be found. Some of them . . . knew where they could hide and stay. . . . We knew what we had to do to survive. We were the first Navy Seals. Why? Because we could hide in a river and learn to breathe. We could hide in the woods. . . . They knew how to blend in. . . . So to look at everybody and say that all Natives went to the reservation is the first lie. What happened is, a lot of times, those individuals went out, they hid their families, they followed to see where [the soldiers] were taking the others, and when the coast was clear, they snuck in. And when they knew something was happening, they snuck back out.

"So not everybody signed up on that reservation," Kurt concluded indignantly. "Not all names are there, I don't care what they tell you!"

This story, in one form or another, is repeatedly recalled and retold and passed from one generation to the next. It *becomes* recollection to people who hear it, learn it, and are socialized to believe it. Mnemonic socialization, in fact, is so powerful that it creates jointly remembered memories even when the remembered events are not jointly experienced. Personal biographies, according to social-memory scholars, fuse with the histories of groups to which people belong (familial and organizational), creating sociobiographical memories vital to people's social identities. For these reasons, it is always critical to interpret collective memories, i.e., the collectively *constructed* memories of mnemonic communities, like public opinion polls. They highlight only *commonly shared* recollections, which, of course, are reinterpretations of others' recollections.[2] As such, people can share memories of events that never happened.

It is foolish to insist Kurt's story about a Native family in hiding never happened. Indigenous peoples have been dispossessed of their territories, communities, and identities for centuries. But it is equally foolish to accept this collective memory as reality for all people, or even a majority of people, espousing it. Herein lies one of Kurt's struggles as director of the reclaimer community organization. Kurt knows that some people, despite having Indigenous heritage, are unable to trace their Indigenous lineage back to nineteenth-century censuses of Indigenous communities. Preventing these people "from claiming their nationalities," according to Kurt, is unethical. "I'm sorry," Kurt said. "To me that's wrong. . . . If they keep on like they're doing right now," Kurt continued glumly, "the only way you're going to learn about Native Americans is in the Smithsonian Institute behind a glass window."

At the same time, Kurt is responsible for affirming the Indian identities of the few reclaimer community members seeking access to benefits designated for Indigenous people in the urban environment. For instance, Kurt's approval can help a small business owner obtain their minority-owned business certification, which increases marketing opportunities and access to government contracts. "Trust me," Kurt said, "I don't take that stuff lightly." Approved individuals, said Kurt, must be active in the reclaimer community and accepted as a community member—"not somebody who just knocks on my door out of the blue and says, 'Hey, can I have a paper?' And, no matter what, we all know certain individuals will take advantage of situations," Kurt continued, "so it's my job as the executive director of this agency to filter those individuals out."

Kurt works too hard for the organization's scant resources to waste them. "We are limited on funds here and we are limited on what we can do for individuals," Kurt said, so he focuses on "helping urban American Indians connect with services, or at least connect with their own tribes. You know, we always hear, 'I'm Cherokee, I'm Cherokee!'" Kurt said. "Well then, for God's sakes, go! Learn from the Cherokee. Don't just keep saying, 'I'm Cherokee.' I can't help you, I'm Choctaw." Kurt said he encourages all community participants to learn about their ethnic and national heritages. He provides community members with (donated) Internet-enabled computers (in donated office space) to assist with genealogical research, and "if you're not Native," Kurt said, "then my motivation for you is learn *who* you are and be *proud* of who you are and be accepted as such. Then you're part of *our* community." Non-Natives, Kurt explained, are identified as "community supporters" on membership cards, and Kurt truly appreciates their participation. Such individuals, said Kurt, "understand us, understand what our needs are, and want to help us get those needs and reach our goals."

The "Métis-Making" Phenomenon

Unlike some organizations comprised of newcomers to Indigenous identities, neither the leadership nor the members of the reclaimer community have a "neotribalist" ethos. Métis scholar Adam Gaudry uses this term to describe formerly white, now Métis-identified Canadians who exploit DNA tests indicating distant descendancy from First Nations people to establish their own "Métis" tribes. This "Métis-making" phenomenon, also studied by French-descended Indigenous studies scholar Darryl Leroux, shares numerous similarities with revelations about the Cherokee "race shifters" studied by Circe Sturm. These scholars discuss Métis- and Cherokee-identified groups engaged in legal efforts to obtain federal or state-level recognition as sovereign and self-determining tribal nations. In each case, group members are not recognized as Indigenous by recognized *Indigenous* communities, so they petition settler authorities for collective Indigenous statuses that will provide them with rights reserved for long-standing Métis and Cherokee communities.

Among Canadian Métis-identified groups, many members' claims to indigeneity rest on DNA testing alone. For instance, the Quebecois Métis Nation of the Rising Sun was founded in 2006 on the basis of twenty genetic tests indicating trace amounts of Indigenous ancestry. Rather than embrace long-standing Métis (whose lands are located nearly three thousand miles away in western Canada) or long-standing regional groups like the Mi'kmaw, members of the Métis-identified group claim to be "the only direct descendants of Quebec's First Peoples" because they were not "killed by microbial shock." Further, the group asserts superiority over reserve-based Indigenous peoples because their "ancestors refused the reserves" and "remained free." Another Quebecois Métis-identified group, Nation Métisse Autochtone de la Gaspésie, similarly intimates that their "authentic" culture more fully captures the "essence of the Indigenous spirit" than the cultures of Indigenous peoples living on reserves. Though less tied to genetic ancestry tests, Cherokee "race-shifting" participants in Sturm's research also suggest that their authenticity as Cherokees is somehow strengthened or intensified by their ancestors' resistance to removal to reservations, i.e., group members' abilities to escape the physical and mental restraints of colonialism.

Such sentiments (unsurprisingly) reveal white-supremacist logics embedded in group members' claims to indigeneity. Each of these Métis-identified groups assumes superiority over enrolled and reservation-based Indigenous populations due to their racial and cultural "hybridity." The stories they tell cohere with stories they learned as (previously) white-identified people living in white settler societies— that white people (settlers) are superior to Indigenous peoples, who are anachronous, brutish, unfit, and inferior. These stories positively orient white/settler identities in racialized societies with dichotomized understandings of racial realities. As Meusburger maintains, when "mutually contradictory assertions of identity" occur in "divided societies," "one identity *only* can be validated, or at worst, constituted by a suppression of another."[3] Accordingly, white settlers' superiority complexes lead them to believe that their white, mixed-blood (or "new Métis") identities, due to their hybridity, are superior to the identities of long-standing Métis and/or members of other long-standing (ostensibly less hybrid) Indigenous communities. Whites/settlers with hybrid identities, thus, believe they are justified in suppressing the identities of Indigenous peoples purported to have less genetic admixture.

In contrast to "indigenized" groups described in the literature,[4] NE Ohio reclaimers do not claim to be a "tribe" deserving of sovereignty or resources set aside for sovereign Indian nations. Reclaimers recognize and respect community members' pan-Indian identities and cultural diversity. When they are able, members encourage and assist each other with learning cultural practices specific to the heritages they claim. Moreover, NE Ohio reclaimers do not focus on family *histories* only. They sometimes fetishize the historical traumas of Indigenous peoples (whom they claim as their ancestors), but they more often express regret about family members' willingness to leave Indian identities and practices behind. Collectively, reclaimers do not endorse DNA testing as evidence of Indigenous ancestry.[5] When reclaimers focus on ancestry or "commune with the dead" (as Gaudry says of the "new Métis"), they generally do so for two reasons: they desire *proof* or *recognition* of their Indian identities. They rarely (if ever) question *whether* they are Indians because they generally believe stories about their Indigenous ancestries shared with them by relatives.

Reclaimers most serious about reclaiming Indian identities prefer to interact and engage with living Indigenous communities. Several reclaimers interviewed for this study sought mentors enrolled in recognized, long-standing Indigenous communities because they perceive such communities as vital to the persistence of Indigenous peoples and traditions. (As shown in previous chapters, reclaimers tend to romanticize reservation-based Indigenous peoples *and* the "old ways." They are more likely to wish their whiteness away than to aggrandize their mixed-race heritages.) Reclaimers with ties to reservation-based Indigenous communities are grateful for the urban, pan-Indian reclaimer community that recognizes them as Indigenous people, but they do not pretend their reclaimer community membership cards convey anything more than the fact that they participate in an urban pan-Indian community.

Reclaimers: "One Word: Community"

Most reclaimers did not grow up in Indian communities. Their families did not socialize them to practice Indian ways. Now they are committed to reclaiming Indigenous identities and practices and they need a space where they can experience *belonging* as Indigenous people. As Sadie (Lenape- and Blackfoot-identified) suggested, the reclaimer community offers respite from the "stupid dumb dog looks" her family receives when they assert Indian identities in public places. "For the most part," Sadie said, "we can go [to community events] and we can be ourselves." Sasha (Lakota-identified) agreed, saying the community is "a comfort." It is "very much about being there for each other," Sasha said. "It's *mitaku oyasin*, we're all related."

The community's openness is exhilarating and life-changing for many reclaimers, who have learned to expect and even accept rejection of their Indigenous identities. Valerie (Cherokee-identified) spent much of her adult life searching for belonging. After failing to obtain validation of her Cherokee identity, participating in the reclaimer community offers Valerie some consolation. "They always made me feel so accepted, that I was special," Valerie said. "All the things I wanted people to see me for, they saw." Now Valerie engenders these feelings in others. "[I] embrace everyone positively," Valerie said, "so they feel more comfortable." To Valerie, the reclaimer community's affirming ethos makes people feel content and confident.

The reclaimer community also provides members with a place to *practice* the "old ways" together. As twenty-something Matu (multitribally identified) stated, "If you are Native and you don't know how to do it, come! We'll teach you!" Reclaimer community activities are structured around this idea. Monthly community meetings, for instance, expose reclaimers to an array of pan-Indian practices like drumming, singing, praying, smudging (cleansing the environment by burning sage), and the dedication of spirit plates (food set aside for the ancestors) at mealtime. Most meetings include a keynote speaker sharing Indiancentric information with the group, from traditional storytelling to harvesting wild herbs to buying and caring for authentic Navajo rugs. The latter was presented by a Cherokee-identified reclaimer with a small minority-owned, Internet-based business. She sells rugs made by Diné women she befriended while living in the Southwest. She claims her business provides the women rug weavers with a less exploitative option for moving their merchandise than their local (sometimes white/settler owned) general stores.

More recent activities added to the community's previous mainstays (i.e., monthly community meetings, an annual holiday party, and participation in local parades) include twice-monthly drum circles and craft and regalia nights. Drum night tended to be more popular, but both events frequently attracted thirty or more attendees. "That's the kind of stuff that helps me," said Sadie (Lenape- and Blackfoot-identified). "It's good to have that 'there's-other-people-out-there' type of support." Sasha (Lakota-identified) agreed, saying that it is important to "come together with other people who are also isolated." Both women have reservation-based mentors, but visiting them is time-consuming and expensive. The reclaimer community's cultural activities provide a feasible everyday alternative. "It's nice," said Sadie about the community drum circle, "because . . . it helps us learn those songs better." Floyd (Blackfoot- and Ojibwa-identified) helps Sadie and her family pronounce words that are unclear in Sadie's low-quality recordings of songs her mentor suggested she learn. At drum night, reclaimers also discuss things like different types of songs, appropriate times to sing different songs, and accepted ways of asking permission to sing others' songs. Valerie (Cherokee-identified) often worked evenings, but she looked forward to the craft and regalia nights she was able to attend. She particularly appreciated the nonjudgmental way other reclaimers mentored her. "They make you feel that, you know, the regalia you have on is fine," Valerie said, "but if you *want* to make it better, [they] actually [help] you do that rather than saying, 'Oh, that isn't appropriate.'" For Sadie, Sasha, Valerie, and other reclaimers, it is liberating to engage in Indigenous practices knowing they can stumble over words or accidentally wear "inappropriate" regalia and the people around them will still accept them as Indigenous people.

The Resurgence of (Reclaimed) Indianness in NE Ohio

Reclaimers expressed excitement about the community's progress under Kurt's leadership. They credited Kurt with the resurgence of Indigenous identities and practices in the NE Ohio region. Sadie (Lenape- and Blackfoot-identified), for instance, noted that people who comprised the "Indian community" of her youth walked away from the community due to unchecked "Indian politics." Now that Kurt occupies a stronger leadership role, the same people are once again "talking and hanging out" and "exchanging spiritual ideas and concepts and beliefs." The best part, said Sadie, is that they are having these conversations "without this, 'I'm right, you're wrong' type of mentality." Floyd (Blackfoot- and Ojibwa-identified) agreed. "Kurt's doing a good thing," he said. "He's taking one of the teachings and living it, you know what I mean?" Floyd swallowed hard before continuing. "I got a lot of respect for Kurt. He's a really good person. And he's humble about everything is the other thing, you know?" Floyd's eyes welled with tears. "I kind of like to think he makes me a better person, you know, because he reminds me, oh, yeah, I'm supposed to be living a certain way."

Such effusive praise for Kurt was common among reclaimers. They extolled Kurt's warm leadership style and inclusive philosophy. Many reclaimers, like Floyd, suggested that Kurt modeled *their* teachings—the things they had learned from Indian-identified family and friends and mentors both on- and off-reservation. The mnemonic communities that nourish reclaimers' Indian identities taught them that *everyone* benefits from Indian ways of thinking and acting in the world. "Too much [emphasis] is put on religion and nationality," Floyd said. "Why can't we all just be humans?" he asked. "As long as we share [our spiritual beliefs] . . . and we just make it a *human* religion, everybody will thrive." According to Floyd, this harmonious message was delivered by a "medicine man in modern times." Similarly, Neville (multitribally identified) said Indigenous prophecies suggest "dropping the racial boundaries" and "saying we are people, we are one. We bleed the same, we're pink on the inside. Let's get over our differences. Let's stand up and be a people."

Like the Cherokee-identified race shifters in Sturm's study, many reclaimers enthusiastically share their Indian practices with Indian- and *non*-Indian-identified people.[6] Kurt's son Daniel (Choctaw-identified) believes that sharing is critical to preserving Indigenous cultures. "Even if I don't teach Natives," Daniel explained, "if I teach Peter and Paul, as long as they know it, then what I know lives on that much longer." Other reclaimers suggest that they need to "walk the walk" if they "talk the talk" that celebrates acceptance of *all* others. They know how it feels to be called a "wannabe," and they want to "pay forward" the feelings of assurance they experience as participants in the reclaimer community.

"To me, there are no wannabes," Tabatha (Cherokee) said adamantly. "Evidently these people think you're special enough to want to be like you. What's wrong with wanting to learn Indian heritage? . . . I don't see where being a 'wannabe,' or you know, embracing 'wannabes,'" Tabatha continued, "is a bad thing." "They have a need for knowledge and why shouldn't we help with that?" Floyd (Blackfoot- and Ojibwa-identified) said. He agreed that "wannabe" is a "messed-up term" but admitted to using it occasionally. "There are people out there who try too hard," Floyd said. "They don't do things right." Obviously flustered and perhaps feeling guilty, Floyd frowned and shook his head disapprovingly. "Those people shouldn't be ridiculed, you know what I mean? We should go approach them in a good way and try to teach them," he said earnestly. Floyd sighed. "We're all just humans," he offered as justification for his own and "wannabes'" bad behaviors. Sasha (Lakota identified) also agreed that "wannabes" require guidance rather than ridicule. "For the most part, if I encounter people who some people would call wannabes," Sasha said, "I think it's more important to teach and share with them. Why would you want to exclude someone because they want to learn more, you know? It doesn't make sense to me." Sasha, however, also stated that some people have dishonorable intentions: "I understand there have been cases of exploitation and I understand some people are shy of that and I—I am somewhat shy. I kind of feel someone out, you know? Are they trying to use me for their own selfish reasons? Or are they actually trying to do something good?"

Layers of Wannabeness

Whether or not they use the label, most reclaimers agree that wannabes exist. They disagree about *who* fits the description of a wannabe, but the matter is not discussed at reclaimer community meetings due to its "political" nature. Unlike many relocators, who unapologetically swap stories about wannabes at fundraisers, meetings, potlucks, and powwows, individual reclaimers merely raise an eyebrow, lock eyes with a friend, or engage in some other slight gesture to indicate their disapproval of someone's behaviors. The reclaimer community's open-door policy, after all, means that *everyone* is welcome. Even if the "wrong" people enter, the necessarily inclusive philosophy undergirding the reclaimer community's existence prevents community members from turning them away. If someone new to the community, for example, announces that they are the great-great-great-great-great-granddaughter of Chief Joseph, reclaimers—whether they are merely skeptical or outright offended—say nothing. (This announcement, however, provoked at least one unambiguous eye roll.)

As director of the reclaimer organization, Kurt strives to provide community participants and the general public with opportunities to learn about Indigenous peoples and Indigenous affairs. More people listening means more people learning, from Kurt's perspective, so limiting any person's participation in reclaimer community meetings or events is counterproductive. If a non-Native "community supporter," for instance, wants to sing, drum, make regalia, or powwow dance, they are invited into the powwow circle. "Because if you notice at the powwow," Kurt said, "that's one of our things. Come dance! Enjoy life!"

Kurt also knows that some people take advantage of such situations, and he firmly maintains that only people with Indigenous ancestry exerting genuine effort to learn their Indigenous traditions have the right to claim Indigenous identities. Kurt admits he gets frustrated with people who identify as Indian, but "have no clue about their culture at all." These people, according to Kurt, differ from people who *know* they have Native blood and are trying to follow tradition, but just "don't know where or how. And that, sometimes, is your urban American Indian," said Kurt, "whether you want to accept that or not." The fine line distinguishing the former Indian-identified person from the latter complicates things, and Kurt can only encourage reclaimer community participants to represent themselves honestly. Kurt explained, "Because I know individuals who . . . get to a certain point where they've intermingled with us, learnt the culture, learnt the traditions, and the next thing you know, they're [claiming to be] Native! . . . And *then*, next thing you know, they're teaching everybody! And that's fine, but then you start noticing they're putting their own agenda in there somehow, and it becomes like that person in Arizona who was leading the sweat lodge." For Kurt, the bottom line is: everyone is welcome to learn, practice, and even teach Indian ways, but it is *never* okay to exploit Indian identities for personal gain—financial, emotional, or spiritual—and individuals need to be up-front and honest about their *specific* relationship to Indigenous peoples (e.g., ancestry, adoption, culture).

Not all reclaimers, however, share Kurt's perspective on Indian identity claims. For instance, Oda, a formerly white-identified woman in her sixties who only recently began identifying as Indian, said people who "honestly and truly" want "to live and practice the Native ways . . . should be able to and they should be given credit for that." Several reclaimer interview respondents agreed that non-Indian people who practice Indian culture are commendable, not contemptible. Oda further stated, however, "If you walk the Red Road and you want to be a part of the center and you do all the different functions and help and do all those kinds of things, if you want to call yourself a Native, then call yourself a Native because that's what you believe." This interpretation of Indian identity—i.e., people of any ancestry can and should claim Indian identities if they feel like it—is neither representative of reclaimers' perspectives nor completely anomalous. It certainly contradicts Kurt's beliefs and the identity-related customs he tries to nurture among reclaimer community members. By making Indian identity an identity option for *all* people, Oda's statement denationalizes and deracializes indigeneity. Her perspective expunges all past, present, and future experiences of

Indigenous people who are citizens of Indian nations. It falsely reduces indigeneity to spirituality, and though spirituality is central to Indigenous communities, it is multiform and fluid and frequently affixed to Indigenous landscapes that most non-Native people and many urban Native people practicing (pan-)Indian ways will never visit.

Because Oda holds a somewhat esteemed position in the reclaimer community, her interpretation of indigeneity matters. She runs the powwow planning committee and assumes ownership of the powwow. "My powwow is an educational powwow," Oda said assertively. "The more we educate people," Oda continued, "the more people will understand and the better treatment our urban Natives are going to get." Powwow attendees learn, for instance, that Indians live in unexpected places (e.g., Ohio) and have unexpected appearances (e.g., fair skin). Though Oda does not broadcast her interpretations of Indianness at powwows, she undoubtedly impresses her beliefs upon people within and beyond the reclaimer community. In other words, when Oda tells *her* stories, people listening may believe her, and they may pass her stories on to others, who may pass her stories on to others, until the stories assume some semblance of truth to people who know only *untruths* about Indigenous peoples.

And herein lies one problem with the reclaimer community's openness in combination with its fundamentally political "nonpolitical" stance: the collectivity practically encourages ignorance of Indigenous nationhood. Further, it engenders confidence in people who claim Indian identities and assert "Indian" opinions, but due to their lack of knowledge about Indigenous peoples, Indigenous beliefs, Indigenous sovereignty, and/or Indigenous conceptualizations of community and belonging, neither their Indian identities nor their opinions are grounded in *Indigenous* stories and understandings.

The Reclaimer Community's Expansive Boundaries and Too Many Fake People

Reclaimers' interpretations of indigeneity are grounded in their (collective) memories and experiences. Regardless of their families' impacts on their Indian identities, their identification with Indigenous peoples is strengthened by participation in the reclaimer community, a mnemonic site that affirms the memories, stories, and histories of Indian-identified people without (other) Indigenous communities to call home. Community participants' commitments to developing deep, multilayered understandings of their specific Indigenous histories and cultures vary widely. Inevitably, some reclaimers remain committed to Indian identities despite their low levels of commitment to understanding what identifying as an Indigenous person means.

In private conversations, two reclaimers with long-term reservation-based mentors pointed out the problematic behaviors of some reclaimer community members. "There's a lot of people there that are kind of off-kilter," Floyd (Blackfoot- and Ojibwa-identified) said. "Those are the 'wannabes' that you hear talk about, you know?" he continued. "Where they're wearing the felt that looks like leather and the fake eagle feathers," Floyd said gruffly, "and they're out there, going in the parades, going, 'Oh, we're Indian!'" Visibly agitated, Floyd admitted he used to call the community's core members "the Geritol crew."[7] Prior to Kurt's directorship, this core group skewed older. During my participant observation of reclaimer community events, these reclaimers still participated in monthly meetings but did not attend the newly launched drum circle or crafting events. Two of them, a married couple named Harold and Flo, served on the board of directors and agreed to an interview.

Snippets from the interview: Harold's "great-great-great-great grandmother" was "full-blooded. I think it was either Cherokee or Navajo," he remarked. "I'm pretty sure Cherokee, but there was Navajo blood mixed in somewhere along the line." His grandmother had "coal black hair." Flo is "only probably an eighth of Cherokee" but she does not have documentation. "My dad always teased us that he was half coyote and half Indian," Flo said, "but the coyote part wasn't true, but the Indian part, yes." Her grandmother "had this long, beautiful hair that she'd always wear in braids." Sometimes she told Flo stories "about the Indians" and said "she always wanted to live in those teepees."

Harold and Flo do not claim Indian identities on the US Census. They identify as Indians at reclaimer community events and at church, however, and Flo's quilting friends at church ask her endless questions about it. "I explained the Cherokee tear dress to them, and the Trail of Tears. . . . They asked me about the powwows . . . and just different things," Flo recalled. They asked why Flo does not wear her tear dress more often. "They think because you're Cherokee or whatever, they think you should dress like that every day." Flo continued: "I said, on the reservations, I think they do dress like that." "And then we've been in parades," Flo remembered, "so they ask me about the parades. We just ride on the float," Flo said. She and Harold smiled and nodded.

Floyd (Blackfoot- and Ojibwa-identified) and Kenai (Lakota-identified) both insisted that Harold and Flo are "olders," not "elders." Sadly, they said, the couple is not unique among the reclaimer community's senior participants. True elders "stay away from the center," said Kenai, because they will not bring their spiritual practices into a space fraught with "fake people." "They're *here*," Kenai said, affirming the presence of elders in the region, "but they don't advertise it." Floyd agreed, stating that respected elders "[keep] an eye on things" happening in the community, but maintain their distance. "Hopefully Kurt can change that," Kenai said, but conceded, "Kurt's in a bad spot because he can't turn people away." Kenai appreciates Kurt's conundrum. He understands why the reclaimer community is open to everyone and why Kurt is committed to helping (Indigenous) people reclaim Indigenous identities. "That's why I like Kurt, because he puts himself out there," Kenai said. "He takes a lot of hits from a lot of people and I back him up from the background."

But, Kenai said, he will remain in the background because "too many fake people" participate in reclaimer community events. "Because at the Indian Center meeting," Kenai said, "you hear people go [twangy, sing-song falsetto], 'I'm wearing my first Indian dress.'" His mocking tone is moderated by the defeated sigh that escapes from the back of his throat. "I don't know how to feel," Kenai said earnestly. "I mean, there are some people there who are really offensive," he said. "The community *should* be my family," Kenai continued, "but there are just people who don't understand." For instance, Kenai is making a bustle for his son's pow-wow regalia. Theoretically, the bustle is an ideal project to work on during craft and regalia night. Realistically, however, Kenai is not willing to bring his eagle feathers around "those people." "Those people," Kenai said, "don't need to have those things near them. They just don't. So right there, then what do you do?" "And the sad thing is—the *Indians* don't even know," Kenai said, shaking his head. "That's what kills me, like, they don't even know who they are. It just blows me away." But Kenai understands *why* the "really offensive" people get away with acting in "really offensive" ways. "There's too much out there keeping us stereotyped,"

Kenai said, shaking his head. "But that's why I stay away from the community. And that's why a lot of really good people stay away from the community. The community pushes them away."

The Relocator Community Is a Place of Refuge

The nonprofit relocator community organization provides refuge to relocated Northeast Ohio Indians. At community-sponsored events, relocators can relax and be themselves without anyone "bothering [them] about it," as Berta (Lakota) said. "I don't tell people how to be white. I don't tell people how to be black. And, you know, I don't like people telling me how to be Indian," Berta said indignantly. Imposed memories of Indianness in US settler society so completely replace realistic portrayals of Indians that Indigenous people, like Berta, feel stymied in thought, word, and deed. Outsiders' expectations of them as Indians sometimes leave little room for relocators to define and simply *be* themselves. "Like I tell people," said Berta (Lakota), "it's always good just to be with your own people, you know, because you can be free. You don't have to be under a spotlight, you know? People are usually looking at you under a spotlight, saying, 'Oh, Indians do this! Indians do that!' You know, looking at us . . . differently," Berta said, shaking her head. "Then when you're with your friends, you can be yourself, you know? You can be crazy, talk crazy, whatever!"

The relocator community provides space for relocators to be whoever and however they want to be. They are accepted and respected as Indians by other relocators regardless of their appearances, attitudes, cultural aptitudes, or spiritual beliefs. Within the boundaries of the relocator community setting, relocators practice the lesson they impart to their children—there is no right or true or singularly "authentic" way to be Indian. One simply *is* Indian, by birth, blood, and *community recognition*, which is absolutely necessary to being accepted *as* Indian by relocator community members. This constriction of the boundaries of relocator community membership is necessary because relocators cannot risk the infiltration of *their* protected space by non-Indians or non-allies. Except for an occasional new Indian transplant to the Northeast Ohio region, the relocator community primarily expands when relocated families add new members, like the spouse of a recently married grandchild or a newborn great-grandchild.

Relocators, thus, are a fairly tightly knit group. Most families who participate in the community have known each other for decades, and relocators frequently call one another familiar terms like "auntie" and "cousin." They share similar pasts and remembrances that shape their collective identities. As with reclaimers, relocators comprise a mnemonic community, or thought community, that influences the way community members across generations think about and differentiate themselves from Northeast Ohioans and other Indigenous peoples. First-generation relocator elders are "the de facto custodians"[8] of the community's memories, and thereby influence later generations' interpretations of their urbanness and indigeneity. Despite the various reasons relocators migrated to Northeast Ohio—e.g., participating in Indian Relocation, following a relative who participated in Indian Relocation, trailing a spouse with some connection to Northeast Ohio—the story repeatedly told and retold, the jointly remembered story, centers on the painful necessity of leaving home reservations to escape brutal poverty and discrimination. It is a story of forced eviction rather than voluntary migration, though the truth for many relocator families lies somewhere in between. For many first-generation relocators, it is also a story of community building, community support, and community continuity.

Relocators: Family off the Rez

Upon migrating from reservations to Northeast Ohio, first-generation relocators missed the closeness of extended family and friendship networks back home. Participants in the government's Indian Relocation program did not need to look far to find other Indians because the BIA tended to house them in close proximity to one another, in poor, somewhat run-down, "ethnic" (meaning nonwhite) neighborhoods. Many relocators were unhappy with the downtrodden neighborhoods into which their families were placed by BIA authorities. At the same time, however, they felt fortunate to reside near other Indian individuals and families. First-generation relocators reported experiencing homesickness upon moving to the urban environment. They also talked about the crucial support they received from other Indian relocators. Susan (Dakota), for instance, was only nineteen when she came to NE Ohio alone on relocation. She initially shared an apartment with other "girls from different reservations and nations," but all of them eventually moved back home. Susan said she does not think she would have stuck it out in Ohio if she had not found other relocated Indians who made her feel as though she belonged.

Bly (Sioux) was twenty when she moved to Northeast Ohio with her now ex-husband. "I didn't like it," Bly said, "and the reason was because I didn't have no family here . . . so I basically was real lonely and homesick." Bly did not come to Ohio as a participant in the federal Indian Relocation Program, and consequently did not live with or near other Indians. It took her about five years to finally find and connect with the growing network of relocated Indigenous people in the region. "That's when I started realizing that [Native companionship] was something I really needed," Bly said. She needed to be connected with other people to whom she could relate, people who understood her, who shared some of her perspectives. Bly explained, "Because even though we're different nations, we all have the basic teachings from our grandpas and our grandmas. We're told that even though we are from different nations, that we have to respect each other. . . . We know it's important for community, that's number one. We're not supposed to be at all complacent. We're supposed to think of others all the time. It's not about us. That's what has been a problem with the European way of thinking and us. . . . You're only *one*. That one is important, yes, but it's better to be part of everybody." "That's why you have to be part of a community," Bly said. "You're supposed to think of yourself as being little, little. Just barely a small part of the whole." Bly still relies on the family-like support she receives from members of the pan-Indian relocator community. "I've always wanted to go back [home] and be around my mom and my dad," Bly said. "What happens, though, of course, as we live here, we raise our families here, we establish roots. We have more roots here."

Second-generation relocators who regularly communed with other Indians agreed: there is something special about their relationships with other Indians, whether or not they share specific cultural customs. "I think when you identify with your group," said Samantha (Cherokee, second generation), "then you don't even have to talk about it, being Indian, but you just feel that. I don't know how to explain it. You just feel inside that there's some kind of connection." Melissa (Native Hawaiian–identified, second generation) said that urban Native people need "a place to get together, where you identify with other people and can be yourself and be comfortable." Her vision for the future is a "self-sustaining" relocator community organization that permanently provides urban Native children with a space of belonging, a place where, in Melissa's words, "our kids aren't part of a minority, they feel they're more of the majority." A place where young people never have to hear people say things like, "Wow! There's still Indians out there?!" "I've heard it I don't know how many times over the last twenty years!" Melissa said, throwing up her hands.

The Relocator Community and Necessary Continuity

Many relocators share Melissa's concerns regarding the community's children and community continuity. After centuries of struggle to maintain indigeneity, assimilation into settler culture is not an option. Several relocators said that the community exists for their children, their grandchildren, and their great-grandchildren (etc.). Yes, adult community members depend on one another for social, emotional, and financial support, but the relocator community must continue for the sake of past, present, and future urban Indian people. They want their children to be proud to be Indian. And they want them to pass their Indian belief systems and Indian identities to future generations. Continuity is everything, and many early-generation relocators agree that continuity requires instilling Native pride in the community's young people and eliminating pretendians.

Relocator community gatherings occurred at regular intervals throughout the calendar year. A core group of mostly women elders led by Berta met monthly to organize the community's biggest events, primarily holiday parties, a back-to-school barbecue, and a small powwow when financially feasible. The women elders, all first-generation relocators, were the community's movers and shakers. Melissa (Native Hawaiian–identified) was the only second-generation community member who regularly participated in planning meetings. She assumed more and more responsibilities as Berta's health declined. The women's husbands usually accompanied them to meetings, but the men stayed in the background, often babysitting grandchildren. Activities and events were planned with utmost consideration for the community's children, even when children did not participate. Protests against the Cleveland MLB team's Native-themed mascotry (i.e., the most visible form of pretend Indianness in Northeast Ohio), were frequently child-free because many relocators chose not to expose young children to the abuses of Cleveland baseball fans. The point of the protests, however, was to transform the NE Ohio environment in ways that enabled Indigenous young people to thrive in the future. Nevertheless, most community events are child-friendly because adult relocators understand how important it is for their children and "grandbabies" to engage in the warm, safe space of an all-Indian (and a few allies) gathering—a place where they are not outsiders called "chiefs" or "wahoos," but where they feel like part of a "majority," as Melissa said.

Relocators celebrated major (frequently religious) US holidays together, just as many of them would celebrate these occasions with extended kinship networks back home. The holiday mainstays included an Easter egg hunt, Harvest Dinner, and two Christmas parties, a smaller, more intimate potluck attended primarily by first-generation relocators and a bigger pizza party and gift giveaway for anyone with children, grandchildren, and/or great-grandchildren. With the exception of the former (adult) Christmas party, each event typically had between eighty and one hundred attendees who varied not only ethnically across tribe and nation but also across myriad other social demographics, including age, race, class, religion, sexuality, and dis/ability. The racial diversity primarily came from out-dating and out-marriage in relocators' families—the children and grandchildren of first-generation relocators frequently partnered with white-, Hispanic-, or black-identified people, creating multiracial families and an increasingly multiracial pan-Indian community. Non-Indian members of the multiracial protest group also added some racial-ethnic diversity to relocator community events.

The Harvest Dinner and Christmas parties are community events that occur annually regardless of resource availability. Relocator women elders hustle to make them happen. For instance, the Harvest Dinner, held the Wednesday before Thanksgiving, often requires donated church space and donated turkeys. Collectively, a handful of women elders spend weeks preparing for this event. They cook all the turkeys and hams, make the stuffing, boil and mash the potatoes, and acquire all the needed coffee, soda, and gallon jug "juice." The evening of the dinner, while the majority of community members sit around tables, leisurely chatting about the latest community news and gossip, the women elders—who shoo nearly everyone else out of the kitchen—labor intensively. They sort all the side dishes and desserts donated by community members, serve the entire community their meals, sort the leftovers and create care packages for the neediest relocator families, and clean up after everyone—all before many of the women head home to carry out the same tasks on a smaller scale the next day.

The Christmas parties also require some work. The adult party is a potluck with plenty of games and giveaways and a Secret Santa gift exchange. The children's party entails acquiring, mostly through solicited donations, gifts for the community's young people. Upwards of thirty children, 'tweens, and teens attend the party each year, and everyone receives one or more presents. One year, for instance, the younger children unwrapped Curious George and Raggedy Ann books, dolls, Legos, and lip gloss, and the teenagers received ten-dollar movie theater gift cards. Everyone in attendance was treated to pizza, chips, soda, and swimming.

The Easter egg hunt is also a big hit with adults and children. Community members, Melissa (Native Hawaiian–identified) suggested, "probably" like this springtime event so much because it gives them an opportunity to "see how everybody's been doing, what babies were born, and what we missed over the winter." Weather permitting, the Easter gathering is held in a Cleveland-area metro park. Hamburgers, hot dogs, and other barbeque necessities (e.g., buns and condiments) are provided by the multiracial protest organization, while the relocator community organization supplies Easter baskets and monetary prizes for egg hunt winners. Event attendees are asked to bring side dishes or desserts to share or, alternately, a dozen decorated hard-boiled eggs to hide. To spice things up, both hard-boiled eggs and plastic eggs with cash inside are hidden all over the park grounds. After the community prays and eats together, approximately eight different egg-hunting expeditions ensue—one for each age group, starting with mere babes (who must be carried around the grounds by parents or siblings) and ending with the adult hunt, for which the competition is just as fierce as any of the youths' groups. Each round of hunts garners the enthusiasm of onlookers who cheer, taunt, and tease participants scrambling around the park grounds searching for money-filled eggs.

Aside from (most) participants' indigeneity, these relocator community gatherings may appear (to the non-Indian onlooker) indistinguishable from holiday celebrations of (Christian) non-Native people in the Northeast Ohio region. As Bly stated, non-Indians attending these events might think, "Okay, this is just a dinner. We're gonna eat, munch down, whatever, gifts will be involved maybe. But it's more than that," Bly explained. "Physically we sit and talk and whatever, but . . . it's more spiritual." Because relocators hail from diverse Indian nations across the United States, each relocator family's traditional spiritual ceremonies and cultural celebrations are unique. It is somewhat impractical to practice these traditions alone, so far from home, and doing so does not foster *pan-Indian* community. Yet, for many relocators, community is central to indigeneity and key to urban Indian continuity. If relocators want their children and grandchildren "to think of others all the time," to understand that they are "a small part of the whole" (as Bly stated), the community must be a true collectivity. Creating and maintaining the collective identity of diverse members of an intergenerational pan-Indian community, however, means finding common ground—and due to the centuries-long imposition of settler customs and memories on Indigenous peoples and communities, culturally homogeneous US celebrations provide a sense of home and a source of comfort for many Indigenous people, whether they grew up in reservation, rural, suburban, or urban environments.

As discussed in chapter 5, powwows also constitute "common ground" in the pan-Indian relocator community. Adult relocators enjoy powwows and generally agree that powwow dancing benefits the community's youth by improving their cultural proficiency and increasing their Native pride. After receiving a small grant, John (Diné) organized monthly dance classes for relocator youth. The classes were a community affair, with relocator men drumming and singing and relocator women chatting and observing while John taught the children "western-style" dancing in a musty church basement. That all the children, regardless of tribal affiliation, learned western dances was a point of contention for some relocator community members, but John was Diné, so western style was the only style he knew.

The fact of the matter is that communal lessons for young relocators primarily contained pan-Indian content. Community elders resigned themselves to this reality years ago. Second- and later-generation relocator youth were collectively socialized to be proud of their Indigenous heritages, but many of these youth were estranged from their specific tribal cultures. As Sandra (Native- and Mexican-identified), a third-generation relocator, stated, "We're all kind of the same *because* we're here in Ohio. It's a weird part of the country for Natives."

Relocators: Promoting Counterstories

In addition to community gatherings meant to foster and maintain relationships between relocated Indians in Northeast Ohio, relocators strategically participate in numerous (non-Native) regional events each year. The same group of women elders who organize the former also determine community participation in the latter. The women almost always choose events that accomplish two or three community goals simultaneously, usually some combination of fundraising, educational outreach, and nurturing pride in the community's youth. Participating in such events means stepping outside the safe space of the community's restrictive boundaries, but the women elders who comprise the community's unofficial "steering committee" understand that resistance goes hand in hand with persistence. Relocators need money to fund community gatherings. To raise money, they need Northeast Ohio individuals and institutions to recognize their *existence* as twenty-first-century, urban Indian *people*. To obtain recognition, relocators must strategically counter the settler-constructed, imposed memories that distort most Northeast Ohioans' perceptions and understandings of Indigenous peoples.

Relocators know they must create and promote countermemories[9] that challenge dominant discourses about Indianness, including deceptive "memories" of Indians as historical relics and ferocious (or, in the case of Cleveland, happy-go-lucky) mascots. Relocators contest these ideas by asserting their Indigenous identities in white-dominated spaces. Sometimes they attend long-standing regional events like the small-town Heritage Days festival (briefly discussed in chapter 6), replete with actors in cowboy costumes engaged in "Wild West"–style theatrics. Relocator adults come as they are—as urban Indigenous people wearing everyday clothes—and sell Indian foodstuffs like fry bread, Indian tacos, and *wojape* (berry pudding) to raise money for the community. The mere *presence* of relocators, who intentionally assert their Indian identities in "unexpected places," is educational for many Ohioans.

Relocator youth powwow dance in full regalia at some regional events. In some years they participate in Cleveland's IngenuityFest, for instance, dubbed an exploration of "the boundaries of art and technology." For many IngenuityFest attendees, Indigenous people dancing at a celebration of innovation and entrepreneurship seems counterintuitive.

Similar to the sale of Indian foodstuffs, the youth's public performances show event attendees that Indigenous peoples and cultures continue to adapt and persist, even in colonized urban (and suburban) spaces. Further, Indian youth get an opportunity to practice their culture in a relatively friendly space, which boosts their confidence. Such opportunities, said Berta, are necessary to instill Native pride in children descended from people who "survived over five hundred years in the Americas with our language and our religion." Though Northeast Ohio relocators are no longer able to speak their Indigenous languages, this sentiment coheres with the remembered and retold stories of US Indigenous peoples more generally, some of whom, like many of Berta's reservation-based kin, primarily speak their Indigenous languages.

Relocators also work with community partners to create new fundraising and educational events. They partnered with the Native American Student Association (NASA) of a regional liberal arts college, for instance, to sponsor a cake walk fundraiser that included Indigenous dancing demonstrations by relocator youth. At the time, this particular NASA chapter had no Indigenous (or Indigenous-identified) members, so the cake walk was held to raise money exclusively for the relocator community's (almost) annual powwow. One year, the relocator community and the (Native-themed mascot) protest organization cosponsored a psychic fair benefit. Though some relocators disapproved of inhabiting a "new age" space, others determined that the potential profits outweighed the potential pitfalls. The latter relocators spent the day selling Indian goods—everything from Indian tacos to cookie pops decorated with the American Indian Movement logo to Berta's beaded jewelry—alongside a white woman selling self-help books, crystals, semiprecious stones and pendants, sage, and tobacco pouches for "spiritual use" decorated with the silhouette of an Indian smoking a long pipe. On the upside (according to relocators who championed this fundraising opportunity), the three-dollar entrance fee paid by every psychic fair attendee (predominantly middle-aged white women) was pure profit for the relocator community. Additionally, relocator youth demonstrated powwow dancing styles to a crowd of enthusiastic onlookers. Between dances, John (Diné), the youths' dance instructor and the community's ad hoc emcee, talked about how hard the children practice to learn the different dances and how they are encouraged to improvise, taking cues from the drummers and moving in ways that feel right to them. John also informed spectators about the origins of different dances and explained the importance of the children's participation in the dance troupe to the Northeast Ohio (relocator) Native community's persistence.

The relocator community's cosponsored psychic fair provides an interesting illustration of the clever means by which relocators teach NE Ohioans important lessons about indigeneity. Adult relocators know that most people's fascination with Indianness is based on stereotypical, settler-constructed stories about Indigenous people. These romanticized fictions associate Indigenous people and spiritualities with mysticism, witchcraft, and other "new age" practices that go hand in hand with psychics and other mediums. Relocators cleverly manipulate audience members' expectations by hosting a psychic fair, and then they use the opportunity to engage Northeast Ohioans in deeper conversations about Indigenous realities. Anthropologist Laura Peers discusses this phenomenon in terms of a "Native performers' gaze" that counteracts the "tourists' gaze."[10] Peers's ethnographic research at living historical sites featuring Native interpreters revealed that Native interpreters' public performances *seem* to reinforce stereotypes about Indianness but are actually quite strategic. Native interpreters are not, as previous scholars suggested, colonial pawns dutifully enacting the roles settler society constructed for them. Rather, Peers argues, Indigenous people use "bait and switch" tactics, basically "playing Indian" as audience members imagine they should, and then pursuing educational agendas once the audience is hooked.

Another illustration of this strategy in action comes from relocators' participation in a "family day" event at one of the region's premier art museums. Relocators seize such opportunities to occupy influential spaces while challenging dominant discourses about Indigenous people. This particular event coincided with the opening day of an exhibition of North American Indian art spanning two thousand years. Exhibit items, grouped according to region (e.g., Alaska, California, Great Plains, Northeast), included cascading warrior headdresses and medicine masks, ladles, pottery, statues, daggers, regalia, beads and feathers, hunting gear, robes, moccasins, and jewelry. Relocators' agreed-upon roles at this event included crafting and dancing demonstrations. Just outside the art exhibition entrance, "live" Indians exhibited their crafting skills and wares. Marla, a Diné elder, beaded on a loom. Eleanor, a middle-aged Cherokee woman, stretched leather across the wooden base of a drum. Berta, unable to craft that day because she had recently had (a second) surgery to accelerate the flow of filtered blood returning to her body during dialysis treatments, sat near half-beaded moccasins and numerous dream catchers. Occasionally she explained her temporary inability to work on the moccasins to a museum guest, concluding, "And wouldn't you know it, everyone is in need of new moccasins right now and I'm the only person who can make *and* bead them!"

Adults meandered through this live exhibition space while children attended hands-on activities. Though some children's activities were supervised by members of the relocator community, one of the more popular sessions was directed by (non-Native) museum employees. During this arts-and-crafts "workshop," children used scissors, glue, crayons, and markers to construct "Indian" masks. The juxtaposition of the children's paper masks and the exhibit's medicine masks elucidates the "Native performers' gaze." Relocators strategically tolerated the former to ensure museum goers' (and their children's) exposure to the latter. At the workshop's conclusion, parents and guardians retrieved their chortling, shrieking, paper-mask-wearing children and escorted them down the crowded hallways toward the next exhibit. Many rushed upstairs toward the museum auditorium where one of the main exhibits, live Native dancing, began anew every hour on the hour. A surprising number of exhibit attendees unabashedly wore Wahoo on baseball hats, t-shirts, sweatshirts, and socks. One woman sported a leather jacket adorned with a sparkling applique Wahoo face.

The Native dancing exhibition, emceed by John (Diné), also elucidates the Native performers' gaze. Consider the following scene:

Audience members file into a dark auditorium. They hear shrill vocals and steady drumbeats. A spotlight shines on a large drum, encircled by Indian men. The music stops abruptly and John slowly rises from his seat. A spotlight follows John as he walks, stern-faced, across the stage. The audience, mesmerized and holding its collective breath, waits to see what happens next. The only sounds are the swishing and tinkling of John's regalia. Suddenly, the auditorium brightens and John grabs the microphone. Smiling broadly, he welcomes the audience and asks—"Did I look stoic? Because that is the look I hoped to achieve," he says, giggling, "but it's hard! We Indians prefer to laugh!" The audience chuckles.

As with the psychic fair, John regales the audience with stories about different dances performed by the dance troupe. When announcing the jingle dance, for instance, he explains that American feminism started in the 1920s, but feminism began earlier for US Indigenous women, who began dancing jingle around the turn of the twentieth century. "It was their way of telling the men," John begins, then he thrusts his hip to the side, wags his finger, and in his best falsetto, says, "You are not so special! We can dance fancy, too!" The audience erupts in laughter. When they settle, John gives them a lesson on this style of dance, elaborating on its history and its regalia. As John explains how jingle dancers' clockwise movement around the powwow circle, like the rising and setting sun, keeps them in harmonious balance with the earth, his captivated audience hangs on every word. "And you won't learn these things in school," John says, "or attending Cleveland Ind–." After a pregnant pause, John pretends to regain his composure, then resumes, "attending *games*." The audience gets the joke and responds positively with laughter and applause. John warns audience members to be wary of Cleveland's other "Indians," who are much less friendly than the Indians here today. Again the audience laughs, and John thanks them for coming.

"Family day" at the art museum reveals numerous tensions intrinsic to celebrating urban Indigenous cultures in twenty-first-century cities. Museum administrators' inclusion of relocators in planning the art exhibition's opening-day festivities indicates a constructive attempt to highlight the perspectives of a marginalized group.[11] Relocators were *invited* to present their truths to museum goers, many of whom were white, middle- to upper-class Northeast Ohio residents with more exposure to fraudulent Indianness than actual Indigenous peoples. One might suggest, however, that relocators' live exhibitions, which demonstrated traditional and ceremonial activities, may have reified tropes about anachronistic Indianness. Museum goers arguably might have benefited from candid conversations with relocators discussing their daily struggles, like resisting the negative impacts of stereotypes about Indigenous peoples. Because museum personnel perceived numerous topics (e.g., the Cleveland MLB team's inappropriate use of Native-themed mascotry) as potentially offensive to museum patrons, relocators had to improvise. While celebrating the Indigenous cultures on display at the museum, relocators shared stories countering dominant ideas about

Indigenous peoples. And they were sure to make several pointed statements about the region's problematic Native-themed imagery.

Weeding Out Wannabes: Contracting Relocator Community Boundaries

In addition to organizing community gatherings and participating in public exhibitions, relocator adults see another practice as essential to community building and community persistence: weeding out wannabes. For decades, relocator elders purposefully contracted the boundaries of their urban Indian community to protect themselves, their children, and their grandchildren from outsiders and other threats (e.g., pretendians). Relocators across generation shared some weariness about Indian-identified people they did not know through *some* Indigenous network, but first-generation relocators were most vigilant about monitoring community boundaries. Pretend Indianness had been a problem for relocators for decades. Over the years, some relocators even accused other relocators of being pretendians. Bly (Sioux), for example, talked about some relocators' suspicions about a former relocator community director. "There was always a discrepancy about [him] because they said he was a wannabe Indian," Bly said. "Because if you walked to the door, he looked like a white guy. And I guess he changed his name to Clement Thunderclap. . . . Some of our Native people were having a heartburn about that. Personally," Bly continued, "I didn't feel that way. I said, 'Well, he's doing something for the community. Who else is going to do it?'" A final verdict regarding the (pretend) Indianness of many of the accused, including Clement Thunderclap, was never reached.

With respect to some individuals, however, relocator elders' misgivings were substantiated, as in the case of another man who once (decades earlier) occupied a leadership position in the community. Due to community disharmony, the man split off from the relocator community and founded a different, competing nonprofit organization for Native people in NE Ohio. Though first-generation relocators accused the man of being a wannabe for decades, his duplicitousness was not publicly revealed until 2018, when he pleaded guilty in federal court to embezzling seventy-seven thousand dollars in grant money meant for Northeast Ohio's Indigenous people via the nonprofit he founded and served as executive director. (Whether or not this man could document his Indian identity claims became a moot point for relocator community members. Notably, local news writers reporting on his embezzlement conviction stated unambiguously that he was from the tribe that *he* claimed but that did not claim him.) Neither this man's indictment nor his guilty plea surprised relocator elders, who always said he was "underhanded," "unscrupulous," and "exploitative."

Though later-generation relocators did not share the first generation's complicated history with this particular man, they unfortunately shared with each other the disheartening experience of growing up in a divided Native community. As a result, later-generation relocators did not perceive the community's exclusiveness as an effective maintenance strategy. Rather, they disapproved of what they saw as the community's divisiveness. In fact, every relocator interview respondent under fifty who grew up in NE Ohio expressed interest in quelling disputes between differently aligned groups of Indigenous and Indigenous-identified people in the Northeast Ohio region.[12] Keep in mind, however, that I captured their perspectives on the issue *prior to* the federal indictment of the Indian-identified man discussed above. From first-generation relocators' perspectives, he was the man primarily responsible for discord in the community.

Sandra (Native- and Mexican-identified, third generation) summed up her experiences as a young person in the relocator community this way: "If there's one thing that should be said for the Native people in this area, there needs to be some sort of togetherness." Samantha (Cherokee, second generation), approximately the same age as Sandra, remembers feeling a sense of "togetherness" in her childhood, but said things changed by the time she reached her teens: "As I've gotten older, it seems the different groups in Cleveland, the different Native organizations, are more politically divided. And some of them are very hostile toward each other. So I think that makes it very uncomfortable. . . . And that is disappointing because I would like to be around other Native people, but that uncomfortable feeling is not worth it." Unlike Samantha, who participates less often in the community due to what she perceives as community disunity, Melissa (Native Hawaiian–identified, second generation) participates more than she had previously. Her deeper level of involvement, however, did not give her a different perspective on the issue. Melissa explained why she thinks the community needs to quash old disputes and move forward:

> Maybe because I've been a part of [the relocator community] for twenty years, I see the turmoil between everybody? And I'd like to see that dissipate and I'd like to see everybody finally get along and strive for one common objective: our kids. And it's always been our kids, but we've been sidetracked here and sidetracked there and forgot what the focus was. . . . And if they could just, I don't know—just all get along [laughing], it would be, *we'd* be a stronger community. Our kids wouldn't have to hear, "For real?! You're Indian?" They wouldn't have to hear that anymore.

In contrast to many later-generation relocators, Melissa was fully committed to the continuation of the relocator community—for her child, and for the community's children. And she was willing to work for it.

Later-Generation Relocators' Community Involvement

Young people between twenty and fifty years of age attended large functions, such as the annual Easter egg hunt and the Harvest Dinner, but generally did not help with the organization or administration of relocator community events. Melissa (Native Hawaiian–identified), who was like a daughter-in-law to Berta and also mother to one of Berta's grandchildren, was the exception to this general rule.[13] As Berta's health failed, Melissa took on more and more responsibilities regarding the administration of community affairs. During our interview, Berta expressed disappointment in young relocators' (general) lack of involvement. "Like I tell people, we [elders] can't be here all the time," Berta said. "I don't mind doing some of the stuff, but the whole big portion of it, I want to go to some of the younger people, you know, so they can learn." Berta praised Melissa for taking "initiative" and working to keep Indigenous culture part of "everyday life" for Indigenous residents of NE Ohio: "One girl I was teaching—you know Melissa—I would take her with me to every meeting with the city, just to get her [acclimated], and she was scared. She was scared to talk, she was scared to do anything. And she's doing *really* good now! She can speak up and do a lot of the stuff herself. But when I first got her in it . . . I used to have to go to everything with her. But now she goes to a lot of stuff, initiative on her own. So I wish more of our children were like that," Berta said with a sigh, "getting more involved in it. I mean, it is hard to survive in the city because you have to work to survive." Berta was proud of Melissa's commitment to the community, and of the progress she had made in her new (quasi) leadership role. "You know," Berta said, "that part of our culture is still pretty much part of our everyday life."

Melissa continued her efforts to bring community members together, but admitted she occasionally felt discouraged. Melissa said she tried but failed to engage more of the community's young people—specifically, later-generation relocators in their twenties, thirties, and forties. She was hesitant to share her discoveries. "How do I say this?" she asked, equivocating. "They don't like some people," Melissa said, "or they've had bad experiences with some people from [the community]. So they tend to step back and be in the background more." Gertrude (Cayuga, first generation), a community elder, said she had similar conversations with people about their lack of participation in community affairs. Although "there's plenty of Indians in [the] area," Gertrude said, "a lot of people . . . have been there, they've tried it, and they don't like what they see, so they get out."

Across generations, relocators feared their community organization, in its current configuration, was in danger of collapse. Their concerns revolved around community elders' degenerating health and community young people's lack of engagement. In casual conversation at a Harvest Dinner, Marla, a Diné elder, articulated both concerns. Marla noted that her children were at the dinner, but did not help with any preparations necessary to make it a success. In her opinion, she said, her children take too many things for granted. More importantly than prepping community dinners, they recuse themselves from learning crucial Indigenous knowledges. They seem to think community elders like herself will retain the needed stories, the stories she learned from her grandmother and grandfather. But Marla knows she will not be around forever. She expressed concern about the (potential) failure of the next generation to pick up where community elders eventually must leave off. Two community elders nodded in agreement as Marla spoke. With Berta ill and first-generation relocators advancing in age, the two elders speaking with Marla agreed it was past time for young people to "step up."

Melissa (Native Hawaiian–identified) described the community's situation as "a changing of the guards." "It's up to my generation to take up the slack," she explained. Her failed efforts to engage people her age, however, made her somewhat apprehensive about the community's future. Melissa knew she needed a community of people behind her and she was disappointed by younger relocators' lack of interest and/or engagement. Some, like twenty-something Sandra (Native- and Mexican-identified, third generation), noted the increasing age of community elders, yet seemed unwilling even to consider themselves responsible for the community's continuity: "Everyone's getting old. They are. Everyone keeping it [the community] together is now in their sixties. I mean, in another ten years, who is going to be doing it? So that's the big question. What's going to happen in the next ten to fifteen years? And I don't think they [community elders] like to think about that. I'm sure they know it, but they don't say anything." Sandra did not know that community elders, including her grandparents, talked frequently about this issue. She did not know because she was not involved in community affairs. Moreover, Sasha seemed to think "they," meaning community elders, were responsible for keeping the community alive. "I don't know if they'll be able to keep it alive forever," she concluded matter-of-factly.

This question of why second- and later-generation relocators (aside from Melissa) were not "taking up the slack" created by aging community leaders is critically important and utterly complex. Perhaps, as a few relocator elders suggested, the community's young people simply were not motivated to exert themselves for the greater good of the community. This explanation parallels Theresa O'Nell's accounts of elders on the Flathead Reservation. In the course of O'Nell's research, she discovered that Flathead elders blamed the disappearance of "really Indians" on "the younger generations' rejection of the [elders'] teachings." Recall from my discussion of Indian identities in chapter 1 that "really Indians," according to O'Nell, are conceptualized as Indians who fill the "empty center" of the concentric-circles heuristic used to indicate more or less "authentic" Indian identities. Youths' "lack of obedience," Flathead elders suggested, was responsible for fault lines in the structure and substance of Indigenous identities.

I suggest that the problem is more elaborately *entangled* with O'Brien's "empty center." Due to serious threats to the relocator community caused by pretendians and other people intent on exploiting Indigenous identities and resources, first-generation relocators justifiably espoused "rhetoric" regarding who (within and outside the community) is "more or less" Indian. Second- and later-generation relocators who feel *less* Indian because aspects of their existence are misaligned with points along the (settler-constructed) "really Indian" yardstick—e.g., they live in urban environments, they are multiracial ("mixed blood"), they cannot speak Indigenous languages—may believe they are too far removed from the "empty center" to adequately fulfill community leadership roles.

Melissa's story is illustrative. Melissa (Native Hawaiian–identified) did not think she was the "right" person to represent the community because she did not know her Native Hawaiian culture. Melissa's mother was only nineteen when she married Melissa's white father, who was stationed at a Hawaiian Army base. When she moved with him to the "mainland" and had children, she did not think it worthwhile to teach her children her language (though she regrets this decision now). According to Melissa, her mother did not practice any elements of Hawaiian culture. "My mom's family [in Hawaii] has forgotten their traditional roots," Melissa explained. "They're just Christians now. They don't easily identify with being traditional Hawaiians." When Melissa *really* thinks about how she was raised, however, she realizes that her mother engrained in her a sense of responsibility to something greater than herself, to a *community* of people. At her mother's house, Melissa's friends were always welcomed and cared for. Her mother cared for other children, too, like her cousin when he needed a place to stay. "That could go back to the way *she* was brought up," Melissa said thoughtfully, "being a Native Hawaiian, having that 'it takes a tribe' mentality." Melissa connected this idea to her own understandings and experiences. She explained that she had recently assumed guardianship of a small girl child, her friend's daughter. "I never gave it a second thought to take her in when she needed me," Melissa said.

The more deeply Melissa became involved in relocator community organizing, the more she understood her perspective, her "sense of community," as a value passed down to her from her mother. "That's what she brought with her [from Hawaii]," Melissa said. "And that's what she gave us. And this is what we're giving our kids." Melissa sees connections (that she previously could not see) between her perspective and the perspectives of relocator elders. "Even though we're all different nations, we're all still one community. If one person needs help and we can offer it, then that's what we do," Melissa explained. Melissa expressed gratitude to relocator elders whose mentorship taught her that her identity experiences paralleled the experiences of unknown numbers of Indigenous (and Indigenous-identified) people who yearned for more understanding and deeper engagement with their Indigenous heritages. Relocator elders taught her that she mattered to the relocator pan-Indian community, that she *belonged*.

> They just, the people of [the relocator community], I guess, made it okay that I didn't know. And they let me know it was okay to want to know more. I don't know if that sounds crazy! And to be wary of *how* I learn, like I said, [because of] what people did with Native culture in books, history books, and stuff like that. It's okay that I don't know, and I understand that . . . I'll probably never know the whole story, never know *my* whole history. And, it's okay. And I guess I've learned that from the people here.

For Melissa, providing the community's young people with this sense of community and belonging is the most important thing relocators can do. In fact, when asked about the specific needs of urban Native people, Melissa responded, "I think, in Cleveland, just having a place to get together, to know where you can identify with other people and be yourself and be comfortable is what the original plan was. You know, someplace for our kids to be comfortable, to not have to feel the pressures of 'Are you *this*? Are you *that*?' They can just be themselves with their people." Most relocators agreed that this goal—providing urban Indigenous people with a warm, hospitable gathering space— necessitated *some* constriction of community boundaries. Relocators did not *want* to spend time delineating between "more or less" Indians and pretendians, but they also understood the necessity of doing so in a society that ostracizes, invisibilizes, and romanticizes Indigenous peoples in ways that create blurred boundaries between Indigenous people and Indian impersonators. These blurred boundaries result from settler-colonial structures and processes set in motion centuries ago and still working continuously to eliminate Indigenous peoples. Like members of long-standing Indigenous communities, members of the NE Ohio pan-Indian relocator community continue to bend and adapt, modify and shift their practices and perspectives just enough to maintain the vitality of their stories, memories, and identities.

Postscript

Despite relocators' concerns regarding community persistence, at the time of this writing (a decade following my participation and interviews with community members), the relocator community continues working to provide relocated Indians with a home away from home—a space for communion, connectedness, support, and celebration. Relocator community members' investments of time and energy, both with respect to resisting false memories of Indianness and infusing Northeast Ohio spaces with countermemories that elucidate more authentic Indigenous realities, have succeeded in making the NE Ohio region a more habitable, less hostile place for Indigenous people to live. Relocator elders' constriction of community boundaries did not cause a mass divestment of second- and later-generation relocators from the community. Rather, the community remains a safe space for Indigenous people to be Indians (as Berta stated) "without people bothering them about it."

The reclaimer community, in contrast, primarily served Indian-identified people working to reclaim Indigenous traditions. In attempts to provide a welcoming environment for reclaimers across tribal enrollment statuses, this community strategically expanded its boundaries. Though the point of full inclusivity was to educate a broader swath of the region's Native and non-Native residents, some reclaimer community members, including people claiming Indian identities, unwittingly said and did things that perpetuated rather than diminished ignorance and untruths about Indigenous peoples. A small number of reclaimer community members suggested that problematic, disinvested "reclaimers" stifled the community participation of much-needed Indigenous elders. These community members also said they understood why some reclaimers, i.e., persons more invested in their Indigenous identities, wished neither to associate with fake Indians nor to share their sacred stories with them. Due to financial difficulties, the reclaimer community's 501c3 nonprofit organization did not survive the COVID-19 pandemic.

Conclusion

History is not a book, arbitrarily divided into chapters, or a
drama chopped into separate acts: it has flowed forward. . . .
What has accumulated in this place acts on everyone, day
and night, like an extra climate.
—Elizabeth Bowen, *A Time in Rome*

The stories, memories, and remembered histories of Indigenous and
Indigenous-identified people in Northeast Ohio occupy the pages of this
book. They are stories accumulated across generations. Over time they
shifted, twisted, merged, and changed in ways that both reveal and veil
subtle truths of the past and present. Relocators' and reclaimers' stories
are personally experienced, but socially composed. They emerge from
different social realms—families, organizations, communities, geo-
graphical regions, and nations—where they uniquely are refashioned
and reformed, remembered and repeated. These stories and memories
ultimately flow forward as collective truths, almost imperceptibly acting
on the people they touch and furtively revising associations between the
past and its entangled present.

This project draws on social-memory and settler-colonial studies to
elucidate the various ways distant and adjacent pasts shape the distinct
stories, memories, and perspectives of relocator and reclaimer community members. As Indians who relocated to urban environments
(relocators) and urban residents reclaiming Indian identities (reclaimers), their stories and memories are often eclipsed by other accounts
of indigeneity in the United States. Yet, as Foucault noted, memory is
"an important factor in struggle" because controlling a people's memory
inevitably "controls their dynamism."[1] Unveiling and understanding the
stories and memories of relocators and reclaimers, therefore, helps expose the persistence of Indigenous peoples and communities in spite
of US settler colonialism. It also reveals some of the *density*[2] of indige-

neity by exploring the subject positions of Indigenous people who live in urban settings and participate in pan-Indian communities. Finally, it uncovers problematic Indian identities created by racializing forces and settler-imposed memories that falsely construct Indianness in the United States.

The continuing structure of US settler colonialism is central to the identity experiences described in this book. White settlers racialized Indigenous people to justify innumerable acts of violence against them, including genocide, forced migration, and forced assimilation into US society. Aside from resistance efforts of Indigenous peoples themselves, these acts of physical violence endure relatively unobstructed due to the erasure of Indigenous peoples' stories and memories. Carefully constructed mythologies about Indians exoticize their pasts and remove them from contemporary landscapes. "Official" versions of US history replace Indigenous peoples' past and present realities with settler-imposed memories that reify US settler society's assumed "legitimacy." These imposed memories naturalize Indigenous peoples' oppression and departicularize Indigenous peoples' experiences, amalgamating diverse Indigenous peoples, communities, and cultures into an immutable, ahistorical "Indian Imaginary" that masquerades as Indianness today.

This imagined Indian remains dominant in the Northeast Ohio environment, where the logics of white possession operate at a fever pitch. The near total erasure of the region's Indigenous histories, coupled with the inculcation of regional space with settler-constructed images of (romanticized) Indianness, create an environment that objectifies Indigenous peoples and obfuscates their realities. These phenomena also inspire non-Indians (and some Indians) to "play Indian," which creates ambiguous boundaries between Indian people and Indian impersonators. Amid this cultural clutter, relocators and reclaimers assert different understandings of indigeneity and countermemories that overlap, intersect, and contradict settler-imposed images and memories of Indianness. Taken together, relocators' and reclaimers' dissimilar but interconnected stories provide needed insights into the continuing impacts of settler colonialism and white supremacy on urban Indigenous people living in the United States today.

Different Pathways

This project empirically demonstrates important differences in how Indigenous and Indigenous-identified people in Northeast Ohio think about "Indianness" and (consequently) experience "Indian" identities. These distinctions generally align with respondents' routes to "urban" *and* "Indian" identities (i.e., relocation or reclamation). First-generation relocators, for instance, experience their identities as something they simply are, an identity born of blood and experience. Their families *persisted* despite the traumas inflicted on them as Indigenous peoples, and relocator elders remember these traumas because they experienced them and/or learned about them from siblings, parents, and grandparents. They also remember many of their traditional ways. They lost some things, like their Indigenous languages, and cannot always participate in other things (like ceremonies on reservations). They maintain their Indigenous perspectives, however, and aspire to pass them to their children, their children's children, and so forth.

Reclaimer adults, in contrast, experience Indian identities as something they are *and* something they can become. Despite being two or more generations removed from the Indigenous communities they claim[3] (but that less frequently claim them), they believe their Indian blood—documented or not—and their dedication to reclaiming Indian traditions substantiate their Indian identities. Some reclaimers' identities were passed down from Indian grandparents, but other reclaimers refer to intuitive remembrances of their indigeneity. Several reclaimers purported to spontaneously remember specific practices of their Indigenous ancestors (e.g., tanning animal hides, carving wooden flutes). Determined to remember more, some reclaimers seek the mentorship of Indigenous elders with uninterrupted ties to long-standing Indigenous communities. From mentors on and off Indian reservations, reclaimers learn "Indian ways" they painstakingly practice and meticulously teach their children.

Pan-Indianness

Both relocators and reclaimers necessarily rely on pan-Indian ethnic traditions and community formations in the Northeast Ohio environment, but for different reasons. Whereas relocators live too many miles from Indigenous homelands to return with any frequency, reclaimers are too far removed *generationally* from territories they consider their ancestral homes. Despite this distinction, pan-Indianness has some similar impacts on each community's traditions and practices. Whether the long-term effects of pan-Indian ethnicity are beneficial or harmful is debated by Indigenous people and scholars. Northeast Ohio Indians, however, are resigned to pan-Indian collaborations and events because the only other option available is engaging in Indigenous practices as individuals or single families without the support of local communities of belonging. As Bly (Sioux, first-generation relocator) pointed out, this option is really no option at all because, from an Indigenous perspective, *community* is the number one priority. Without an urban Indigenous community, pan-Indian or not, Indigenous perspectives may be lost to future generations of urban Indians.

Pan-Indian ethnic traditions are deemed beneficial when perceived as strategic resistance to oppressive structural circumstances meant to destroy Indigenous customs. For centuries, banding together and celebrating the things Indigenous people have in common despite their tribal differences have empowered Indigenous peoples and aided their struggles for sovereignty, dignity, and resources. In the last century, organizing across national and tribal differences enabled Indigenous peoples and cultures to survive federal assimilationist policies like Indian boarding schools and Indian (urban) relocation. Prior to that, pan-Indian coalitions formed the very roots of Indigenous resistance to colonial oppression in Northeast Ohio and across the United States. Since Europeans invaded the Americas, pan-Indian organizing has been an adaptive survival strategy for Indigenous peoples.

According to Indian and Indian-identified people living in Northeast Ohio today, the persistence of Indigenous peoples and cultures in this region is *still* dependent on the strength and staying power of pan-Indian communities. Urban Indian communities' reliance on "intertribal," or pan-Indian, powwows, is an example. Though not traditional to Indigenous cultures,[4] intertribal powwows are central sites for sustaining Indigenous identities and cultures "off the reservation"—a location that, importantly, describes the residency of a vast majority of enumerated American Indians in the United States. Both relocators and reclaimers discussed the importance of Ohio's intertribal powwows to socializing urban Indigenous children (and reclaimer adults) with limited access to tribe-specific ceremonies, festivals, and events. In addition to socialization, twenty-first-century urban pan-Indian powwows can be used strategically to impart the countermemories of Indigenous people to a predominantly non-Indigenous population. Powwows can be used, for instance, to abrogate tired tropes that situate Indigenous peoples in an ahistorical past because they spotlight Indigenous people in the present—where Indians make music that is broadcast electronically and dance in regalia decorated with plastic seed beads (rather than porcupine quills) available at any corporate crafting store. And, when the music stops, powwow attendees will see powwow dancers *outside* the powwow circle, checking cell phones and (perhaps) changing into Adidas before satisfying their appetites with Indian tacos made from canned chili.

Critics of pan-Indian ethnic practices, however, suggest that they are precursors to the wholesale destruction of Indigenous customs and communities due to threats to tribal sovereignty. To many people unfamiliar with sovereignty struggles, Indigenous cultural practices and Indigenous sovereignty seem *disconnected* because their relatedness is socially constructed, meaning that it results from settler-constructed memories of Indigenous peoples (and nations) as entirely *distinct* from other (white-settler) peoples and nations. Artfully crafted depictions of Indians as an entirely different and utterly inferior "type" of human define Indigenous peoples in many US sociocultural contexts, including legal and political realms in which tribal nations' sovereign statuses are negotiated. Because "pure" Indianness (a social construct) has been used by US courts as a yardstick against which to measure the indigeneity of a people, and correspondingly, Indian *tribes'* rights to sovereignty, the socially constructed relationship between cultural practices and sovereignty has *tangible* material and political consequences for Indian nations. From this perspective, the pan-ethnic tendencies of Ohio's Indian and Indian-identified communities, which muddle "Indianness," are potentially dangerous and destructive. Moreover, pan-Indianness—a mash-up of Indigenous cultures—oversimplifies the complexities of Indigenous ways of thinking and being. Such oversimplifications easily transmute into stereotypes that feed false understandings of Indianness already dominant in US society. These false understandings seem to encourage non-Indian people to "play Indian" because superficial proxies of Indigenous cultural traditions are more easily accessed, adopted, and adapted by pretendians.

Urban Indians (in Northeast Ohio and beyond) are caught in the middle of this debate over the benefits or harms of pan-Indian communities' pan-Indian practices. Though members of both NE Ohio pan-Indian communities report that pan-Indian events are not *enough* to sustain their Indigenous cultural traditions, they also reluctantly accede that participating in pan-Indian communities is better than the alternative: no local Indigenous community at all. Some relocators and reclaimers willingly sacrifice time and resources to stay connected to long-standing Indigenous communities, but ultimately they reside in Ohio, where pan-Indian communities are essential to the construction of (pan-Indian) Indigenous identities. Despite being an amalgamation of different Indigenous traditions, pan-Indian practices are still the practices of some contemporary Indigenous people. In the Northeast Ohio context, they are the compromise to which many Indians living "urban realities" agree for the sake of community and continuity.

Urban Indians Matter, Urban Indian Matters

Some Indigenous people and scholars question whether pan-Indian identities *should* be maintained, but Northeast Ohio's Indigenous elders, those with the longest, strongest connections to Indian nations and knowledge of tribe-specific customs, guardedly say *yes*. Though Indigenous people in NE Ohio represent some of the substance, or *density*, of Indigenous identities in the United States, their urban Indian perspectives frequently are marginalized in discussions of Indigenous peoples and communities. Neither relocators nor reclaimers fit false notions of "authentic" indigeneity. Their locations in time (the twenty-first century) and space (a metropolitan environment) position them far outside the "empty center" reserved for "really Indians."[5] Consequently, *urban* Indigenous stories, perspectives, and needs—such as those of (Indigenous) relocators and reclaimers—too often disappear from view in conversations about Indigenous sovereignty. Sovereignty is gravely important to the autonomy of Indian nations. It is crucial to Indigenous peoples' persistence and resistance to settler colonialism. Sovereignty issues, however, are not neatly confined to the bounded (recognized) territories of Indian nations. As Mishuana Goeman[6] (Tonawanda Band of Seneca) brilliantly articulates, Indigenous space extends far beyond the boundaries of Indian nations, which are themselves settler-colonial constructions. Struggles to "defy colonial categories," Goeman insists, cannot be contained within particular spaces. These struggles must move fluidly across false spatial dichotomies like "authentic" and "inauthentic" Indigenous contexts. Indigenous people living in urban spaces—people who, throughout much of their lives, moved fluidly across reservation and nonreservation contexts—undoubtedly have a wealth of knowledge to offer people engaged in tribal sovereignty struggles and broader decolonization movements. Their stories and memories will add depth and insight to critical conversations about Indigenous peoples' futures.

Community Boundaries

The primary and interrelated concerns of relocators and reclaimers include maintaining their respective urban pan-Indian communities, securing the future of Indigenous people in the region, and challenging settler-constructed memories of Indianness. Relocators' and reclaimers' distinct histories and memories, however, lead to different interpretations of these issues. They also lead to different boundary formations used to determine in-group and out-group members in their respective communities. Relocators share experiences of urban relocation and resulting feelings of isolation from family and friendship networks they left behind on Indian reservations. For relocators, it is essential for their community to feel like home away from home—a safe place where they are surrounded by people who understand their Indigenous perspectives *and* their Indigenous cultural diversity. Accordingly, relocators strategically contract the boundaries of their urban pan-Indian community to provide members with a counterspace where they are not expected to perform indigeneity in particular ways and they do not encounter discrimination or judgment. This community space, relocator elders believe, will enable the Indigenous identities of later-generation relocators to flourish and thereby support the persistence of Indigenous people and cultures in Northeast Ohio. Relocator community members also engage in visible actions, like psychic fair benefits and protests against the Cleveland MLB team's "Indians" imagery (prior to the team's name change), to introduce non-Indigenous residents of the region to countermemories of Indianness. By reducing discrimination against Indians, relocator elders hope to increase Native pride in the community's youth. During my time with relocators, many members of the second and third generations were not particularly invested in maintaining the community their elders built. Despite expressed concerns about the community's future sustainability, the community remains strong more than a decade later.

Reclaimers, in contrast, share experiences of longer-term isolation from Indigenous peoples and communities, frequent dismissals of their Indian identities, and lack of socialization into Indian ways. They strategically expand the boundaries of their urban pan-Indian community to provide all people, Indian-identified or not, with a space to learn about Indian people, engage in Indian practices, and (in the case of individuals who identify as Indians) assert Indian identities without fear of being discounted or dismissed. Reclaimers believe that teaching Indian and non-Indian people Indian ways helps sustain Indigenous cultures and increases knowledge about Indigenous people in Northeast Ohio. Reclaimer community members also engage in visible actions, including parade appearances and powwows, to educate Northeast Ohio residents about contemporary urban Indian people and cultures. Despite reclaimers' general optimism about the community's future, some reclaimers expressed serious concerns about the community's open-door policy. Weary reclaimers admitted that the community's openness attracted Indian wannabes who ignorantly embodied Indian stereotypes. They also suggested that the community's openness discouraged the participation of respected Indigenous elders able to mentor reclaimers who were genuinely committed to reclaiming Indigenous ways. As noted in the previous chapter, the reclaimer community 501c3 nonprofit organization could not sustain financial troubles exacerbated by the global COVID-19 pandemic. Its doors closed in 2020.

Collective Memories

Within their respective communities, relocators and reclaimers develop collective identities and memories that transform their experiences of oppression into feelings of solidarity and strength with other members of their respective pan-Indian(-identified) community. In turn, participating in either community affirms a particular perspective that deepens divisions between the two community groups. For instance, relocators collectively remember the reservation-based struggles (e.g., poverty, discrimination) that prompted their migrations to Northeast Ohio. They moved away from home reservations in hopes of creating "fuller" lives for their families, unaware of the degree to which their urban residences would alter their and later-generation relocators' relationships with home reservations and tribal cultures. The progression of relocators' own lives illustrates that some aspects of culture loss occur without willful abandonment of Indigenous identities. Due to stories passed down from parents and grandparents, however, first-generation relocators and their children (and their children) "remember" that people become disconnected from Indigenous communities when they abandon their Indianness for the privileges of whiteness. Relocators less often remember Indigenous people who, much like themselves, made difficult decisions (e.g., moving away from Indigenous communities) to survive in settler society. Moreover, second- and later-generation relocators—some of whom have not spent much or any time immersed in tribal communities—collectively remember being from Indian nations. This collective memory strengthens their assuredness in their Indigenous identities, but for many later-generation relocators, it does not strengthen (at least not directly) their situatedness in long-standing Indigenous communities.

As a result, urban Indigenous people living in environments saturated with settler-constructed understandings benefit from reflecting on how their relationships with Indigenous peoples and perspectives bend, brace, and/or shift over time. Indigenous elders in the relocator community are essential to this reflective process. The "continuous, ongoing storytelling" of relocator elders grounds the *Indigenous* perspectives of younger relocators. Stories of centuries-long struggles to survive settler-colonial erasure, passed down over generations in relocator families, connect relocators to the past, situate them in the present, and provide lessons for the future. Such ongoing storytelling enables the development of *living traditions*. This concept, formulated by Mishuana Goeman (Tonawanda Band of Seneca), captures the dynamism of Indigenous perspectives and practices that adjust and ever-so-slightly transform over time to accommodate the needs of Indigenous communities. Living traditions necessarily emerge from Indigenous stories binding "fragile, complex, and important relationships to each other."[7] They are necessary to ensure Indigenous peoples' persistence and aid Indigenous peoples' resistance to twenty-first-century settler-colonial projects.

The collective remembrances of reclaimers, in contrast, are concerning. Many reclaimers' Indian identities likely are based on incorrect interpretations of the past. Reclaimers learned they were Indians from stories passed down from parents and grandparents, but (as noted in the introduction and illustrated in various passages throughout the book) the veracity of familial stories about reclaimers' Indigenous origins varies wildly. Some stories are rooted in Indigenous soil.[8] Others, however, inevitably stem from myriad interactions between (settler) families and US settler-colonial society. For centuries, settler-colonial institutions intentionally manipulated US residents' memories of US Indigenous peoples, replacing more authentic forms of indigeneity with symbolic images of Indianness and replacing Indigenous peoples' memories with nostalgic settler-constructed remembrances of brave warriors and Indian princesses.[9] These imposter memories then transmuted into some families' Indigenous origin myths.

Thus, an analysis of fraudulent Indianness grounded in social memory studies provides additional, nuanced insight into the pretendian phenomenon. From a social memory perspective, some people (including some reclaimer community members) whose Indigenous ancestry claims are untenable do not intentionally manipulate interpretations of the past, but rather, interpret their pasts based on their experiences and the cultural frameworks available to them.[10] In other words, their mnemonic socialization in familiar and cultural realms inevitably creates "selective memories" of Indigenous ancestors. These memories, accepted as real, are the basis of some reclaimers' Indian identity claims. A central sociological tenet, the Thomas Theorem (1928), indicates that *if people define situations as real, they are real in their consequences.* Accordingly, if people wrongly believe they have Indian ancestries, they identify as Indians *and their false identities have real, harmful consequences* to Indigenous peoples. I highlight this nuance not to deny that settlers claiming Indianness is a form (perhaps the ultimate form) of erasure or to absolve unwittingly fraudulent reclaimers of harms caused by their erroneous identities. Rather, I do so to draw attention to the fact that memory manipulation undergirds and co-constitutes settler-colonial structures intent on Indigenous erasure. Many fraudulent Indians, thus, are pawns in the continuous reproduction of destructive settler-colonial processes set in motion centuries ago and continuously compelled to destroy Indigenous peoples, cultures, communities, and nations. Many reclaimers, I suggest, are unaware of the devastating potentialities of their Indian-identity claims, and do not realize that the problem of Indian-identity fraud extends far beyond the vast numbers of people perpetuating it.

Reclaimers' participation in an urban pan-Indian community tailored to their specific desires (as Indian-identified people predominantly unclaimed by long-standing Indigenous communities) affirms not only their Indian identities but also their faulty definitions of numerous situations related to their Indianness. In other words, they collectively share "selective memories" about Indigenous peoples. Reclaimer community members, for instance, generally do not remember large swaths of Indigenous peoples' histories, including their interactions and treaty negotiations—and more specifically, the outcomes of treaty negotiations—with white colonizers. Though they occasionally reference Indian Removal (1830), many reclaimer community members' remembrances focus on (romanticized) pre-settler-colonial eras—when (according to many reclaimers) "Natives were Natives" who lived in harmony with the environment and did not police the boundaries of Indianness. Collectively, reclaimers know little about tribal sovereignty beyond some reclaimers' recognition that any path to tribal citizenship is *through* Indian nations. When reclaimers discuss "Indian politics," however, even this bit of knowledge collapses under the weight of their collective antipathy toward Indians concerned about "a piece of paper from the government." When reclaimers make this statement, they erroneously refer to the federal government, which does not play a role in adjudicating tribal citizenship claims. Moreover, reclaimers generally believe that reclaiming Indianness is an exceptional act of *individual-ized* resistance against settler-colonial society. With a few exceptions, reclaimers collectively misremember the Red Power Movement and other *collective* acts of resistance engaged by members of historically oppressed groups that opened space in US society for a "resurgence" of Indigenous (and other marginalized) identities.[11]

Reclaimers also cannot comprehend the degree to which they misunderstand many Indigenous people's realities. Notably, a majority of reclaimers are fair-skinned, yet do not acknowledge their white privilege. Reclaimers frequently espouse color-evasive ideologies, saying things like "everyone is human," "we all bleed red," and "skin color is irrelevant." Contrarily, they bemoan their white skin because it does not match societal expectations of Indianness. They do not reflect on how darker skin would negatively impact their lives in white-supremacist US society. White settlers racialized Indigenous peoples to justify their genocide, enslavement, forced migration, hypersegregation, and compulsory assimilation, and these racialized understandings of Indianness are *still used* today to identify and oppress Indigenous people. Skin color, for racially "othered," nonwhite Indigenous people, can be a matter of life or death. Like the Cherokee "race shifters" in Sturm's work, however, most Northeast Ohio reclaimers fail to recognize that *choosing* to identify as Indians, rather than being identified as Indians by others, is "a subtle marker of [their] whiteness."[12] They also fail to reflect on how their whiteness protects them from dangerous and damaging discrimination in their day-to-day lives.

Additionally, the endless stream of subtle and not-so-subtle messages about Indianness to which reclaimers have a lifetime of exposure deeply influences reclaimers' understandings of what being and acting Indian means. Many reclaimers, for example, have a tendency to think about Indians as guardians of the natural environment and people equipped with wilderness survival skills, but (despite claiming Indian identities themselves) they do not also think of Indians as construction workers, dentists, and small business owners. As discussed in chapter 5, many reclaimers' attachments to idealized, settler-constructed images of Indians lead them to perform Indianness in superficial, stereotypical ways that perpetuate misinformation and misunderstandings about contemporary Indigenous peoples and issues. Consequently, reclaimers respond to their marginalization as urban Indian and Indian-identified people in ways that reinforce rather than resist settler-colonial formations. Reclaimers' exaggerated "Indian" performances, ironically, also distinguish reclaimers from Indigenous people with stronger ties to tribal nations (e.g., relocators).

Relative to relocators, reclaimers' fuller, lifelong immersion in the dominant settler society influences not only their perceptions of Indigenous peoples but also the *structure* of their perceptions more generally. That is, reclaimers are ontologically oriented to settler structures of thought. Reclaimers' search for "an authentic past outside of settler colonialism," for instance, indicates the *static* ways in which they construct indigeneity.[13] Their attitudes and behaviors often point to a collective commitment to returning to a (fictitious) precolonial era when "pristine" Indigenous cultures existed. They fail to recognize how Indigenous ways of knowing persist in contemporary society.[14] Furthermore, reclaimers' behaviors are aligned with dichotomous understandings of the world that position (their claimed) indigeneity as oppositional to (their discarded) whiteness and Indigenous culture (not pluralized to elucidate the perspective of too many reclaimers) as oppositional to contemporary US culture. Such polarized understandings lead reclaimers to distance themselves from their "prior" (socialization into) whiteness and emphasize their Indianness instead. From an Indigenous perspective, however, "calling on the past" is necessary "to define the future."[15] Reclaimers' refusals to reflect on how their prior socialization and experiences in settler-dominated spheres impact their current understandings prevent them from acting in ways that assist rather than obstruct Indigenous peoples' decolonization movements.

Challenging Pretendians, Resisting Indigenous Erasure

Appropriated, pretend Indianness abounds in settler-colonial societies like the United States because white people's possession of Indianness is normalized and legitimized.[16] In Northeast Ohio, the MLB team's former "Indians" identity is an extreme example: the baseball franchise named itself "the Indians," identified as *the* tribe, and glorified a red-faced "chief" named Wahoo. For more than a century, Cleveland baseball fans played Indian on game day, wearing war paint and feathers while performing war whoops and tomahawk chops. These mocking behaviors (which remain firmly in place in other sporting realms) dehumanize Indigenous peoples, deny their oppressions, and erase their contemporary existences. Though less exaggerated than the behaviors of Cleveland baseball fans, the collective behaviors of Northeast Ohio reclaimers are also damaging to Indigenous peoples and communities. Despite claiming Indian identities, many participants in the Northeast Ohio reclaimer community are not committed to learning about Indigenous peoples' collective realities. They assert Indian identities without reflecting on how their lives are different from the lives of members of long-standing Indigenous communities. Rather than considering the reasons why some people label them "pretendians" and "wannabes," many reclaimers dismiss these remarks and console themselves by participating in a community of otherwise isolated Indian and Indian-identified people like themselves. They are largely ignorant of myriad complexities of Indian identities, including relationships between unverified Indian identity claims and Indian nations' struggles to obtain and/or maintain tribal sovereignty. Importantly, sorting reclaimers according to tribal enrollment status does not reveal any patterns with respect to reclaimers' reflections of or commitments to Indigenous communities outside the Northeast Ohio region.

"Pretendians," Rebecca Nagle (Cherokee) states in an opinion piece in *High Country News*, "must be challenged and the retelling of their false narratives must be stopped."[17] I agree, and my research empirically demonstrates how many NE Ohio reclaimers' identity strategies, rooted in static (mis)understandings about Indigenous peoples, reinforce rather than resist Indigenous peoples' oppression. Reclaimers' incomplete understandings and false narratives are rooted in settler-imposed memories of Indianness, disseminated across US institutions to legitimize settler possession of Indigenous territories. Strategies for *uprooting* pretend Indianness, then, must focus on overwriting fabricated US histories with more truthful accounts of this nation's past. In the words of Malissa Phung, "Mobilizing all settlers to become aware of the ways in which their settler privileges are anything but natural and well deserved can constitute a first step in supporting Indigenous activism against settler domination."[18]

Finally, I urge caution regarding summary dismissals of the claims of *all* people working to reclaim Indigenous identities in urban and other nonreservation contexts. Settler-constructed and settler-maintained definitions of Indianness continue to create the unfortunate need to discover and expel *pretend* Indian participants from urban pan-Indian communities. Sometimes blurry boundaries exist, however, between pretend Indians and people with legitimate claims to Indian identities. Indigenous people are exposed to the same stereotypes of Indianness as everyone else in US settler society, and Indigenous people dislocated from their tribal communities may not have elders or other mentors to teach them Indigenous stories and help them unlearn settler-constructed stories. Accordingly, I suggest that dismissing all reclaimers' claims of indigeneity potentially *assists* rather than resists settler-colonial processes of Indigenous erasure. Settler-colonial structures that distanced Indigenous people from long-standing Indigenous communities also "disappeared" their routes back. Rejecting their stories not only expunges the existence of Indigenous people separated from Indigenous communities but also censors information necessary to understanding the full impacts of settler colonialism on Indigenous peoples and communities.

Still Pushing Indigenous People "under the Rug"

As I completed this book manuscript, the necessity of replacing settler-imposed understandings of Indianness with countermemories rooted in the histories and realities of US Indigenous peoples could not have been more urgent. In fall 2021, the novel coronavirus continued to disproportionately impact communities of color in the United States. Major media outlets granting attention to pandemic-era inequalities affecting black and Hispanic communities were less likely to highlight similarly devastating impacts of COVID-19 on US Indigenous populations. Weekly data from the Centers for Disease Control (CDC) indicated, however, that (as of October 2021) racial disparities in case numbers and death rates narrowed for black and Hispanic people while US Indigenous people continued to suffer higher rates of infection and death than other US racial/ethnic groups.[19] AIAN death rates, in fact, consistently outpaced rates in other US communities of color since May 2020.[20]

Importantly, Indigenous peoples' struggles to contain the virus and treat infected citizens were undercut by settler-colonial structures impacting Native governments and people contemporaneously. Infrastructural insufficiencies throughout Indian Country, for instance, created limited access to clean water, sanitation services, electricity, and the Internet. The federal government's failure to honor treaty obligations also resulted in woefully inadequate health care on many Indian reservations.[21] Consequently, disproportionate numbers of Indigenous people had preexisting health conditions (e.g., asthma, cancer, diabetes) that exacerbated the effects of the virus, and Indian nations (due to their reliance on Indian Health Services, or IHS, which is federally operated) were ill equipped to care for citizens once they contracted the virus. As a sixteen-year-old Diné (Navajo) child, Larry Jackson, pointed out in a viral social media post, the Navajo Nation is roughly the size of West Virginia, yet the latter boasted sixty-three hospitals while the Navajo Nation had only six. Jackson also noted the lack of media attention granted Indigenous communities. "Why is there no news coverage for us, or any Native Americans?" he asked. "It's really disappointing," Jackson continued. "It's really sad to think that people would push a whole group of people under the rug and just pretend that they are not there."[22] US Indigenous peoples are also "pushed under the rug" in discussions of police violence against black and brown communities. The back-to-back murders of Breonna Taylor, Ahmaud Arbery, and George Floyd by police authorities in 2020 sparked a new wave of Black Lives Matter activism, along with important conversations challenging the nature of police work. Indigenous peoples are also disproportionately killed by police officers,[23] but despite the efforts of Native Lives Matter activists, the impacts of police violence on Native lives continue to be unnoticed by the broader US public.

Inadequate health care and police brutality are life-and-death matters in Native communities. Throughout 2020 and 2021, in the midst of the global COVID-19 pandemic and a resurgence of racial-justice activism in the United States, these issues were headline news in every major media outlet. Yet, the impacts of the novel coronavirus and police violence on Native communities received relatively little media attention. US Indigenous peoples continue to be "pushed under the rug" because that is where settler-imposed stories of Indianness leave them—out of sight and out of mind. Most Americans do not think about Indigenous peoples because they are socialized to forget that Indigenous people are *people*. They learn instead that Indigenous people are historical relics and sports team mascots that spark feelings of nostalgia and excitement. As Cleveland "Indians" baseball fans at the stadium on opening day made abundantly clear, they were not interested in engaging with or understanding the perspectives of Indigenous people. They wanted Indigenous people to move out of the way so they could remain firmly entrenched in and attached to their own memories of Indianness—settler-constructed fictions and fantasies that granted them possession of caricatured Indianness and that thoroughly displaced living Indigenous peoples.

> There is a reciprocal relationship between truth about the
> past and justice in the present. Telling the truth about the
> past helps cause justice in the present. Achieving justice
> in the present helps us tell the truth about the past.
> —James Loewen, *Up a Creek, with a Paddle*

Honoring Indigenous Peoples, Their Stories, Memories, Histories, and Realities

Cultivating respect and concern for Indigenous peoples necessitates the reversal of centuries of disinformation about Indianness—a reversal that upends the settler-colonial perspectives that continue to justify settler domination and Indigenous oppression. This burden belongs to whites/settlers and the settler institutions they/we created and maintain. In the twenty-first century, US institutions perpetuate the same false memories and stories of Indianness generated in the eighteenth century. An overhaul of these institutions—which, ironically, serve neither settlers nor Indigenous peoples—is long overdue. I cannot address the totality of changes required here, but instead conclude with a few thoughts on the interrelated issues of education and representation. Not only did Indigenous residents of NE Ohio emphasize the need for change in these areas, but these areas also present opportunities for people disconnected from Indian nations to engage in actions that can improve the circumstances of Indigenous people living on and off Indian reservations. Changing erroneous understandings of Indigenous peoples can powerfully shift perceptions in ways that elucidate Indigenous peoples' contemporary realities and spur empathy and action on their behalf. None of these ideas are new, but they are not being implemented either, so they (apparently) bear repeating.

Every US institution reifies and affirms whites' possession of Indianness, but for many people in the United States, schools are initial sites of exposure to fraudulent memories and stories of Indianness. Rather than lying to children, we must demand that educators discuss more truthful histories of this composite of territories now called the United States. It is crucial for children to learn that our collective history did not begin in 1492 or 1776. Imposing this false memory on US children—settler, Indigenous, and immigrant—indoctrinates them into settler mindsets and socializes them to disregard US Indigenous peoples. Consider the implications of instituting new "rules of remembrance" that shift the eras deemed relevant to this nation's history. If US history lessons begin with Indigenous peoples and highlight Indigenous perspectives, it follows that children will learn about the experiences of Indigenous peoples, both pre- and postcontact, with settlers who eventually became colonizers and negotiators of ill-begotten and often broken treaties. They will learn about sovereignty and Indian nations. They will also learn about Indigenous people's *racialization* and how it was used to justify white supremacy and the oppression of all people of color in the United States. These lessons will provide the foundation children need to reflect on the relationships between settler colonialism and systemic inequalities that diminish the life chances of people who belong to racialized groups today.

Educational institutions, of course, do not perpetuate false memories of Indianness in isolation. They operate in conjunction with other US institutions to establish false memories of Indianness as taken-for-granted truths. We must demand that Indigenous peoples be represented more accurately in the past and *much* more often in the present. It is (past) time to remove allusions to whites' possession of the landscape. In addition to acknowledging the Indigenous territories on which US villages, towns, and cities are built, it is time to tear down statues, memorials, and other tributes to settler-colonial authorities who mercilessly abused and murdered Indigenous people. This issue finally received more attention in 2020 due to renewed calls for racial justice in the United States. Christopher Columbus statues (along with Confederate statues) were targeted, and cities across the United States—including Boston, Chicago, Detroit, Philadelphia, Sacramento, and even the capital of Ohio, named after the brutal colonizer himself—removed Columbus's figure from prominent locations in city centers. In recent years, several cities and states across the United States also changed Columbus Day to Indigenous People's Day—an important step forward in recognizing and attempting to reckon with US settler colonialism. Plenty of statues and buildings, parks, and streets with colonizers' names remain to be reclaimed, however, and those with Indian names also require revisions that recognize present-day Indigenous peoples and communities rather than acting only as tributes to nondescript Indians from a past era.

It is also (past) time to eradicate references to whites' possession of Indianness and Indian identities. Sports team mascots and corporate logos are among the most visible, and again, some progress in these areas is being made. According to the National Congress of American Indians (NCAI), no professional teams have adopted racially discriminatory mascots since 1963.[24] Native people and their allies scored a big win in 2020, when Washington football team owner, Daniel Snyder, finally announced a change to the team's racist R-word name. Snyder's long-overdue reversal on the name change was not spurred by a sudden change in *his* consciousness, but rather, investment firms', shareholders', and lawmakers' threats of disinvestment if he did not replace the team's unconscionable name.[25] Notably, national attention to the Washington team's name change resulted in pressure on the Cleveland MLB franchise to change its name as well. The Cleveland MLB franchise finally announced its name-change decision in December 2020. Though I argue elsewhere that the franchise's denials of *intentional* harm is an intentional deflection of responsibility that silences Indigenous people (Cleveland-area relocators, specifically) by refusing to recognize their half-century of struggle to eradicate Cleveland's "Indians" identity, the name change still represents a (baby) step in the right direction.[26] The franchise's strategic verbalization of white innocence, however, illustrates that the settler-colonial logics that spawned Native-themed mascots remain firmly embedded in US sociocultural spheres. Almost a thousand "Indian" references that reproduce notions of white settler supremacy remain unchanged across all levels of sports, including K–12, amateur, and professional teams. On the up side, however, the NCAI reports that this number is only one-third the total that existed in the United States prior to 1995.[27] The century-old trend of using Indian imagery to market corporate products is also losing its edge. In 2020 Mutual of Omaha and Land-o-Lakes both announced the retirement of their stereotypical Indian imagery—an Indian head and a "butter maiden," respectively.[28]

Another development in recent years involves Indigenous political representation. More Native people than ever ran for office in 2018, including twelve candidates for statewide offices (including governor and lieutenant governor), seventy-eight candidates for state legislatures, and ten candidates for the US House of Representatives. Democrats Deb Haaland (Pueblo of Laguna) of New Mexico and Sharice Davids (Ho-Chunk Nation) of Kansas made history as the first Native women elected to Congress. They joined two Republican Native men members of the House, Tom Cole (Chickasaw Nation) and Markwayne Mullin (Cherokee Nation), to establish the 116th Congress as the Congress with the most Indigenous representation to date.[29] Additionally, in August 2020, Cherokee Nation citizen, Kimberly Teehee, was unanimously confirmed to be the Cherokee Nation's first (nonvoting) representative in the US House. This long overdue representation was negotiated by the Cherokee Nation in the Treaty of Echota (1835).[30] In March 2021, former US representative Deb Haaland (Pueblo of Laguna) made history a second time when she became the first Native woman to hold the position of US secretary of the interior. In this US Cabinet role, the Honorable Deb Haaland oversees numerous government agencies, including the Bureau of Land Management, the US Geological Survey, the National Park Service, and the Bureau of Indian Affairs.[31]

These changes barely skim the surface of what must be done to upend settler-colonial structures and improve the conditions of Indigenous peoples' lives, but they at least indicate movement in the right direction. In addition to working toward the removal of false memories of Indianness, we need to insist on the dissemination of countermemories that come from Indigenous people themselves. It is critically important for Americans to recognize Indigenous peoples as remarkably diverse twenty-first-century global citizens. Some Indigenous people practice their traditions while others do not, but for all Indigenous people, the passage of time has created changes in habits and lifeways. Denying the transformation, growth, and movement of Native people dehumanizes them and devalues their experiences. It also denies the authenticity of Indians living in urban and suburban spaces outside Indian reservations, who account for the vast majority of enumerated Native people in the United States today.

Removing romanticized Indianness from US social and cultural spheres and deepening understanding of Indigenous realities will also discourage people from playing Indian. When people acquire deeper understandings of Indigenous peoples' histories and contemporary realities, they will be better able to recognize that Indigenous people who historically suffered and continue to be impacted by US settler colonialism and white supremacy occupy a unique social location only *Indigenous people* have the right to claim. They will be better equipped to honor Indigenous perspectives without coopting them. The eradication of fraudulent Indians will enable Indigenous people to organize across difference—including across the intersection of location (e.g., Indian reservations, rural areas and border towns, suburban and urban locales). Rather than wasting time, energy, and resources weeding out wannabes, Indigenous communities will be able to assist one another in realizing their collective needs. US Indigenous peoples will be free to focus on more important matters, like securing tribal sovereignty, maintaining and revitalizing Indigenous cultures, and maintaining the health and happiness of Indigenous peoples.

ACKNOWLEDGMENTS

My heart is full with gratitude for the people who made this book possible. I am deeply humbled by the generosity of people who shared their stories with me. Thank you for welcoming me into your communities, lives, and homes. Your stories transformed me. I cannot repay the debt I owe, but I hope I have relayed your stories in ways capable of transforming others.

A special thanks to "Berta," who loved to tell stories. The world is a better place because you were in it. I am also grateful to "Kurt," who supported me and my work in numerous ways. Thanks also to the NE Ohio pan-Indian community participants who read and commented on my manuscript-in-progress. Your feedback was invaluable.

To Faye, Ferne, Margie, Chris, "the Committee," and everyone else involved in eradicating Cleveland's dehumanizing mascot, YOU DID IT! The struggle was *real*, but you persisted and the future of Indigenous people in NE Ohio is brighter than ever. To all people still working to eliminate Native-themed mascots and other caricatures of "Indianness," your work is valued and appreciated and necessary and *seen*. Thank you.

This project could not have happened without the friendships I made in Tó Naneesdizí, Dinétah (Tuba City, Navajo Nation). I learned and unlearned so many valuable lessons during my time there. Special thanks to Sarah Slim and my colleagues at the Tuba City community center. I am also exceedingly thankful for the education imparted by Mr. Ed Little, my "Foundations of Navajo Culture" teacher at Diné College. I can still hear you say, "This really happened, Jacobs!" My heart swells with gratitude for the Nez family, and especially my friend Norris, aka "Junior." I still struggle to understand why your time on earth was so small when your heart was so big. Many heartfelt thanks and warm wishes to his daughter, Naliyah. I am so grateful we are connected. Thanks also to Kendrick, the spaghetti master. Ahéhee'.

I have many people to thank for helping me become the sociologist I am today. I am so fortunate to draw on the insights and experiences of a remarkable group of scholars, mentors, and friends. I extend my sincere appreciation to (alphabetically) Carolyn Behrman, Katrina Bloch, C. André Christie-Mizell, Laurel Davis-Delano, Joanna Dreby, Kathryn Feltey, Jim Fenelon, Elaine Hall, David Kaplan, Matt Lee, Thomas Michael Norton-Smith, Clare Stacey, Tiffany Taylor, and Linda "Tess" Tessier. Your compassionate guidance taught me so much about research, responsibility, and reciprocity, and your ways of being in academia continue to inspire me.

I am grateful to colleagues who read and commented on various pieces of this work. It has been too long since our paths crossed, Lauren Eastwood and Kirsten Isgro! I miss our writing accountability sessions at SUNY Plattsburgh. I am very fortunate to have phenomenal colleagues at Wayne State University as well. Special thanks to Krista Brumley for reading and commenting on endless drafts of this work and related others. Many thanks also to Zachary Brewster, my "champion" and friend. Nicole Trujillo-Pagán, thanks for rallying with me at the end! To my Productive-Academic-Writing pals—your camaraderie and encouragement kept me going. I also owe heartfelt thanks to David Pitawanakwat and Regan West, two lovely humans who read my book-in-progress and provided much needed and much appreciated feedback.

My students also sustained me through this process. Many thanks to Kearabetswe Mokoene, for sharing such beautiful and inspiring stories, to Harmandeep Kaur, for your energy and commitment to *unsettling* sociology, and to Zunaira Imran, for buoying my spirits on so many occasions. You inspire me to be a better teacher, colleague, mentor, and friend.

I extend my sincere appreciation to my editor, Ilene Kalish. Your commitment to my book project helped me persevere. I also thank New York University Press staff, whose work behind the scenes made this book possible. I am truly indebted to several anonymous reviewers who introduced me to important authors and scholarship in the field and whose knowledgeable and perceptive feedback helped reshape and refocus my ideas. This book is much improved as a result.

A shout-out, also, to the beautiful friends in my life whose loving support, thoughtful advice, and collective wisdom have sustained me through the years. Many thanks to (alphabetically) Emma Arnott, Jessica Penwell Barnett, Mario Cariñes, Daniela Jauk, Jodi Ross, and Anabel Stöckle (and others who have gifted me their time, energy, compassion, and presence). Words cannot express how grateful I am to have you in my life. Thank you for being there, for broadening my outlook, for loving me unconditionally, and for making me a better, braver, brighter, kinder, and more joyful person.

And finally, to my family, my heart. Your love and support make me everything I am today. To my parents, Roy and Karen Jacobs—thank you for always believing in me, always encouraging me, and for giving me so much love and guidance over the years. To my brother, Roy—I love you to the moon and back. I am so grateful for your bear hugs and belly laughs and your sense of humor that makes big problems seem less heavy. To my Aunt Sharon—your support over the years has meant the world to me. Your many kindnesses are impressed upon my heart. And to my sister, Karen, and my cousins, Tanya and Brian—I love you! We don't see each other enough! Finally, I am so grateful for my life partner and spouse, David Merolla, my best friend, mentor, and colleague. Words cannot convey what your support contributed to this project, or what inspiration, peace, joy, and wonder you bring to my life. I love you.

APPENDIX

Community Participants

TABLE A.1. Reclaimer Community Participants

Reclaimers	Primary Tribal Affiliation/Identification	Age at Interview
Casey	Cherokee-identified	63
Cheryl	Odawa	54
Daniel	Choctaw-identified	22
Danna	Odawa	33
Dean	Choctaw-identified	75
Flo	Cherokee-identified	57
Floyd	Blackfoot- and Ojibwa-identified	40
Harold	Cherokee- and/or Navajo-identified	66
Kenai	Lakota-identified	37
Kurt	Choctaw-identified	47
Matu	Arapaho-, Blackfoot-, Cherokee-, Cree-, Gros Ventre-, Shoshone-, Ute-identified	26
Neville	Anishinaabe-, Cherokee-, Lakota-, Lenape-, Nanticoke-identified	33
Oda	Delaware- and Blackfoot-identified	67
Sadie	Lenape- and Blackfoot-identified	30
Sasha	Lakota-identified	32
Starla	Cherokee-identified	55
Tabatha	Cherokee	52
Valerie	Cherokee-identified	48

TABLE A.2. Relocator Community Participants

Relocators	Primary Tribal Affiliation/ Identification	Generation of Urban Residence	Age at Interview
Barbara	Cherokee	first	58
Berta	Lakota	first	59
Bly	Sioux	first	52
Gertrude	Cayuga	first	72
Greg	Lakota	first	59
John	Diné	second	32
Marla	Diné	first	68
Melissa	Native Hawaiian–identified	second	37
Monica	Diné- and Mexican-identified	first	60s
Sam	Diné- and Mexican-identified	first	60s
Samantha	Cherokee	second	23
Sandra	Native- and Mexican-identified	third	24
Susan	Dakota	first	64

NOTES

INTRODUCTION

1 Pseudonyms are used in place of participants' names.

2 Throughout the book I use numerous terms to refer to people who identify as members of Indigenous communities in the United States: "(US) Indigenous people," "Natives," "Indians," and "American Indian and Alaska Native" ("AIAN"). I recognize that contestation over appropriate terminology exists and hope readers do not take offense to my choices, which I briefly explain here. I prefer the referent "Indigenous peoples." It is commonly used in scholarship and activism on Indigenous issues and also helps elucidate commonalities in experiences of diverse Indigenous populations around the world. My work, however, is restricted to US Indigenous peoples. I use the referents "Natives" and "Indians" because these terms were used frequently by the Indigenous and Indigenous-identified people who participated in the research that forms the basis of this book. Finally, I use "AIAN" when discussing US Census counts and other statistical data describing US Indigenous peoples because it is the designation given to US Indigenous peoples by the US government.

3 Barker 2017; Goldstein 2014; Veracini 2010; Vimalassery, Pegues, and Goldstein 2016.

4 Veracini 2010.

5 Glenn 2015; Moreton-Robinson 2015.

6 Omi and Winant 2014.

7 Moreton-Robinson 2015.

8 Vimalassery, Pegues, and Goldstein 2016: 7.

9 Moreton-Robinson 2015: xiii.

10 Moreton-Robinson 2015: xix.

11 Moreton-Robinson 2015: xx.

12 Lipsitz 1998; Brunsma and Wyse 2019.

13 Bhambra 2014; Brunsma and Wyse 2019; Collins 2007; Rabaka 2010; Sousa Santos, Nunes, and Meneses 2007.

14 Meusburger 2011; Olick and Robbins 1998; Zerubavel 1996.

15 Zerubavel 1996.

16 Mills 2014.

17 Mills 2014.

18 Mills 2014: 31.

19 Mills 2014: 39.
20 Moreton-Robinson 2015: 51.
21 Veracini 2010.
22 Moreton-Robinson 2015: 50.
23 Vimalassery, Pegues, and Goldstein 2016.
24 Vimalassery, Pegues, and Goldstein 2016.
25 Vimalassery, Pegues, and Goldstein 2016: 1.
26 Mills 2007: 7 (emphasis his).
27 Vimalassery, Pegues, and Goldstein 2016: 3.
28 Vimalassery, Pegues, and Goldstein 2016: 3.
29 Tuck and Yang 2012; Vimalassery, Pegues, and Goldstein 2016.
30 Moreton-Robinson 2015: xiii.
31 To "portage" means to haul the canoe out of the water to shoulder and carry it.
32 George n.d.
33 Tully 2016: 11.
34 The arrowhead statues were created by Onondaga-Seneca artist Peter Jones.
35 Meusburger 2011.
36 Tully 2016: 12.
37 It took twenty to thirty minutes for a fireboat, the *Anthony J. Celebrezze*, to put out the flames.
38 Souther 2017.
39 This nickname is used interchangeably with "the Mistake *by* the Lake."
40 The Cleveland Electric Illuminating Company used this tagline in a 1940s-era public relations campaign.
41 Staurowsky 1998.
42 Staurowsky 1998.
43 Sheinin and Bonesteel 2018.
44 Major League Baseball 2020.
45 Cleveland Indians Twitter page 2020.
46 Meusburger 2011; Zerubavel 1996.
47 These incredible land sculptures were used for burials, ceremonies, residences, and protection. The largest earthwork encloses eighty acres of land within walls twelve feet high and fifty feet wide.
48 Baires 2018; Lepper 2020.
49 No one really knows why the French called them "*chat sauvage*" (wildcat) or the Iroquois called them "*Erieehronones*" (people of the long tail), but educated guessers suggest they may have ornamented themselves with cougar skins and/or raccoon tails.
50 This brief history of Indigenous peoples in Northeast Ohio is composed from multiple, sometimes contradictory sources.
51 White 1991: x, xiv.
52 White 1991: xiv.
53 Bloetscher 1981.

54 Tully 2016.
55 Tully 2016: 90.
56 Bureau of the US Census 1920: 34, 37.
57 Goeman 2008: 296.
58 Tuck and Yang 2012: 9.
59 "Rez" is slang for (Indian) "reservation."
60 Goeman 2008: 297.
61 Rosenthal 2012; Shoemaker 1988.
62 Between 1940 and 1960, about 122,000 Indians moved to cities (Philp 1985).
63 Philp 1985.
64 Laukaitis 2005.
65 Burt 1986: 89.
66 Philp 1985.
67 Burt 1986.
68 Miller 2013.
69 Miller 2013: 59.
70 Rosenthal 2012.
71 Philp 1985: 188.
72 Blackhawk 1995.
73 Willard 1997.
74 Blackhawk 1995: 18–20.
75 Miller 2013: 55.
76 Philp 1985.
77 Miller 2013.
78 Rosenthal 2012: 119.
79 Anderson 2016; Kovach 2009; Wilson 2008.
80 Wilson 2001: 177.
81 Wilson 2001: 177.
82 Tallbear 2014; Wilson 2008.
83 The town name is not pronounced like Louisville, Kentucky, but rather like the name Lewis with "ville" tagged on the end.
84 Loewen n.d.
85 Smith 1999: 144.
86 US Interagency Council on Homelessness 2012.
87 Harjo 2018.
88 These definitions are from Wiktionary's (online) entry for "go off the reservation," available at https://en.wiktionary.org.
89 Goeman 2008: 297.
90 Goeman 2008: 300.
91 Goeman 2013: 3.
92 Goeman 2008: 300.
93 Meusburger 2011: 52.
94 Meusburger 2011: 51.

95 Meusburger 2011: 53.
96 Meusburger 2011: 53.
97 Zerubavel 1996: 290.
98 Meusburger 2011: 53.
99 Zerubavel 1996: 290.
100 Zerubavel 1996: 294.
101 Lobo 2003.
102 Kathleen Fitzgerald first used the "reclaimer" designation in her book, *Beyond White Ethnicity: Developing a Sociological Understanding of Native American Identity Reclamation* (2007).
103 Alba 1990; Waters 1990.
104 Saldaña 2009.
105 Olick and Robbins 1998: 111.
106 Olick and Robbins 1998: 133.
107 Khanna 2010.
108 Said 1978.
109 Olick and Robbins 1998: 126.
110 Schwalbe and Mason-Schrock 1996; Snow and Anderson 1987.
111 Olick and Robbins 1998; Zerubavel 1996.
112 Bradley 1996.
113 Morris 1999; Owens, Robinson, and Smith-Lovin 2010; Taylor and Whittier 1999.
114 Hall 1990: 227.

CHAPTER 1. TOWARD A MORE "SOPHISTICATED" SOCIOLOGY OF COMPLEX URBAN INDIAN IDENTITIES

1 Biolsi 2005: 254.
2 Akers (2014) reveals numerous "corrupt and dishonorable practices" used by US authorities to steal Indigenous lands during the so-called treaty period, including but not limited to threatening to annihilate entire tribes, using unauthorized signatories when tribal leaders refused to sign, changing treaty terms immediately prior to ratification, and refusing to litigate the cases of Native nations whose leaders protested the violent and deceitful tactics of treaty negotiators.
3 Akers 2014: 59.
4 Akers 2014: 59.
5 Cherokee Nation v. Georgia.
6 Krakoff 2017: 498.
7 Omi and Winant 2014.
8 Tallbear 2013.
9 E. Davis 2008.
10 Akers 2014.
11 US Department of State, Office of the Historian n.d.
12 Akers 1999; Foreman 1932.
13 Akers 1999.

14 Cherokee, NC, n.d.

15 Sturm 2011.

16 Hirschfelder and Kreipe de Montano 1993.

17 Wilbur and Keen 2019.

18 Garroutte 2003: 42.

19 Excluded nations (n = 61) did not have publicly available citizenship information. Federally recognized Alaskan tribes (n = 227) were intentionally excluded from the sample due to their unique "structures of tribal belonging and citizenship."

20 Rodriguez-Lonebear 2021.

21 Blood quantum criteria vary across "type" (tribal blood only or Indian blood more generally) and proportion, with proportion requirements ranging from five-eighths to one-thirty-second blood quantum in this sample.

22 The last published research (Gould 2001) utilized 1991 data.

23 For an example, see M. Annette Jaimes, "Federal Indian Identification Policy: A Usurpation of Indigenous Sovereignty in North America," pp. 123–38 in *State of Native America: Genocide, Colonization, and Resistance*, edited by Annette M. Jaimes (Boston: South End Press, 1992). For more recent scholarship grounded in this perspective, see Galanda and Dreveskracht (2015) and Hill and Ratteree (2017).

24 According to Gover (2010), more than two hundred Native nations were still using federally created base rolls, while less than twenty nations used tribally created rolls. Kirsty Gover, *Tribal Constitutionalism: States, Tribes, and the Governance of Membership* (Oxford, England: Oxford University Press, 2010).

25 Garroutte 2003: 24.

26 Biolsi 1995: 28.

27 TallBear 2013.

28 Elizabeth Cook-Lynn and Beatrice Medicine are two prominent scholars who maintain that blood concepts have always indicated belongingness in tribal communities.

29 Tallbear 2013: 64.

30 Straus and Valentino 1998.

31 Rodriguez-Lonebear 2021.

32 Krakoff 2017: 534.

33 O'Nell 1996: 51–53.

34 Interestingly, according to the 2010 Census, non-Indians outnumbered Indian-identified persons only three to one.

35 This example draws directly on the work of legal scholar Sarah Krakoff. Krakoff (2017: 492) uses "color-blind" challenges to the Indian Child Welfare Act (ICWA) and the Indian Gaming Regulatory Act (IGRA) to untangle "the legitimate constitutional basis for tribal recognition . . . from the racial logic that nearly eliminated tribes from the continent."

36 Krakoff 2017: 515.

37 Krakoff 2017: 545.

38 Lawrence 2003: 24.

39 Lawrence 2003: 21.

40 Spivak 2010.
41 Omi and Winant 2014: 22.
42 Omi and Winant 2014.
43 Goeman 2008.
44 Liebler and Zacher 2013; Liebler, Bhaskar, and Porter 2016; Nagel 1997, 2000.
45 Jones 2006.
46 Prior to 1960, census enumerators determined the race of people they enumerated. As a result, the implementation of racial *self*-identification in the 1960 census may account for some of the 46 percent growth in the AIAN population between 1950 and 1960. This change, however, cannot explain the following periods of growth.
47 Nagel 1997.
48 Steiner 1968.
49 Straus and Valentino 1998.
50 Kelly 2011: 247.
51 Rosenthal 2012: 138.
52 Straus and Valentino 1998: 103.
53 Liebler 2004.
54 Liebler and Zacher 2013.
55 Liebler, Bhaskar, and Porter 2016.
56 Fitzgerald 2007.
57 Fitzgerald's perspective, originally published in 2007, may have changed over time.
58 Quoted in Sturm 2011: 181.
59 Sturm 2011.
60 Sturm (2011: 26) uses "citizen" in reference to federally recognized Cherokees not to "make a fetish of federal recognition" or "question other forms of Indigenous identification" but rather "to clarify historical, political, and legal differences that are important to interpretations of tribal politics and sovereignty."
61 Sturm 2011: 17.
62 Currently there are sixty-three state-recognized tribes in eleven states. Nearly two dozen additional states are considering legislative criteria for state recognition. Martha Salazar, "State Recognition of American Indian Tribes," National Conference of State Legislatures, October 2016. Available at www.ncsl.org, accessed February 2, 2022.
63 Moreton-Robinson 2015.
64 Elmahrek and Pringle 2019.
65 My earlier work (Jacobs 2014) and works by Sturm (2011) and Fitzgerald (2007) are examples.
66 Sturm 2011: 86.
67 Andersen 2009.
68 Hokowhitu 2009.
69 Andersen 2009: 94.
70 Andersen 2009: 94.
71 Moreton-Robinson 2015: xviii.

72 In part, this lack of consideration is methodological. American Indians and
    Alaska Natives comprise only approximately 1.2 percent of the US population.
    AIAN are difficult to enumerate and difficult to survey, and their small population
    size does not lead to particularly robust quantitative findings.
73 Robertson 2015.
74 Omi and Winant 2014.
75 Feagin 2014.
76 Feagin 2014: 225.
77 Quoted in Robertson 2015: 118.
78 Robertson 2015: 120–21.
79 Robertson 2015: 141.
80 Moreton-Robinson 2015: xviii.
81 Glenn 2015; Bonilla-Silva 2015.
82 Blauner 1972.
83 Konishi 2019.
84 Blauner 1972: 84–85.
85 American Sociological Association n.d.
86 Unfortunately, this important article fixates on "white sociology" versus "black so-
    ciology" and mentions Indigenous peoples only once—in one sentence that serves
    as a territorial acknowledgment. As Moreton-Robinson (2015: 54) elucidates,
    the black/white binary "places the literature out of [settler] colonial history, and
    thereby, reifies white possession of knowledge and the academy."
87 Brunsma and Wyse 2019: 8.
88 US Interagency Council on Homelessness 2012.
89 Schilling 2018.
90 National Center for Education Statistics n.d.
91 National Congress of American Indians 2020.
92 National Center for Education Statistics n.d.
93 Indian Health Service 2019.
94 National Congress of American Indians 2020.
95 Tribal Epidemiology Centers 2018.
96 US Interagency Council on Homelessness 2012.
97 Rosay 2016.
98 Hansen 2017.
99 US Census Bureau 2019.
100 O'Nell 1996: 61.

CHAPTER 2. STORIES OF RELOCATION
1 McCarty, Romero, and Zepeda 2006: 28–29.
2 Weeks and Metzger n.d.
3 Fixico 2000: 27.
4 Fixico 2000.
5 Fixico 2000.

6 Fixico 2000: 132.
7 National Library of Medicine n.d.
8 Means and Wolf 1995.
9 Means and Wolf 1995: 140.
10 O'Keefe and Reger 2017.
11 US Department of Veterans Affairs 2012.
12 Matthiessen 1991: 36–37.
13 Jones 2006: 2126.
14 Jones 2006: 2129.
15 Conti 2017.
16 "Scrofulous" is in scare quotes because it *literally* means relating to tuberculosis but also was used to describe people who appeared sickly and/or acted immorally.
17 Conti 2017.
18 Moffatt, Mayan, and Long 2013.
19 Stevenson 2014.
20 The IHS claims, for instance, that it "reduced tuberculosis [among US Indigenous populations] by 96 percent" between its establishment in 1955 and 1989.
21 Burich 2007.
22 Burich 2007: 104.
23 Burich 2007: 104.
24 Fixico 2000: 97.

CHAPTER 3. STORIES OF RECLAMATION

1 US Department of Veterans Affairs 2012.
2 Tate 1986: 427.
3 Fitzgerald 2007; Garroutte 2003.
4 Sturm 2011: 132.

CHAPTER 4. BEING AND BECOMING INDIAN

1 Deloria 1969.
2 Deloria 1969.
3 Deloria 1969: 106.
4 Deloria 1969: 109.
5 Public Law 95–341 1978.
6 Hoefnagels 2007.
7 Garroutte et al. 2009.
8 Lucero 2010.
9 Krouse 1999.

CHAPTER 5. DOING AND DISCOVERING INDIGENEITY

1 Admittedly, Kurt's and Tabatha's "apocalyptic scenarios" seemed more far-fetched pre–COVID-19.
2 Dunaway 2017.

3 Meusburger 2011: 57.

4 Indigenous people still wear such adornments and outfits, but generally not as a matter of course in their day-to-day lives.

5 O'Barr 2013.

6 Cheshire 2001; Kelley 2012; Lerch and Bullers 1996; Sanchez 2001.

7 Hoefnagels 2007.

8 Nagel 1997; Snipp 1997; Sturm 2011.

9 Lawrence 2003; Spivak 2010; Tallbear 2013.

10 This phenomenon also occurs in other racialized groups who experience oppression in US settler society (Demo and Hughes 1990).

11 I was on more familiar terms with young adult relocators who felt more (as opposed to less) committed to Indigenous peoples and communities because these young people more frequently participated in relocator community meetings and events.

12 In addition to Shawn Wilson (2001), these ideas are credited to A. J. B. Johnson (1993), who, in an unpublished manuscript, states that Native people "may well want to talk more about their world view and less about the 'things' to which its culture has often been reduced." Johnson's finding was based on interviews conducted with First Nations scholars about Park Canada's portrayals of Indigenous histories.

13 Meusburger 2011.

CHAPTER 6. URBAN INDIAN TROUBLES

1 Portions of this discussion appear in my 2021 publication, "'You Should Be Proud!' Native-Themed Mascots and the Cultural Reproduction of White Settler Space."

2 This idea (white settler space) builds on Brunsma and colleagues' (2020) examination of white space, conceptualized as settings that normalize whiteness and white possession.

3 Davis-Delano 1993.

4 Moreton-Robinson 2015.

5 I provide a more thorough discussion of this diversity in the Cleveland metropolitan area in an empirical article: Michelle R. Jacobs, "Race, Place, and Biography at Play: Contextualizing American Indian Viewpoints on Indian Mascots." *Journal of Sport and Social Issues* 38 (2014): 322–45.

6 For a succinct review of this research, see Davis-Delano, Gone, and Fryberg 2020.

7 Fryberg et al. 2008; LaRocque et al. 2011.

8 Fryberg et al. 2008: 216.

9 Angle et al. 2017; Burkley et al. 2017; Chaney, Burke, and Burkley 2011.

10 Freng and Willis-Esqueda 2011.

11 Clark et al. 2011; Steinfeldt et al. 2010.

12 Neville et al. 2011; Steinfeldt and Wong 2010.

13 In an earlier work, sociologist Laurel Davis-Delano (1993) similarly asserts that mascot portrayals of Indianness are necessarily stereotypical because stories about

the noble warrior defeated by heroic white men who ultimately conquered the West are central to US national identities.

14 Staurowsky 1998.
15 Staurowsky 1998.
16 Staurowsky 1998: 306.
17 Ricca 2014.
18 Waldstein 2018.
19 King 2003: 10.
20 United Press International 1972.
21 Associated Press 1972.
22 McQuade 2014.
23 White people claiming Indian identities to assert authority in Indian mascot debates is a phenomenon documented in the literature (Springwood 2004).
24 The polls are problematic for a number of reasons, including failure to report polling methods (e.g., how participants were recruited, how Native identity was defined) and failure to discuss how poll findings compare with other public opinion polls on Indian mascots. Moreover, the polls' findings are not contextualized with historical information about Indigenous peoples or Indian mascots, and therefore, do not explicate how or why the polling results cohere with centuries of systems and structures that reproduce colonial unknowing (Fenelon 2016; King et al. 2002).
25 Matias 2016.
26 Although Pewewardy uses this concept to discuss Indigenous issues like Indian mascots, he borrows the concept from Joyce E. King and Gloria Ladson-Billings.
27 Pewewardy 2000: 3.
28 Robertson 2015.
29 Robertson 2015: 129.
30 Robertson 2015: 140–41.
31 See Wydemer (2010) for the term "enduring smear."
32 Lara-Cooper and Cooper 2016.
33 Robertson 2015.
34 Sturm 2011.
35 Nagel 2000.
36 Gonzales 1998.
37 Liebler 2018.
38 Tallbear 2021.
39 Barker 2017: 3.
40 I use this term to maintain consistency with current literature on the topic. Given that Indigenous peoples are racialized *citizens* of Indian nations, however, the "race shifting" concept does not fully capture the magnitude and/or consequences of the phenomenon by which previously non-Native-identified people identify as Indians.
41 Sturm 2011: 177.
42 Sturm 2011: 162.
43 Nagle 2019.

44 This type of pretend Indianness evokes pity from Kim Tallbear (Sisseton Wahpeton), who, in a blog about "race shifting red flags," says she "feel[s] really bad" for people whose adornments "look like they were purchased from Amazon.com." Such purchases may include "off-the-shoulder Disney-like 'Pocahontas' dresses" similar to dresses she has seen at some east coast powwows. Kim Tallbear, "Indigenous 'Race-Shifting' Red Flags," September 10, 2021. Available at https://kimtallbear.substack.com.

45 Kenai occasionally refers to full-blood Natives as "skins," which is short for the R-word. He said he learned this lingo from the Lakota men with whom he Sun Dances.

CHAPTER 7. URBAN INDIAN COMMUNITIES

1 Gaudry 2018; Gaudry and Leroux 2017; Nagel 1997; Sturm 2011.

2 Zerubavel 1996.

3 Meusburger 2011: 66.

4 Kurt's professed beliefs contain echoes of Métis- and Cherokee-identified groups' stories—primarily regarding DNA and warriors' avoidance of being removed to reservations—but important differences distinguish Northeast Ohio reclaimers from these other groups.

5 None of the reclaimers interviewed for this study had taken a genetic ancestry test.

6 Sturm (2011) refers to this practice as "spreading the Cherokee gospel."

7 Geritol is a brand-name multivitamin. The prefix "geri" conveys a connection with elderly people.

8 Zerubavel 1996: 291.

9 Foucault 1977.

10 Peers 1999.

11 Olick and Robbins 1998.

12 Though the topic of intercommunity tensions was not included in the interview guide, every later-generation relocator who participated in a formal interview raised the issue.

13 Another exception was a young second-generation, tribally enrolled couple (a man and a woman), both of whom moved to the Northeast Ohio region from different states. Over the years of my involvement, the couple attended established relocator community events, but also tried to branch out and create new methods and models of community building.

CONCLUSION

1 Foucault 1977.

2 Hokowhitu 2009.

3 Kenai, for instance, is a reclaimer who says his grandparents participated in Indian Relocation, "skipped out," "did this and that," and ended up in Northeast Ohio. Still, Kenai did not learn his Lakota culture from his mother because his grandparents

did not teach his mother Indian ways. Referring to his grandparents, Kenai said, "They're not traditional at all, which is weird. It's almost like, when you leave the rez, it starts to go away. It's almost like you forget who you are and your culture. . . . I mean, how many people don't know their families' histories or languages?"

4 Indigenous communities, after all, did not host pan-tribal social gatherings with dancing, drumming, and Indian tacos prior to the European invasion of the Western hemisphere.

5 This idea, introduced in chapter 1, is borrowed from O'Nell's (1996) research conducted on the Flathead Reservation in Montana.

6 Goeman 2008.

7 Goeman 2008: 300.

8 Whereas some reclaimers had tribal identification cards and other documentary evidence to support their Indian identity claims, other reclaimers with seemingly veritable Indian ancestries did not.

9 These "nostalgic" memories are more likely to surface in urban spaces located some distance from places more densely populated with Indigenous peoples. Different "memories" of Indigenous peoples (e.g., drunken, violent Indianness), for instance, infuse environments bordering Indigenous nations.

10 Olick and Robbins 1998.

11 Nagel 1997.

12 Sturm 2011: 54.

13 Arvin, Tuck, and Morrill 2013: 21.

14 Arvin, Tuck, and Morrill 2013.

15 Anderson 2016: xxvii.

16 Moreton-Robinson 2015.

17 Nagle 2019.

18 Phung 2011: 296.

19 Centers for Disease Control and Prevention 2021.

20 In the earliest months of the pandemic (March and April 2020), black people suffered the greatest number of COVID-related fatalities in the United States.

21 In 2019, Indian Health Services (IHS) expenditure per person ($4,078) was only about 40 percent of US National Health expenditure per person ($9,726). Indian Health Service, "IHS Profile," August 2020. Available at www.ihs.gov.

22 Noor 2020.

23 Hansen 2017.

24 National Congress of American Indians 2020.

25 Davis 2020.

26 Jacobs 2021.

27 National Congress of American Indians n.d.

28 Manseau 2020.

29 Trahant 2018.

30 He 2020.

31 US Department of the Interior 2021.

WORKS CITED

Akers, Donna L. 1999. "Removing the Heart of the Choctaw People: Indian Removal from a Native Perspective." *American Indian Culture and Research Journal* 23(3): 63–76.

———. 2014. "Decolonizing the Master Narrative: Treaties and Other American Myths." *Wicazo Sa Review* 29(1): 58–76.

Alba, Richard D. 1990. *Ethnic Identity: The Transformation of White America.* New Haven, CT: Yale University Press.

American Sociological Association. N.d. "Sociology of Indigenous Peoples and Native Nations." Available at www.asanet.org. Retrieved August 12, 2021.

Andersen, Chris. 2009. "Critical Indigenous Studies: From Difference to Density." *Cultural Studies Review* 15(2): 80–100.

Anderson, Kim. 2016. *A Recognition of Being: Reconstructing Native Womanhood.* Toronto: Canadian Scholars' Press.

Angle, Justin W., Sokiente W. Dagogo-Jack, Mark R. Forehand, and Andrew W. Perkins. 2017. "Activating Stereotypes with Brand Imagery: The Role of Viewer Political Identity." *Journal of Consumer Psychology* 27(1): 84–90.

Arvin, Maile, Eve Tuck, and Angie Morrill. 2013. "Decolonizing Feminism: Challenging Connections between Settler Colonialism and Heteropatriarchy." *Feminist Formations* 25(1): 8–34.

Associated Press (AP). 1972. "Real Cleveland Indian Assails Club Symbol." *New York Times,* January 16. Available at www.nytimes.com.

Baires, Sarah E. 2018. "White Settlers Buried the Truth about the Midwest's Mysterious Mound Cities." *Smithsonian Magazine,* February 23. Available at www.smithsonianmag.com.

Barker, Joanne. 2017. "Introduction: Critically Sovereign." Pp. 1–44 in *Critically Sovereign: Indigenous Gender, Sexuality, and Feminist Studies,* edited by J. Barker. Durham, NC: Duke University Press.

Bhambra, Gurminder K. 2014. "Introduction to Knowledge Production in Global Context: Power and Coloniality." *Current Sociology* 6(2): 452–54.

Biolsi, Thomas. 1995. "The Birth of the Reservation: Making the Modern Individual among the Lakota." *American Ethnologist* 22(1): 28–53.

———. 2005. "Imagined Geographies: Sovereignty, Indigenous Space, and American Indian Struggle." *American Ethnologist* 32(2): 239–59.

Blackhawk, Ned. 1995. "I Can Carry On from Here: The Relocation of American Indians to Los Angeles." *Wicazo Sa Review* 11(2): 16–30.

Blauner, Robert. 1972. *Racial Oppression in America.* New York: Harper & Row.

Bloetscher, Virginia Chase. 1981. *Indians of the Cuyahoga Valley and Vicinity*. Akron, OH: North American Indian Cultural Center.

Bonilla-Silva, Eduardo. 1997. "Rethinking Racism: Toward a Structural Interpretation." *American Sociological Review* 62(3): 465–480.

———. 2006. *Racism without Racists: Color-blind Racism and the Persistence of Racial Inequality in the United States*. Lanham, MD: Rowman & Littlefield Publishers.

———. 2015. "The Structure of Racism in Color-blind,'Post-Racial' America." *American Behavioral Scientist* 59(11): 1358–1376.

Bradley, Harriet. 1996. *Fractured Identities: Changing Patterns of Inequality*. Cambridge, UK: Polity Press.

Brunsma, David L., Nathaniel G. Chapman, Joong Won Kim, J. Slade Lellock, Megan Underhill, Erik T. Withers, and Jennifer Padilla Wyse. 2020. "The Culture of White Space: On the Racialized Production of Meaning." *American Behavioral Scientist* 64(14): 2001–15.

Brunsma, David L., and Jennifer Padilla Wyse. 2019. "The Possessive Investment in White Sociology." *Sociology of Race and Ethnicity* 5(1): 1–10.

Bureau of the US Census. 1920. "Contents—Ohio." Available at www2.census.gov.

Burich, Keith. 2007. "'No Place to Go': The Thomas Indian School and the 'Forgotten' Indian Children of New York." *Wicazo Sa Review* 22(2): 93–110.

Burkley, Melissa, Edward Burkley, Angela Andrade, and Angela C. Bell. 2017. "Symbols of Pride or Prejudice? Examining the Impact of Native American Sports Mascots on Stereotype Application." *Journal of Social Psychology* 157(2): 223–35.

Burt, Larry W. 1986. "Roots of the Native American Urban Experience: Relocation Policy in the 1950s." *American Indian Quarterly* 10(2): 85–99.

Carpenter, Les, and Mark Maske. 2020. "NFL Franchise to Go by 'Washington Football Team' This Season, Delaying Permanent Name Change." *Washington Post*, July 23. Available at www.washingtonpost.com.

Centers for Disease Control and Prevention. 2021 (November 6). "COVID-19 Weekly Cases and Deaths per 100,000 Population by Age, Race/Ethnicity, and Sex." Available at https://covid.cdc.gov.

Chaney, John, Amanda Burke, and Edward Burkley. 2011. "Do American Indian Mascots = American Indian People? Examining Implicit Bias towards American Indian People and American Indian Mascots." *American Indian and Alaska Native Mental Health Research: The Journal of the National Center* 18(1): 42–62.

Cherokee Nation v. Georgia, 30 U.S. (5 Pet.) 1 (1831). Available at https://supreme.justia.com.

Cherokee, North Carolina. N.d. "Culture: The People." Retrieved September 28, 2020. Available at https://visitcherokeenc.com.

Cheshire, Tamara C. 2001. "Cultural Transmission in Urban American Indian Families." *American Behavioral Scientist* 44(9): 1528–35.

Clark, D. Anthony, Lisa B. Spanierman, Tamilia D. Reed, Jason R. Soble, and Sharon Cabana. 2011. "Documenting Weblog Expressions of Racial Microaggressions That Target American Indians." *Journal of Diversity in Higher Education* 4(1): 39.

Cleveland Indians Twitter page. 2020 (December 14). "Statement from the Organization." https://twitter.com/cleguardians/status/1338559595774681089.

Collins, Patricia Hill. 2007. "Pushing the Boundaries or Business as Usual? Race, Class, and Gender Studies and Sociological Inquiry." Pp. 572–604 in *Sociology in America: A History*, edited by C. Calhoun. Chicago: University of Chicago Press.

Conti, Kibbe. 2017 (May 1). "The History of Sioux Sanitarium as a Segregated Tuberculosis Clinic." Rapid City, South Dakota: Mniluzahan Okolakiciyapi Ambassadors. Available at www.moarapidcity.org.

Davis, Ethan. 2008. "An Administrative Trail of Tears: Indian Removal." *American Journal of Legal History* 50(1): 49–100.

Davis, Scott. 2020. "The Washington Redskins Are under More Pressure Than Ever to Change Their Name." *(Business) Insider*, July 2. Available at www.insider.com.

Davis-Delano, Laurel R. 1993. "Protest against the Use of Native American Mascots: A Challenge to Traditional American Identity." *Journal of Sport and Social Issues* 17(1): 9–22.

Davis-Delano, Laurel, Joseph P. Gone, and Stephanie A. Fryberg. 2020. "The Psychosocial Effects of Native American Mascots: A Comprehensive Review of Empirical Research Findings." *Race, Ethnicity, and Education* 23(5): 613–33.

Deloria, Vine. 1969. *Custer Died for Your Sins: An Indian Manifesto*. Norman: University of Oklahoma Press.

Demo, David H., and Michael Hughes. 1990. "Socialization and Racial Identity among Black Americans." *Social Psychology Quarterly* 53(4): 364–74.

Department of Veterans Affairs. 2012. "American Indian and Alaska Native Servicemembers and Veterans." Available at www.va.gov/tribalgovernment.

Dhillon, Jaskiran. 2019. "Notes on Becoming a Comrade: Indigenous Women, Leadership, and Movement(s) for Decolonization." *American Indian Culture and Research Journal* 43(3): 41–54.

Dunaway, Finis. 2017. "The 'Crying Indian' Ad That Fooled the Environmental Movement." *Chicago Tribune*, November 21. Available at www.chicagotribune.com.

Elmahrek, Adam, and Paul Pringle. 2019. "Two Tribes Aren't Recognized Federally. Yet Members Won $500 Million in Minority Contracts." *Los Angeles Times*, December 31. Available at www.latimes.com.

Feagin, Joe. 2014. *Racist America: Roots, Current Realities, and Future Reparations*, 3rd edition. Oxfordshire, England: Routledge.

Fenelon, James V. 2016. *Redskins? Sport Mascots, Indian Nations, and White Racism*. Oxfordshire, England: Routledge.

Fitzgerald, Kathleen J. 2007. *Beyond White Ethnicity: Developing a Sociological Understanding of Native American Identity Reclamation*. Lanham, MD: Lexington Books.

Fixico, Donald Lee. 2000. *The Urban Indian Experience in America*. Albuquerque: University of New Mexico Press.

Foreman, Grant. 1932. *Indian Removal: The Emigration of the Five Civilized Tribes of Indians*. Norman: University of Oklahoma Press.

Foucault, Michel. 1977. *Language, Counter-Memory, Practice: Selected Essays and Interviews.* Transl. D. F. Bouchard and S. Simon. Ithaca, NY: Cornell University Press.

Freng, Scott, and Cynthia Willis-Esqueda. 2011. "A Question of Honor: Chief Wahoo and American Indian Stereotype Activation among a University Based Sample." *Journal of Social Psychology* 151(5): 577–91.

Fryberg, Stephanie A., Hazel Rose Markus, Daphna Oyserman, and Joseph M. Stone. 2008. "Of Warrior Chiefs and Indian Princesses: The Psychological Consequences of American Indian Mascots." *Basic and Applied Social Psychology* 30(3): 208–18.

Galanda, Gabriel S., and Ryan D. Dreveskracht. 2015. "Curing the Tribal Disenrollment Epidemic: In Search of a Remedy." *Arizona Law Review* 57: 383.

Garroutte, Eva. 2003. *Real Indians: Identity and the Survival of Native America.* Berkeley: University of California Press.

Garroutte, Eva M., Janette Beals, Ellen M. Keane, Carol Kaufman, Paul Spicer, Jeff Henderson, Patricia N. Henderson, Christina M. Mitchell, Spero M. Manson, and AI-SUPERPFP Team. 2009. "Religiosity and Spiritual Engagement in Two American Indian Populations." *Journal for the Scientific Study of Religion* 48(3): 480–500.

Gaudry, Adam. 2018. "Communing with the Dead: The 'New Métis,' Métis Identity Appropriation, and the Displacement of Living Métis Culture." *American Indian Quarterly* 42(2): 162–90.

Gaudry, Adam, and Darryl Leroux. 2017. "White Settler Revisionism and Making Métis Everywhere: The Evocation of the Métissage in Quebec and Nova Scotia." *Critical Ethnic Studies* 3(1): 116–42.

George, Robert. N.d. "The Cuyahoga, a National Heritage River." Available at www.nps.gov. Retrieved November 9, 2021.

Glenn, Evelyn Nakano. 2015. "Settler Colonialism as Structure: A Framework for Comparative Studies of US Race and Gender Formation." *Sociology of Race and Ethnicity* 1(1): 52–72.

Goeman, Mishuana. 2008. "(Re)Mapping Indigenous Presence on the Land in Native Women's Literature." *American Quarterly* 60(2): 295–302.

———. 2013. *Mark My Words: Native Women Mapping Our Nations.* Minneapolis: University of Minnesota Press.

Goldstein, Alyosha, ed. 2014. *Formations of United States Colonialism.* Durham, NC: Duke University Press.

Gonzales, Angela. 1998. "The (Re)Articulation of American Indian Identity: Maintaining Boundaries and Regulating Access to Ethnically Tied Resources." *American Indian Culture and Research Journal* 22(4): 199–225.

Gould, L. Scott. 2001. "Mixing Bodies and Beliefs: The Predicament of Tribes." *Columbia Law Review* 101: 702.

Gunn Allen, Paula. 1986. *The Sacred Hoop: Recovering the Feminine in Native American Traditions.* Boston: Beacon Press.

Hall, Stuart. 1990. "Cultural Identity and Diaspora." Pp. 222–37 in *Identity: Community, Culture, Difference*, edited by Jonathan Rutherford. London: Lawrence and Wishart.

Hall, Stuart, and Paul Du Gay, eds. 1996. *Questions of Cultural Identity*. Thousand Oaks, CA: Sage.

Hansen, Elise. 2017. "The Forgotten Minority in Police Shootings." CNN, November 13. Available at www.cnn.com.

Harjo, Suzan Shown. 2018. "'Off the Reservation'—A Teachable Moment." *Indian Country Today*, September 12. Available at https://indiancountrytoday.com.

He, Felicia. 2020. "First Native American Congressional Delegate, Kimberly Teehee, Discusses Historic Appointment at IOP." *Harvard Crimson*, November 19. Available at www.thecrimson.com.

Hill, Norbert S., and Kathleen Ratteree, eds. 2017. *The Great Vanishing Act: Blood Quantum and the Future of Native Nations*. Ann Arbor, MI: Fulcrum Publishing.

Hirschfelder, Arlene B., and Martha Kreipe de Montano. 1993. *The Native North American Almanac: A Portrait of Native America Today*. New York: Prentice Hall.

Hoefnagels, Anna. 2007. "The Dynamism and Transformation of 'Tradition': Factors Affecting the Development of Powwows in Southwestern Ontario." *Ethnologies* 29(1–2): 107–41.

Hokowhitu, Brendan. 2009. "Indigenous Existentialism and the Body." *Cultural Studies Review* 15(2): 101–18.

Indian Health Service. 2019 (October). "Mortality Disparity Rates: AI/AN in the IHS Service Area." Available at www.ihs.gov. Retrieved November 9, 2021.

Jackson, Deborah Davis. 2002. *Our Elders Lived It: American Indian Identity in the City*. DeKalb: Northern Illinois University Press.

Jacobs, Michelle R. 2014. "Race, Place, and Biography at Play: Contextualizing American Indian Viewpoints on Indian Mascots." *Journal of Sport and Social Issues* 38: 322–45.

———. 2021. "'You Should Be Proud!' Native-Themed Mascots and the Cultural Reproduction of White Settler Space." *Sociological Inquiry*, November 10. Available at https://doi.org/10.1111/soin.12477.

Johnson, A. J. B. 1993. "Toward a New Past: Reflection on the Interpretation of Native History within Parks Canada." Unpublished manuscript.

Jones, David S. 2006. "The Persistence of American Indian Health Disparities." *American Journal of Public Health* 96(12): 2122–34.

Kelley, Dennis F. 2012. "Ancient Traditions, Modern Constructions: Innovation, Continuity, and Spirituality on the Powwow Trail." *Journal for the Study of Religions and Ideologies* 11(33): 107–36.

Kelly, Casey Ryan. 2011. "Blood-Speak: Ward Churchill and the Racialization of American Indian Identity." *Communication and Critical/Cultural Studies* 8(3): 240–65.

Khanna, Nikki. 2010. "'If You're Half Black, You're Just Black': Reflected Appraisals and the Persistence of the One-Drop Rule." *Sociological Quarterly* 51(1): 96–121.

King, C. Richard, Ellen J. Staurowsky, Lawrence Baca, Laurel R. Davis, and Cornel Pewewardy. 2002. "Of Polls and Race Prejudice: *Sports Illustrated*'s Errant 'Indian Wars.'" *Journal of Sport and Social Issues* 26(4): 381–402.

King, Thomas. 2003. *The Truth about Stories: A Native Narrative*. Minneapolis: University of Minnesota Press.

Konishi, Shino. 2019. "First Nations Scholars, Settler Colonial Studies, and Indigenous History." *Australian Historical Studies* 50(3): 285–304.

Kovach, Margaret. 2009. *Indigenous Methodologies: Characteristics, Conversations, and Contexts*. Toronto: University of Toronto Press.

Krakoff, Sarah. 2017. "They Were Here First: American Indian Tribes, Race, and the Constitutional Minimum." *Stanford Law Review* 69: 491–548.

Krouse, Susan Applegate. 1999. "Kinship and Identity: Mixed Bloods in Urban Indian Communities." *American Indian Culture and Research Journal* 23(2): 73–89.

Lara-Cooper, Kishan, and Sammy Cooper. 2016. "'My Culture Is Not a Costume': The Influence of Stereotypes on Children in Middle Childhood." *Wicazo Sa Review* 31(2): 56–68.

LaRocque, Angela R., J. Douglas McDonald, Jeffrey N. Weatherly, and F. Richard Ferraro. 2011. "Indian Sport Mascots: Affective Difference between American Indian and Non-Indian College Students." *American Indian and Alaskan Native Mental Health Research* 18(2): 1–16.

Laukaitis, John J. 2005. "Relocation and Urbanization: An Educational History of the American Indian Experience in Chicago, 1952–1972." *American Educational History Journal* 32(2): 139.

Lawrence, Bonita. 2003. "Gender, Race, and the Regulation of Native Identity in Canada and the United States: An Overview." *Hypatia* 8(2): 3–31.

Lepper, Bradley. 2020. "Archaeology: Saga of Giant Mound Builders Is a Tall Tale That Won't Go Away." *Columbus Dispatch*, April 21. Available at www.dispatch.com.

Lerch, Patricia, and Susan Bullers. 1996. "Powwows as Identity Markers: Traditional or Pan-Indian?" *Human Organization* 55(4): 390–95.

Liebler, Carolyn A. 2004. "American Indian Ethnic Identity: Tribal Nonresponse in the 1990 Census." *Social Science Quarterly* 85(2): 310–23.

——. 2018. "Counting America's First Peoples." *Annals of the American Academy* 677: 180–90.

Liebler, Carolyn A., Renuka Bhaskar, and Sonya R. Porter. 2016. "Dynamics of Race: Joining, Leaving, and Staying in the American Indian/Alaska Native Race Category between 2000 and 2010." *Demography* 53(2): 507–40.

Liebler, Carolyn A., and Meghan Zacher. 2013. "American Indians without Tribes in the Twenty-first Century." *Ethnic and Racial Studies* 36(11): 1910–34.

Lipsitz, George. 1998. *The Possessive Investment in Whiteness*. Philadelphia: Temple University Press.

Lobo, Susan. 2003. "Urban Clan Mothers: Key Households in Cities." *American Indian Quarterly* 27(3/4): 505–22.

Loewen, James W. N.d. "Louisville, Ohio." History and Social Justice. Retrieved November 9, 2021. Available at https://justice.tougaloo.edu.

Lucero, Nancy M. 2010. "Making Meaning of Urban American Indian Identity: A Multistage Integrative Process." *Social Work* 55(4): 327–36.

Major League Baseball. 2020 (December 14). "Letter from Paul Dolan." Available at www.mlb.com.

Manseau, Peter. 2020. "As the World Churns: Inside the Clarified Butter–Maiden Backstory." *Baffler*, May 6. Available· at https://thebaffler.com.

Matias, Cheryl E. 2016. *Feeling White: Whiteness, Emotionality, and Education*. Boston: Brill.

Matthiessen, Peter. 1991. *In the Spirit of Crazy Horse*. New York: Viking Penguin.

McCarty, Teresa L., Mary Eunice Romero, and Ofelia Zepeda. 2006. "Reclaiming the Gift: Indigenous Youth Counter-Narratives on Native Language Loss and Revitalization." *American Indian Quarterly* 30(1/2): 28–48.

McQuade, Dan. 2014. "Time to Put Chief Wahoo Out to Pasture?" *VICE*, June 26. Available at www.vice.com.

Means, Russell, and Marvin J. Wolf. 1995. *Where White Men Fear to Tread: The Autobiography of Russell Means*. New York: St. Martin's.

Meusburger, Peter. 2011. "Knowledge, Cultural Memory, and Politics." Pp. 51–69 in *Cultural Memories*. Dordrecht, Germany: Springer.

Miller, Douglas K. 2013. "Willing Workers: Urban Relocation and American Indian Initiative, 1940s–1960s." *Ethnohistory* 60(1): 51–76.

Mills, Charles W. 2007. "White Ignorance." Pp. 11–38 in *Race and Epistemologies of Ignorance*, edited by Shannon Sullivan and Nancy Tuana. Albany: State University of New York Press.

———. 2014. "White Time: The Chronic Injustice of Ideal Theory." *Du Bois Review* 11(1): 27–42.

Moffatt, Jessica, Maria Mayan, and Richard Long. 2013. "Sanitariums and the Canadian Colonial Legacy: The Untold Experiences of Tuberculosis Treatment." *Qualitative Health Research* 12(12): 1591–99.

Moreton-Robinson, Aileen. 2015. *The White Possessive: Privilege, Power, and Indigenous Sovereignty*. Minneapolis: University of Minnesota Press.

Morris, Aldon D. 1999. "A Retrospective on the Civil Rights Movement: Political and Intellectual Landmarks." *Annual Review of Sociology* 25(1): 517–39.

Mutual of Omaha. 2020 (July 17). "Mutual of Omaha to Retire Corporate Logo." Available at www.mutualofomaha.com.

Nagel, Joane. 1997. *American Indian Ethnic Renewal: Red Power and the Resurgence of Identity and Culture*. New York: Oxford University Press.

———. 2000. "False Faces: Ethnic Identity, Authenticity, and Fraud in Native American Discourse and Politics." In *Identity and Social Change*, edited by Joseph E. Davis. Boca Raton, FL: Routledge.

Nagle, Rebecca. 2019. "How 'Pretendians' Undermine the Rights of Indigenous People." *High Country News*, April. Available at www.hcn.org.

National Center for Education Statistics. N.d. "Table 104.10. Rates of High School Completion and Bachelor's Degree Attainment among Persons Age 25 and Over, by Race/Ethnicity and Sex: Selected Years, 1910 through 2016." Available at https://nces.ed.gov. Retrieved November 9, 2021.

National Congress of American Indians (NCAI). 2020 (June 1). "Demographics: Indian Country Demographics." Available at www.ncai.org.

———. N.d. "Ending the Era of Harmful 'Indian' Mascots." Available at www.ncai.org. Retrieved November 8, 2021.

National Library of Medicine. N.d. "Native Voices: Timeline / Citizenship, Services, and Sovereignty / 1953: Congress Seeks to Abolish Tribes, Relocate American Indians." Available at www.nlm.nih.gov. Retrieved November 9, 2021.

Neville, Helen A., Jeffrey G. Yeung, Nathan R. Todd, Lisa B. Spanierman, and Tamilia D. Reed. 2011. "Color-Blind Racial Ideology and Beliefs about a Racialized University Mascot." *Journal of Diversity in Higher Education* 4(4): 236.

Noor, Poppy. 2020. "Interview: The Navajo Teenager Who Went Viral Reporting on Coronavirus: 'I Just Want Us to Be Seen.'" *Guardian*, May 22. www.theguardian.com.

O'Barr, William M. 2013. "Images of Native Americans in Advertising." *Advertising & Society Review* 14(1): 1–51.

O'Keefe, Victoria M., and Greg M. Reger. 2017. "Suicide among American Indian/Alaska Native Military Service Members and Veterans." *Psychological Services* 14(3): 289–94.

Olick, Jeffrey K., and Joyce Robbins. 1998. "Social Memory Studies: From 'Collective Memory' to the Historical Sociology of Mnemonic Practices." *Annual Review of Sociology* 24: 105–40.

Omi, Michael, and Howard Winant. [1986] 2014. *Racial Formation in the United States*. New York: Routledge.

O'Nell, Theresa DeLeane. 1996. *Disciplined Hearts: History, Identity, and Depression in an American Indian Community*. Oakland: University of California Press.

Orange, Tommy. 2019. *There, There*. London: Vintage.

Owens, Timothy J., Dawn T. Robinson, and Lynn Smith-Lovin. 2010. "Three Faces of Identity." *Annual Review of Sociology* 36: 477–99.

Peers, Laura. 1999. "'Playing Ourselves': First Nations and Native American Interpreters at Living History Sites." *Public Historian* 21(4): 39–59.

Pewewardy, Cornel D. 2000. "Why Educators Should Not Ignore Indian Mascots." *Multicultural Perspectives* 2(1): 3–7.

Philp, Kenneth R. 1985. "Stride toward Freedom: The Relocation of Indians to Cities, 1952–1960." *Western Historical Quarterly* 16(2): 175–90.

Phung, Malissa. 2011. "Are People of Colour Settlers Too?" Pp. 289–98 in *Cultivating Canada: Reconciliation through the Lens of Cultural Diversity*, edited by Ashok Mathur, Jonathan Dewar, and Mike DeGagné. Ottawa, Canada: Aboriginal Healing Foundation. Available at www.ahf.ca.

Public Law 95–341. 1978 (August 11). "American Indian Religious Freedom." Available at www.govinfo.gov.

Rabaka, Reiland. 2010. *Against Epistemic Apartheid: W. E. B. Du Bois and the Disciplinary Decadence of Sociology*. Lanham, MD: Rowman & Littlefield.

Ricca, Brad. 2014. "The Secret History of Chief Wahoo." *Belt Magazine*, June 19. Available at https://beltmag.com.

Robertson, Dwanna L. 2015. "Invisibility in the Color-Blind Era: Examining Legiti-mized Racism against Indigenous Peoples." *American Indian Quarterly* 39(2): 113–53.

Rodriguez-Lonebear, Desi. 2021. "The Blood Line: Racialized Boundary Making and Citizenship among Native Nations." *Sociology of Race and Ethnicity* 7(4): 527–42.

Rosay, André B. 2016. "Violence against American Indian and Alaska Native Women and Men." *NIJ Journal* 277: 38–45.

Rosenthal, Nicolas G. 2012. *Reimagining Indian Country: Native American Migration and Identity in Twentieth-Century Los Angeles*. Chapel Hill: University of North Carolina Press.

Said, Edward W. 1978. *Orientalism*. New York: Pantheon Books.

Saldaña, Johnny. 2009. *The Coding Manual for Qualitative Researchers*. Thousand Oaks, CA: Sage.

Sanchez, Victoria E. 2001. "Intertribal Dance and Cross-Cultural Communication: Traditional Powwows in Ohio." *Communication Studies* 52(1): 51–69.

Schilling, Vincent. 2018. "Getting Jobbed: 15 Tribes with Unemployment Rates over 80 Percent." *Indian Country Today*, September 13. Available at https://indiancountryto-day.com.

Schwalbe, Michael L., and Douglas Mason-Schrock. 1996. "Identity Work as Group Process." *Advances in Group Processes* 13(113): 47.

Sheinin, Dave, and Matt Bonesteel. 2018. "Cleveland Indians' Removal of Chief Wahoo Reignites Debate over Controversial Nicknames." *Washington Post*, January 29. Available at www.washingtonpost.com.

Shoemaker, Nancy. 1988. "Urban Indians and Ethnic Choices: American Indian Organizations in Minneapolis, 1920–1950." *Western Historical Quarterly* 19(4): 431–47.

Smith, Linda Tuhiwai. 1999. *Decolonizing Methodologies: Research and Indigenous Peoples*. London: Zed Books.

Snipp, C. Matthew. 1997. "Some Observations about Racial Boundaries and the Experi-ences of American Indians." *Ethnic and Racial Studies* 20(4): 667–89.

Snow, David A., and Leon Anderson. 1987. "Identity Work among the Homeless: The Verbal Construction and Avowal of Personal Identities." *American Journal of Sociol-ogy* 92(6): 1336–71.

Sousa Santos, Boaventura de, João Arriscado Nunes, and Maria Paula Meneses. 2007. "Introduction: Opening Up the Canon of Knowledge and Recognition of Differ-ence." Pp. xix–lxii in *Another Knowledge Is Possible: Beyond Northern Epistemolo-gies*, edited by B. de Sousa Santos. New York: Verso.

Souther, J. Mark. 2017. "From 'Mistake on the Lake' to 'Defend Together': The Long (and Amusing) History of Trying to Rebrand Cleveland." *Belt Magazine*, October 3. Available at https://beltmag.com.

Spivak, Gayatri Chakravorty. 2010. "Can the Subaltern Speak?" Pp. 21–78 in *Can the Subaltern Speak? Reflections on the History of an Idea*, edited by Morris Rosalind. New York: Columbia University Press. Available at www.jstor.org.

Springwood, Charles Fruehling. 2004. "'I'm Indian Too!' Claiming Native American Identity, Mascot Debates." *Journal of Sport and Social Issues* 28(1): 56–70.

Staurowsky, Ellen J. 1998. "An Act of Honor or Exploitation? The Cleveland Indians' Use of the Louis Francis Sockalexis Story." *Sociology of Sport Journal* 15: 299–316.

Steiner, Stan. 1968. *The New Indians*. New York: Harper & Row.

Steinfeldt, Jesse A., Brad D. Foltz, Jennifer K. Kaladow, Tracy N. Carlson, Louis A. Pagano Jr., Emily Benton, and M. Clint Steinfeldt. 2010. "Racism in the Electronic Age: Role of Online Forums in Expressing Racial Attitudes about American Indians." *Cultural Diversity and Ethnic Minority Psychology* 16(3): 362.

Steinfeldt, Jesse A., and Y. Joel Wong. 2010. "Multicultural Training on American Indian Issues: Testing the Effectiveness of an Intervention to Change Attitudes toward Native-Themed Mascots." *Cultural Diversity and Ethnic Minority Psychology* 16(2): 110.

Stevenson, Lisa. 2014. *Life beside Itself*. Berkeley: University of California Press.

Straus, Terry, and Debra Valentino. 1998. "Retribalization in Urban Indian Communities." *American Indian Culture and Research Journal* 22(4): 103–15.

Sturm, Circe. 2011. *Becoming Indian: The Struggle over Cherokee Identity in the Twenty-first Century*. Sante Fe, NM: School for Advanced Research Press.

TallBear, Kim. 2013. *Native American DNA: Tribal Belonging and the False Promise of Genetic Science*. Minneapolis: University of Minnesota Press.

———. 2014. "Standing with and Speaking as Faith: A Feminist-Indigenous Approach to Inquiry." *Journal of Research Practice* 10(2): 1–8.

———. 2021 (June 14). "We Are Not Your Dead Ancestors." Available at https://kimtallbear.substack.com. Retrieved October 18, 2021.

Tate, Michael L. 1986. "From Scout to Doughboy: The National Debate over Integrating American Indians into the Military, 1891–1918." *Western Historical Quarterly* 17(4): 417–37.

Taylor, Verta, and Nancy E. Whittier. 1999. "Collective Identity in Social Movement Communities: Lesbian Feminist Mobilization." Pp. 169–94 in *Waves of Protest: Social Movements since the Sixties*, edited by Jo Freeman and Victoria Johnson. Oxford: Oxford University Press.

Trahant, Mark. 2018. "More Native Women Are Running for Office Than Men." *Indian Country Today*, September 4. Available at www.indianz.com.

Tribal Epidemiology Centers. 2018 (March 14). "The Opioid Crisis Impact on Native American Communities." Available at https://tribalepicenters.org.

Tuck, Eve, and K. Wayne Yang. 2012. "Decolonization Is Not a Metaphor." *Decolonization: Indigeneity, Education & Society* 1(1): 1–40.

Tully, John. 2016. *Crooked Deals and Broken Treaties: How American Indians Were Displaced by White Settlers in the Cuyahoga Valley*. New York: NYU Press, Monthly Review Press.

United Press International (UPI). 1972. "Suit Planned against Cleveland." *Star News*, January 16. Available at https://news.google.com.

US Census Bureau. 2019. "Quick Facts: Ohio." Available at www.census.gov.

US Department of the Interior. 2021. "U.S. Secretary of the Interior: Secretary Deb Haaland." Available at www.doi.gov.

US Department of State, Office of the Historian. N.d. "Indian Treaties and the Removal Act of 1830." Available at https://history.state.gov. Retrieved November 9, 2021.

US Department of Veterans Affairs. 2012 (September). "American Indian and Alaska Native Servicemembers and Veterans." Available at www.va.gov.

US Interagency Council on Homelessness. 2012. "Expert Panel on Homelessness among American Indians, Alaska Natives, and Native Hawaiians." Available at www.usich.gov.

Veracini, Lorenzo. 2010. "The Settler-Colonial Situation." *Native Studies Review* 19(1): 101–18.

Vimalassery, Manu, Juliana Hu Pegues, and Alyosha Goldstein. 2016. "Introduction: On Colonial Unknowing." *Theory & Event* 19(4): 1–16.

Waldstein, David. 2018. "Cleveland Indians Will Abandon Chief Wahoo Logo Next Year." *New York Times*, January 29. Available at www.nytimes.com.

Warren, Carol A. B., and Tracy X. Karner. 2005. *Discovering Qualitative Methods: Field Research, Interviews, and Analysis.* Los Angeles: Roxbury.

Waters, Mary C. 1990. *Ethnic Options: Choosing Identities in America.* Berkeley: University of California Press.

Weeks, Philip, and Lynn R. Metzger. N.d. "American Indians." *Encyclopedia of Cleveland History*, Case Western Reserve University. Retrieved November 9, 2021. Available at https://case.edu.

White, Richard. 1991. *The Middle Ground: Indians, Empires, and Republics in the Great Lakes Region, 1650–1815.* Cambridge: Cambridge University Press.

Wilbur, Matika, and Adrienne Keen. 2019. "Can a DNA Test Make Me Native American? Episode #4." *All My Relations* (podcast).

Willard, William. 1997. "Outing, Relocation, and Employment Assistance: The Impact of Federal Indian Population Dispersal Programs in the Bay Area." *Wicazo Sa Review* 12(1): 29–46.

Wilson, Shawn. 2001. "What Is an Indigenous Research Methodology?" *Canadian Journal of Native Education* 25(2): 177.

———. 2008. *Research Is Ceremony: Indigenous Research Methods.* Winnipeg, Canada: Fernwood Publishing.

Wydemer, Gwendolyn. 2010. "The Enduring Smear: Sport Team Names, Mascots, and Native Nations." *Native American Times*, June 6. Available at www.nativetimes.com.

Zerubavel, Eviatar. 1996. "Social Memories: Steps to a Sociology of the Past." *Qualitative Sociology* 19(3): 283–99.

INDEX

accessing resources, 52–54, 199
adoption, 32, 47–48, 123, 126, 128–30; 158; 207
AIAN. *See* American Indian and Alaska Native
AIM. *See* American Indian Movement
Akers, Donna, 39–40, 262n2
alcoholism, 86
Allen, Paula Gunn, 6
American Indian and Alaska Native (AIAN), 26–27, 50, 259n2; military depending on, 73; in population, 265n72; in poverty, 59–60
American Indian Ethnic Renewal (Nagel), 50
American Indian Movement (AIM), 50, 65, 72
AmeriCorps Volunteer in Service to America (VISTA), 18, 22
ancestry: of Kurt, 196–97; race contrasted with, 46; talent crediting, 121–22; of Valerie, 98. *See also* blood quantum; heritage
Andersen, Chris, 2, 54
appropriation, 41, 169
assimilation, 82, 84
autonomy, 40

Banks, Dennis, 74–75
Barbara, 108–9
Barker, Joanne, 181–82
Becoming Indian (Sturm), 182
Belin, Esther, 113
Berta, 33, 147, 211; at American Indian Speaker Series, 65; Bly contrasted with,

115; on Christianity, 118; community honoring, 65–66; on culture, 153–54; events organized by, 214–15; granddaughter of, 159; with Greg, 67, 74; on identity, 1, 27, 71; Indian Relocation Program impacting, 1–2, 69; relocators respecting, 185; on reservations, 149–50; stories of, 27–28, 67
Beyond White Ethnicity (Fitzgerald), 262n102
BIA. *See* Bureau of Indian Affairs
Bird, Gloria, 190
birth certificate, 91, 100
Blackhawk, Ned, 17
Blauner, Robert, 58
blood quantum, 42, 263n21; citizenship criteria, 43–45, 156–57; contestation of, 44; enrollment and, 156–57; politics of, 156–57
Bly, 115, 172, 213, 223
Bonilla-Silva, Eduardo, 57, 58
boundaries, 208–11; citizenship, 43–44; colonialism blurring, 63; of community, 223–25, 237–38; of Indianness, 2–3, 36, 204–6; Métis people and, 200–202; racialization and, 40–41; of reclaimers, 195–200, 202–4; of relocators, 223–25; in sociology, 39; Tallbear on, 44–45; wannabes and, 206–8, 223–25
Bowen, Elizabeth, 231
Brunsma, David L., 267n2
Bruyneels, Kevin, 169–70
Bureau of Indian Affairs (BIA), 16, 53, 99, 250

ABOUT THE AUTHOR

MICHELLE R. JACOBS is Assistant Professor of Sociology at Wayne State University in Detroit, Michigan. Her work focuses on racial/ethnic relations and Indigenous peoples and Native nations. She uses qualitative methods to reveal the impacts of settler colonialism and white supremacy on people's everyday lives and overall well-being.